D0389710

Qualification

I AM A POWERFUL EARNER...
DAVID, YOU ARE A POWERFUL EARNER...
DAVID **IS** A POWERFUL EARNER...

 Pantheon Books, New York

QUALI

THY WILL BE DONE, NOT MINE... THY

OPEN

CATION
DONE, NOT MINE...
XXX
128 CHANNELS
PRIVATE BOOTHS
LIVE GIRLS
FANTASY
OPEN
DAVID HEATLEY

for Rebecca

I can't believe we survived this.

 PUBLISHED IN THE UNITED STATES BY PANTHEON BOOKS, A DIVISION OF PENGUIN RANDOM HOUSE LLC, NEW YORK, AND DISTRIBUTED IN CANADA BY PENGUIN RANDOM HOUSE OF CANADA LIMITED, TORONTO. PANTHEON BOOKS AND COLOPHON ARE REGISTERED TRADEMARKS OF PENGUIN RANDOM HOUSE LLC. A CATALOGING-IN-PUBLICATION RECORD HAS BEEN ESTABLISHED FOR THIS TITLE BY THE LIBRARY OF CONGRESS. ISBN: 978-0-375-42540-0

WWW.PANTHEONBOOKS.COM PRINTED IN THE UNITED STATES OF AMERICA FIRST EDITION 987654321

DISCLAIMER:

THIS IS A TRUE STORY THAT COVERS 40 YEARS OF MY LIFE. I TRIED TO TELL IT AS FAITHFULLY AS I COULD, BASED ON MY MEMORIES, JOURNAL ENTRIES, AND EMAIL CORRESPONDENCE. NAMES HAVE BEEN CHANGED OR OMITTED AND CHARACTERS ARE COMPOSITES OF MANY DIFFERENT PEOPLE TO PROTECT THE ANONYMITY OF MY FRIENDS, FAMILY, AND THE PEOPLE I MET IN THE ROOMS.

THE SPECIFIC SHARES I HEARD AT MEETINGS INSPIRED AND TAUGHT ME, BUT I'VE INTENTIONALLY FOCUSED ON THE ONES THAT TOUCHED ON THEMES I HEARD REPEATEDLY AND COULD HAVE BEEN VOICED BY MANY DIFFERENT MEMBERS OF THE PROGRAM. I'VE DONE THIS TO CREATE A SECOND LAYER OF PRIVACY TO THE ALREADY PSEUDONYMOUS CHARACTERS AND TO HIGHLIGHT THE UNIVERSALITY OF THEIR PERSONAL STRUGGLES, WHICH HELPED ME IDENTIFY WITH THEM.

ALL OF THE FELLOWSHIPS HAVE GUIDELINES PROTECTING THE ANONYMITY OF THEIR MEMBERS AND THEIR MEMBERS' DISCLOSURES, SOMETIMES PHRASED AS "WHAT YOU HEAR HERE, LET IT REMAIN HERE." I WRESTLED WITH THIS GUIDANCE, BUT ULTIMATELY CONCLUDED THAT THESE NARRATIVES WERE A PART OF ME AND I NEEDED TO TELL THEM, IN RECONSTRUCTED FORM, TO A MORE GENERAL AUDIENCE—SOMETIMES PROVIDING EXAMPLES OF HOW TO LIVE, OTHER TIMES SERVING AS CAUTIONARY TALES.

IN THE END, THE STORY I'VE TOLD MOST ACCURATELY, TO THE BEST OF MY ABILITY, IS MY OWN.

♫ ALL I ASK OF YOU IS FOREVER TO REMEMBER ME
AS LOVING YOU... ♪♫
♫ SING HOSANA... ♫
THE CAT IN THE
Bird
MONKS OF
WESTON PR
5H

1979

I DON'T BELIEVE IN HELL.

BUT I THINK HEAVEN IS REAL! YOU CAN CHOOSE WHATEVER AGE YOU WANT TO BE WHEN YOU GET THERE.
ME, AGE 5
VICTOR, 6
LUKE, 5

PFFT! THAT'S EXACTLY WHAT DAD BELIEVES!

IT'S OKAY FOR DAVID TO HAVE THE SAME BELIEFS AS ME.

MY FAITH IN GOD AND MY DAD WAS STRONG.
HOW DO YOU FALL ASLEEP SO EASILY, DAVE?
I JUST CLOSE MY EYES AND IMAGINE I'M ROLLING OVER INTO GOD'S ARMS.

1981
WE MOVED TO A NEW TOWN AND STOPPED GOING TO CHURCH.
OUR HALF OF A TWO-FAMILY HOUSE
THE KIDS ON OUR BLOCK WERE WILD.

EEEW... WHO FARTED?!?
WHAT DOES "FART" MEAN?
HA
HA
HA
HA

MOM, WHAT DO "FUCK" AND "SHIT" MEAN?

MY PARENTS THREW A PARTY ONE NIGHT. THEY GOT A TEENAGE NEIGHBOR TO WATCH US FOR A FEW HOURS.

HE'S BEEN IN THE BATHROOM WITH MY BROTHER FOR A LONG TIME...
KNOCK
KNOCK
KNOCK
KNOCK
JUST LET ME SEE IT

MY DAD CHASED THE BABY-SITTER DOWN THE STREET WHEN I TOLD HIM WHAT HAPPENED.

OVER THE NEXT THREE YEARS, I REENACTED THE SCENE WITH A DOZEN BOYS AND GIRLS MY AGE, INCLUDING OUR NEIGHBOR.

JUST LET ME SEE IT.

JIMMY

COMING OUT OF THE BATH ONE NIGHT
I DO THAT STUFF WITH JIMMY BECAUSE IT'S FUN.
I DO IT BECAUSE I'M GAY...
LUKE

DOES THAT MEAN I'M GAY, TOO?

DO YOU WANT TO PLAY "MASSAGE PARLOR" AGAIN?
OKAY.

MMMMMMM...

WELL! I DIDN'T KNOW I HAD A COUPLE OF FAGGOTS FOR SONS!

I STARTED HAVING TROUBLE FALLING ASLEEP AT NIGHT BECAUSE I WAS WORRYING ABOUT ALL THE PROBLEMS IN THE WORLD. MY MOM SUGGESTED I MAKE A "GOD BOX" TO KEEP UNDER MY BED.

JUST WRITE YOUR WORRIES DOWN AND PUT THEM IN HERE. LET GOD TAKE CARE OF IT. OKAY, ANGEL?

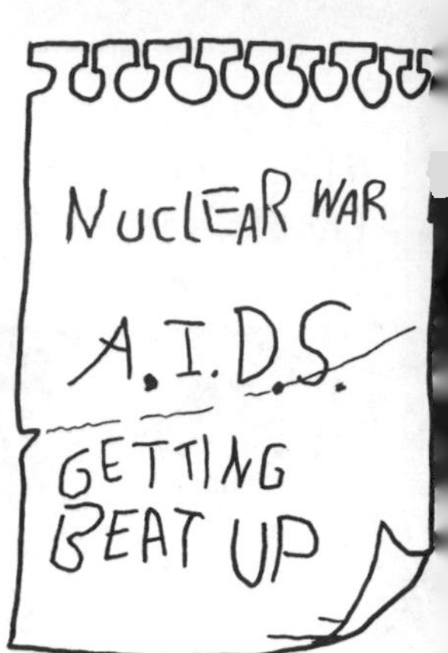
NUCLEAR WAR
A.I.D.S.
GETTING BEAT UP

I THINK IT'S WORKING!

LOOK WHAT I FOUND... YOUR "GOD BOX"!
GIVE IT BACK, ASSHOLE!
LUKE ♂

FINE. BUT FROM NOW ON, ALL I HAVE TO SAY IS "G.B." AND YOU'RE MY SLAVE!
HA
HA
HA

84-86

BOYS!
I'M GOING TO RECORD AGAIN SO I NEED ABSOLUTE QUIET, OKAY?*
SIGH FINE!
VICTOR GOT A "RAT TAIL"

BIRDS FLY OVER THE RAINBOW
HYYY THEN, OH, WHY CANNN'T IIIIII?
VHS
HIS BEST FRIEND, MITCH, MOVED TO OUR TOWN.
HIYA, BUD!
QUICK PECK
!

DID HE JUST KISS MITCH ON THE LIPS?

IT'S PERFECTLY NORMAL FOR MEN TO KISS EACH OTHER, HELLO.
NO, IT'S NOT.

* MY DAD WOULD PERIODICALLY VIDEOTAPE HIMSELF SINGING HIS FAVORITE SONGS ALONE IN OUR LIVING ROOM.

WE WENT UP TO LAKE GEORGE FOR A LONG WEEKEND.

I LOVE IT HERE!
READING WOMEN WHO LOVE TOO MUCH
I'M GOING TO DO SOME SINGING AT THAT STUDIO IN TOWN.

IT WOULD BE NICE IF YOU SPENT SOME TIME WITH US!

♪ HOW GREAT THOU ART... ♫
♫ SOMEWHERE... ♪
♪ DULCINEA... ♫
♫ I LEFT MY HEART IN SAN FRANCISCO ♪ ...
KARAOKE-STYLE

WOW, DAD! YOU SOUND AMAZING! YOU COULD BE A PROFESSIONAL SINGER!

I WENT TO A TALENT AGENT ONCE AND HE SAID I HAVE A "B" VOICE. I COULD DO LOUNGE SINGING, BUT NOTHING BEYOND THAT. I DECIDED NOT TO PURSUE IT.

OH.

WHEN WE GOT BACK, I TOOK A BATH WITH MY BROTHERS.

DAD, CAN YOU USE THE HAIR DRYER ON US?
SURE.
READING ISAAC ASIMOV

IT FEELS SO GOOD!

ESPECIALLY WHEN IT TICKLES MY BUTT.

KISS

KISS

WHAT ARE YOU DOING?!?
KISS

I CAN'T HELP IT. YOU GUYS ARE JUST TOO CUTE!

WHAT WAS **THAT**?!?

I STARTED TO FEEL ASHAMED THAT I HAD A WEIRD DAD.

THEY CAN ALL TELL THERE'S SOMETHING WRONG WITH ME...
HEE
HEE
HA
HA
HA

IT SEEMED LIKE HE WAS DRINKING MORE THAN USUAL.
THIS SHOW IS COMPLETE TRASH, BUT IT'S LIKE A NICE BIG ASPIRIN.
LUKE
IS THAT YOUR THIRD OR FOURTH?

GO DO YOUR HOMEWORK!

I DON'T HAVE TO LISTEN TO YOU. YOU'RE FAT AND BALD!

I AM THE **KING** OF THIS HOUSE!!

NO! MOM IS! SHE MAKES TWICE AS MUCH AS YOU!

HOW CAN LUKE SAY THIS STUFF RIGHT TO HIS FACE ?!?

AAAAAAARRRRRGHHHH!!!!
YOU'RE INSANE!
POUND
POUND
POUND
POUND

I WAS GROOMED TO BE DAD'S UNCONDITIONAL FRIEND – THE ONE WHO FORGAVE HIM NO MATTER WHAT HE DID.

YOU AND I ARE "SYMPATICO."

IT'S NORMAL FOR PARENTS TO HAVE A FAVORITE CHILD. YOU'VE ALWAYS BEEN MINE.
I WISH YOU HAD NEVER BEEN BORN!

JESUS HAD HIS CROSS. I HAVE THE THREE OF YOU!

AAARGHH!
SMAS
TV REMOTE

I ONCE TRIED TALKING BACK TO HIM LIKE LUKE ALWAYS DID.
YOU CAN'T TALK TO ME LIKE THAT! WHY DON'T YOU COME DOWN HERE, AND WE CAN BEAT EACH OTHER BLOODY!
FREE SOUT
ICA

HE WOULD APOLOGIZE AND THEN TALK ABOUT WHAT A VIOLENT MONSTER HIS OWN FATHER HAD BEEN. SOMETIMES HE'D CRY.

BOO HOO HOO HOO HOO
IT'S OKAY, DAD...
PITY ALWAYS OVERPOWERING MY ANGER

BUT HE NEVER GOT BETTER.
I WAS JUST HAVING A LITTLE KNIFE FIGHT WITH GOD...

I TOLD HIM I DID NOT CHOOSE THIS LIFE!

I TOLD JESUS HE COULD TAKE HIS CROSS AND SHOVE IT UP HIS ASS!!!

HE NEEDED HELP.

MY POOR MOM ALWAYS HAD TOO MUCH ON HER PLATE.

PURSUING A MASTER'S DEGREE IN RELIGION

FULL-TIME RELIGIOUS EDUCATOR

RAISING THREE TODDLERS!

WHEN SHE TRIES TO REMEMBER MY EARLY CHILDHOOD, SHE MOSTLY TALKS ABOUT ME SLEEPING.
YOU WERE JUST **DELICIOUS** TO HOLD...
YOU WOULD MOLD YOUR BODY RIGHT INTO MINE.

OTHERWISE IT WAS ALL A BLUR. I DON'T REMEMBER WHICH ONE OF YOU DID WHAT WHEN.

THE REVERSE IS TRUE FOR ME, TOO. MY MOTHER WAS A BLUR.

SO CLOSE AND WARM, ESPECIALLY IF I WAS SICK.

HMM-MM-MM-HMM

AND THEN... GONE.

ON A SCHOOL MORNING, SHE MIGHT STILL BE OUT WORKING FROM THE NIGHT BEFORE.

I'D CRY INTO HER BATHROBE TO SOOTHE MYSELF.

SHE DID A LOT OF JOBS.
IT'S CALLED "SEASONAL COLOR ANALYSIS"...

YEP, YOU'RE AN "AUTUMN" FOR SURE!

WEIGHT WATCHERS
YOU WORK HERE NOW?
I'M THE MANAGER.

ALWAYS REIN-VENTING HERSELF.

I'M NOT A SECRETARY. I'M AN EXECUTIVE ASSISTANT.
AT THE NATIONAL COFFEE ASSOCIATION.
I'M LATE FOR MY BUS!
ALWAYS RUNNING.

BUT HER WEIGHT ALWAYS CAUGHT UP WITH HER.

I'M GOING JOGGING TO THE BAGEL STORE. WANNA JOIN ME?
FIVE BLOCKS AWAY

ISN'T THIS FUN?!? WE SHOULD DO THIS EVERY SUNDAY...

I DON'T REMEMBER HER BINGE-EATING IN FRONT OF ME.

HUFF PUFF

HOT BAGELS

IT MUST HAVE HAPPENED IN PRIVATE.

TWO SALT BAGELS WITH EXTRA CREAM CHEESE.

ALL I KNOW IS, SHE WAS HUGGABLE ONE DAY AND THEN SUDDENLY SO BIG I COULDN'T FIT MY ARMS AROUND HER.

ONE OF HER LOWEST MOMENTS HAD TO HAVE BEEN THE LAST TIME SHE TOOK US ROLLER SKATING.

ARE YOU GONNA SKATE **WITH** US?!?
SURE!

A FEW MINUTES IN...

OWW!
WHAM!!!

SHE LAY THERE CRYING AS BOTH MY BROTHERS TRIED TO HELP HER UP.
SOB

BUT I WAS FURIOUS.
YOU RUINED OUR WHOLE DAY!

THERE COMES A MOMENT IN AN ADDICT'S LIFE...
...WHEN SHE FEELS UTTERLY DEFEATED.
SHE'S READY TO ADMIT THAT HER LIFE IS UNMANAGEABLE.
SHE'S READY FOR STEP ONE.

1987-92

AROUND THE TIME I WAS FIRST DISCOVERING PORN...
CAN YOU BRING THESE WITH YOU EVERY TIME YOU COME OVER?
HA HA
MIDDLE-SCHOOL HAIR

... MY MOM DISCOVERED ST. MARK'S EPISCOPAL CHURCH.
IT'S JUST A FEW BLOCKS AWAY! WE CAN ALL WALK THERE!

DID I TELL YOU THEY HAVE A **WOMAN PRIEST?!?**
VICTOR
LUKE

AND THERE'S A YOUTH GROUP AND A SUMMER CAMP!

MY MOM HAD HIT ROCK BOTTOM, BUT SHE BOUNCED UP OFF THE FLOOR WITH A VENGEANCE!

SOMEHOW SHE GOT US ALL TO ATTEND CHURCH WITH HER EVERY SUNDAY.

YOU HAVE TO GET UP NOW! WE'RE GONNA BE LATE!

GROAN!

AFTER YEARS OF BEING AWAY FROM ITS INFLUENCE, MY BROTHERS AND I HAD A HARD TIME TAKING IT SERIOUSLY.

LOOK! THE HYMNAL IS LEVITATING!
HA
HA
HA
HA
SHHHHHHH!

MY DAD MADE IT KNOWN THAT HE DIDN'T CARE FOR REVERAND GLENDA OR THE ONE OPENLY GAY PARISHONER.

HA HA HA
HE'TH THUCH A THILLY THAVAGE!

OR THE MUSIC.

THE TRUMPET SHALL SOUND!

HA HA HA HA HA HA HA HA

BUT MOM TRIED TO ENDURE ALL OF OUR IMMATURITY WITH DIGNITY AND GRACE.

AMEN.

HER FAITH IN GOD GOT A TURBO CHARGE WHEN SHE DECIDED TO JOIN OA— **OVEREATERS ANONYMOUS.**

WHY DO YOU HAVE TO MEASURE EVERYTHING?

I HAVE AN ADDICTION.
I'M POWERLESS OVER FOOD.

OOPS! I FORGOT TO READ THE LABEL.

SHIT! SUGAR IS THE THIRD INGREDIENT.* I HAVE TO GO BRUSH MY TEETH!

THERE WERE A LOT OF NEW TERMS TO LEARN.
?

MOM CALLED HER "SPONSOR" NIGHTLY TO "TURN OVER" HER FOOD FOR THE DAY.
FOUR OUNCES OF CHICKEN...

* ANY FOOD CONTAINING SUGAR HIGHER THAN FIFTH PLACE ON THE INGREDIENTS LIST WAS FORBIDDEN.

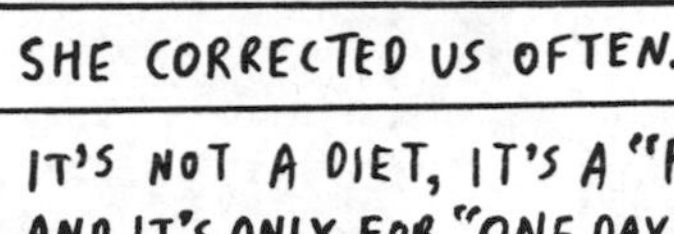
SHE CORRECTED US OFTEN.

IT'S NOT A DIET, IT'S A "FOOD PLAN." AND IT'S ONLY FOR "ONE DAY AT A TIME."

"LET GO AND LET GOD!"

SHE TAUGHT US THE SERENITY PRAYER:
"GOD, GRANT ME THE SERENITY TO ACCEPT THE THINGS I CANNOT CHANGE, COURAGE TO CHANGE THE THINGS I CAN, AND THE WISDOM TO KNOW THE DIFFERENCE."

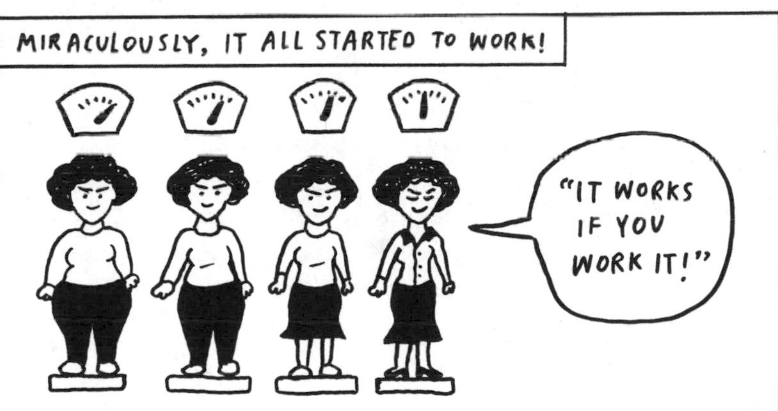
MIRACULOUSLY, IT ALL STARTED TO WORK!
"IT WORKS IF YOU WORK IT!"

MY MOM'S SELF-ESTEEM SKYROCKETED.

SHE GOT A VP-LEVEL POSITION AT A COMPANY IN MANHATTAN!

SHE OFTEN APPEARED ON TV.

SOMETIMES SHE FLEW DOWN TO D.C. TO LOBBY CONGRESS.

HER SALARY TICKED UP INTO THE LOW SIX FIGURES.

I WAS SO PROUD OF HER!

MOM MADE IT THROUGH ALL 12 STEPS AND HER SUCCESS WAS INARGUABLE.

WHO'S WHO IN AMERICAN WOMEN
1987
1987

BUT THERE WAS MORE WORK TO BE DONE.

1:11 AM
DING DONG

THE PRIMARY PURPOSE OF EVERY 12-STEP GROUP IS TO "CARRY ITS MESSAGE TO THE ADDICT WHO STILL SUFFERS."

VICTOR CAUGHT WITH A BAG FULL OF ALCOHOL STOLEN FROM A FRIEND'S PARENTS' LIQUOR CABINET.

AND THE TWELFTH STEP CONCLUDES WITH THE PHRASE "TO PRACTICE THESE PRINCIPLES IN ALL OUR AFFAIRS."

SOMETHING IN MY PARENTS' MARRIAGE HAD TO CHANGE.

WITH HER SUPERHUMAN, GOD-POWERED DETERMINATION, MY MOM CONVINCED MY FATHER TO JOIN THE 12 STEPS, TOO.

ADULT CHILDREN OF ALCOHOLICS

TOGETHER THEY DISCOVERED A LOCAL CHAPTER OF **ADULT CHILDREN OF ALCOHOLICS** AND BECAME MEMBERS.*

"RE-PARENTING ONE'S WOUNDED INNER CHILD WITH LOVE..."
VROOM!
PUKE!

NEW FRIENDS OF MY PARENTS WERE OFTEN IN OUR HOUSE, SOMETIMES JOINING US FOR HOLIDAY MEALS WITH LITTLE WARNING.

BOYS, THESE ARE MY FRIENDS RON AND PERRY!
HI...

*THIS PUZZLED ME AND MY BROTHERS. I HAD NEVER HEARD THEM MENTION THAT ANY OF MY GRANDPARENTS WERE ALCOHOLICS. BUT THEY FELT LIKE THEY BELONGED.

THEY ALL SEEMED A LITTLE BROKEN IN SOME WAY.
THANKS FOR LETTING US JOIN YOUR FAMILY MEAL.

THERE WAS GEORGE.
HE LOVED TO MAKE FUN OF COMMERCIALS
OOH! I NEED TO BUY THAT!
ACNE SCARS
HA
HA
HA
HA HA

LESTER
I HAVE HALF A DOZEN TAPES OF REGGAE RECORDED OFF THE RADIO WHEN I LIVED IN KINGSTON!
WOW!

MARIE
WORKED AS AN EMT
ZERO EMOTIONAL AFFECT
LESBIAN?

AND JOY
YOU'RE LIKE MY SOUL MATE!
??

THESE PEOPLE SLIPPED SO EASILY INTO MY PARENTS' LIVES, IT FELT LIKE THEY'D BEEN THERE FOREVER.

BUT WITHIN A COUPLE OF YEARS, MOST OF THEM DRIFTED AWAY.

I HAVEN'T SEEN GEORGE LATELY.

YEAH... HE STOPPED RETURNING MY CALLS.

IT REMINDED ME OF SOMETHING I SAW IN THE ACOA BOOK:

"I love you."

"Go away."

OF ALL THE CHARACTERS THAT PARADED THROUGH OUR HOUSE, **CHARLES** WAS PROBABLY MY FAVORITE.

OH COOL! TALKING HEADS!

HE SAW THROUGH MY DAD'S BULLSHIT.

MIKE, YOU'RE AN ALCOHOLIC. YOU REALLY NEED AA.

CHARLES BECAME HIS SPONSOR. THEY WORKED THROUGH THE TWELVE STEPS.

"I ADMITTED FOR THE FIRST TIME THAT OF MYSELF, I WAS NOTHING..."
THE BIG BOOK OF AA

WHEN HE MOVED AWAY SUDDENLY AND CUT ALL TIES, DAD WAS DEVASTATED.

I CAN'T LET HIM GO!

UNBEKNOWNST TO MY MOM, DAD CONTINUED TO CALL AND SEND CARDS AND GIFTS REGULARLY.

SHE HATES HIM FOR ABANDONING US.

HE GOT NO RESPONSE IN RETURN.
HOPE YOU'RE WELL. CALL WHEN YOU CAN.

DESPITE THE TRANSIENT NATURE OF THE GROUPS, MY PARENTS WERE STILL ALL-IN, "WORKING" TWO PROGRAMS EACH.

VEREATERS
NONYMOUS

ACA

UNITY
SERVICE
AA
RECOVERY

THEY HAD "SPONSEES" IN DESPERATE SHAPE TO LOOK AFTER.

OOOKAY... LET'S TAKE A DEEP BREATH TOGETHER!

EVENINGS AND WEEKENDS FILLED UP WITH MEETINGS, STEP WORK, AND RETREATS.

BLANK CHECK FOR GROCERIES AND HOTEL INFO IS ON THE KITCHEN TABLE.

I ATE IN FRONT OF THE TV MOST NIGHTS.

MY MAIN FORM OF COMMUNICATION WITH MY MOM WAS HER LONG NOTES WRITTEN ON THE BACK OF JUNK-MAIL ENVELOPES.

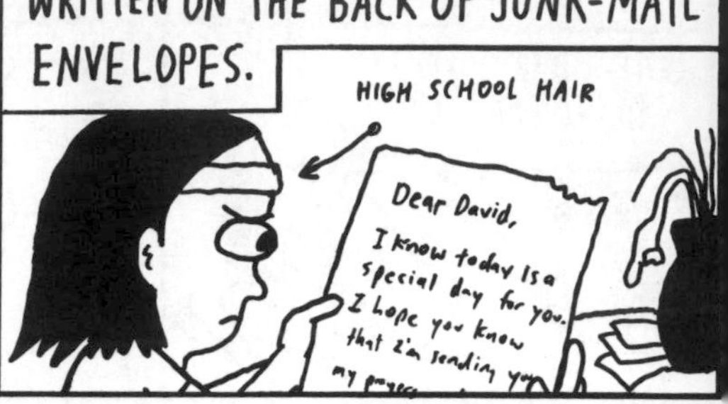
HIGH SCHOOL HAIR
Dear David,
I know today is a special day for you. I hope you know that I'm sending you

MY DAD CREEPED ME OUT, EVEN IN SOBRIETY. HE COULDN'T STOP TALKING ABOUT HIS SPONSEES.*

YOU'D LIKE BOB. HE'S A NICE, ATTRACTIVE YOUNG GUY TRYING TO GET HIS LIFE BACK TOGETHER.

COOL, DAD.

HE REMINDS ME OF YOU AND YOUR BROTHERS.
UGH!

I CAN TELL YOU THIS IN CONFIDENCE...

WHEN BOB WAS SIX, HIS NEIGHBOR RANG HIS BELL, PULLED DOWN HIS PANTS, AND SUCKED HIS DICK. HE WEPT TELLING ME THAT, POOR BABY.

* SOMETHING I KNEW HE SHOULDN'T BE DOING

THIS STORY DAD REPEATED ENDLESSLY:
AN ALCOHOLIC FROM ONE OF MY MEETINGS PASSED OUT UNDER A TRUCK ONE NIGHT.

HE WAS AWAKENED BY A VOICE TELLING HIM TO ROLL OVER, JUST BEFORE THE TRUCK DROVE OVER THE EXACT SPOT WHERE HE WAS LYING!

IT JUST TOUCHES ME THAT GOD CARES ABOUT **ALL** OF US, EVEN THE ONES WHO HAVE MESSED UP THEIR LIVES SO MUCH!

HE DIDN'T HAVE A CLUE THAT I WAS IN A BAD WAY MYSELF.

SNIFF

FUCKING **HATE** YOU!

I HAD BEEN CHOKED IN MY BED BY ANOTHER CAMPER AT OUR CHRISTIAN SUMMER CAMP. I NEVER TOLD ANYONE.

MY COUNSELORS EGGED ME AND MY CABINMATES IN THE MIDDLE OF THE NIGHT AS A "FUN PRANK."

RAPHAEL HUMILIATED ME IN FRONT OF HIS FRIENDS FOR SPORT.

MY "BEST FRIEND" WOULD COVER MY ARMS IN BRUISES WHEN I WENT OVER TO HIS HOUSE.

I PASSED THE VIOLENCE ON TO A COUPLE OF CAMPERS IN MY CARE, BATHING IN SHAME AND SELF-LOATHING AFTERWARD.

STEALING CANDY LED TO STEALING CASSETTE TAPES AND PORN.

POUND
POUND
POUND
POUND
POUND

SINCE I HADN'T GOTTEN CAUGHT, I UPPED THE ANTE. I MASTURBATED IN PLACES WHERE I MIGHT GET DISCOVERED, ONCE ON THE FLOOR OF OUR PUBLIC LIBRARY'S BATHROOM.

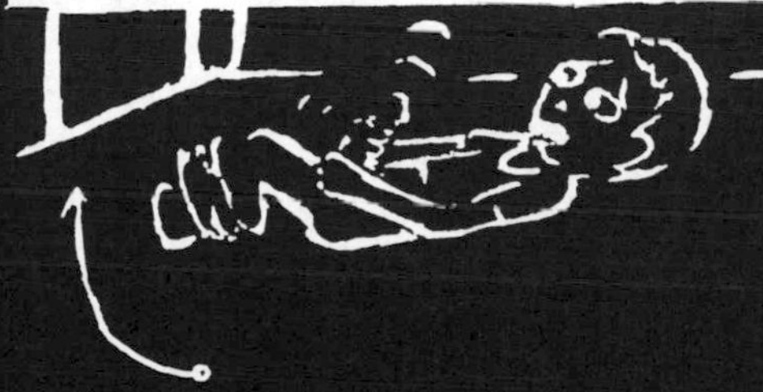

I BIDED MY TIME AND THEN ABRUPTLY DROPPED OUT OF CHURCH.

AND EVEN THOUGH I WAS TOLD ADDICTION RAN IN MY FAMILY, I DECIDED TO BEFRIEND THE BIGGEST POTHEAD I KNEW.

WHAT ARE YOU DOING THIS WEEKEND?
LAIRD

HE SMOKED ME UP FOR FREE.

I DIDN'T KNOW HOW MUCH I'D BEEN LONGING FOR THIS FEELING.

I WISHED I COULD STAY STONED FOREVER.

2
EMPTY METAL
AND MY GUILTY BURNING EYES TELL THE STORY
JAMES JOYCE
FLAN
Invisible

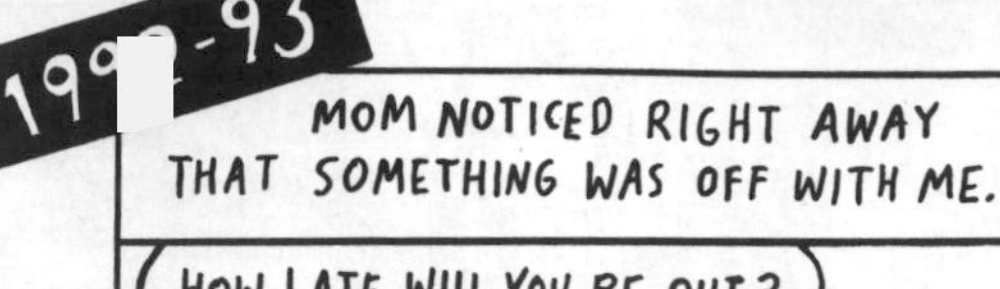
199 -93
MOM NOTICED RIGHT AWAY THAT SOMETHING WAS OFF WITH ME.
HOW LATE WILL YOU BE OUT?
I'M NOT SURE...
SHE STARTED WAITING UP UNTIL I GOT HOME.

COME HERE... LET ME SEE YOUR EYES.
I'M JUST TIRED.

THROUGH LAIRD I HAD FOUND THE OTHER WEED-SMOKING HIPPIE KIDS AT SCHOOL. I GOT INVITED TO THEIR PARTIES.
HOMEMADE PVC PIPE BONG, A.K.A. "THE OCTOPUS"

I QUICKLY ADVANCED TO SMOKING ALL WEEKEND LONG WHENEVER I COULD.
WAKE 'N' BAKE!
IT WAS EXHILARATING!
BIRD SANCTUARY

POT FREED THE ARTIST IN ME THAT HAD BEEN DORMANT SINCE EARLY CHILDHOOD.

LAIRD AND I STARTED A BAND.

HI, CAN I BORROW YOUR BABY?
DICTATING LYRICS TO EACH OTHER
Can I borrow your

WE RECORDED DOZENS OF SONGS ON HIS FOUR-TRACK.

BOOM
CARD-BOARD BOX DRUM

AND WE STARTED PERFORMING AT AN EAST VILLAGE OPEN MIC. THEY LOVED US!

"NOT I," SAID THE BLIND MAN TO THE VERTICALLY CHALLENGED WOMAN!

I DREW SURREAL CARTOONS FOR OUR FLIERS. IT ALL JUST POURED OUT OF ME.

VELVET CACTUS SOCIETY
SAT. OCT. 1 8PM

SO DID MY ANGER.

YOU **FUCKING IDIOT!**

THINGS GOT BAD PRETTY FAST. I CUT CLASS AND FOUGHT WITH MY BAND TEACHER.

YOU CAN LEAVE!

OH! I CAN LEAVE?!? GREAT! BYE!!!

AND I STARTED HANGING OUT WITH WEIRD PEOPLE.

I STOLE SOME FROM MY PARENTS.

DON'T WORRY! I WAS STONED WHEN I GOT MY LICENSE. IT'S LIKE I HAVE A LICENSE TO DRIVE **STONED!**

HA HA HA HA

POUND POUND POUND

I SHOPLIFTED RECKLESSLY.
HARDCOVER SPIDER-MAN BOOK

UNTIL IT FINALLY ALL UNRAVELED.

WE GOT YOU ON VIDEO!

YOU'RE BANNED FROM ALL OF OUR STORES FOR LIFE!
CLICK!
THAT GOT THROUGH TO ME.

I SURRENDERED AND TOLD MY MOM EVERYTHING.

SOB!

MY DAD WAS HURT THAT I HAD LIED TO HIM ABOUT USING DRUGS.

WHO GIVES A FUCK WHAT YOU FEEL?!?

AFTER DELIBERATING FOR A FEW DAYS, THEY GAVE ME TWO CHOICES.

YOU CAN GO TO THERAPY OR 12-STEP MEETINGS.

I HAD ALWAYS BEEN CURIOUS WHAT HAPPENED AT MEETINGS, SO I COMMITTED TO TRYING AA.*

MY FIRST MEETING WAS IN A DIMLY LIT CHURCH BASEMENT IN HACKENSACK.

CREEPY...
POUND
POUND
POUND
POUND

* AS THE ORIGINAL 12-STEP PROGRAM, AA IS HOME TO MANY TYPES OF ADDICTS. MY PARENTS FELT I'D BE SAFER THERE THAN AT NARCOTICS ANONYMOUS

OKAY, LET'S GET STARTED.

WHAT THE HELL AM I DOING HERE?!?

THESE GUYS ALL LOOK LIKE CONSTRUCTION WORKERS.

OR SAILORS.
LET'S START WITH THE SERENITY PRAYER.

THE CHAIRPERSON READ FROM A MEETING FORMAT THEN ASKED ME IF I WANTED TO INTRODUCE MYSELF.

HI, I'M DAVID.

HI, DAVID

HI, DAVID

I'M BRAND-NEW TO AA. I'M NOT REALLY AN ALCOHOLIC, BUT I'VE BEEN HAVING SOME TROUBLE WITH MARIJUANA. I'M GONNA LISTEN TODAY AND SEE WHAT I THINK.

THANKS.

KEEP COMIN' BACK...!

AS THEY SHARED THEIR STORIES, MY WORST FEARS WERE CONFIRMED.

I'LL GO FIRST.

ONE GUY TALKED ABOUT HOW HE USED TO GET INTO BAR FIGHTS.

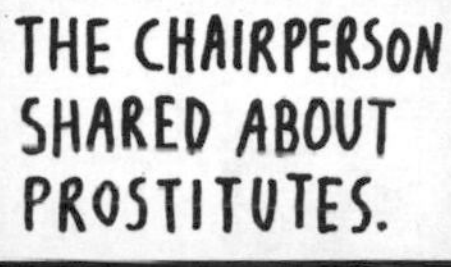
THE CHAIRPERSON SHARED ABOUT PROSTITUTES.

THE ONE WOMAN AT THE MEETING SAID HER SON HAD STARTED SMOKING CRACK.

I HAD ABSOLUTELY NOTHING IN COMMON WITH THESE PEOPLE!

A TATTOOED GUY APPROACHED ME AFTER THE MEETING ENDED AS I BOLTED FOR THE DOOR.

HEY, DAVID...

THIS IS A GOOD GROUP. IT'S A LITTLE QUIET TONIGHT, BUT WE GOT SOME PEOPLE HERE WITH REALLY GOOD SOBER TIME.

YOU SHOULD DO WHAT THEY SAY AND CHECK OUT A FEW MORE MEET-INGS BEFORE YOU DECIDE ANYTHING.

IN THE CAR RIDE HOME...

THERE'S NO WAY I'M GOING TO AA!!!

AFTER MORE DELIBER-ATING, MY PARENTS DECIDED I SHOULD TRY THEIR SATURDAY MORNING **ACOA** GROUP. WE WOULD ALL GO TOGETHER.

IT COULDN'T HAVE BEEN A STARKER CONTRAST.

WHOA...!

THERE MUST HAVE BEEN OVER A HUNDRED PEOPLE IN THE LIGHT-DRENCHED PARISH HALL. THE PODIUM NEAR THE STAGE WAS FLANKED BY ENORMOUS BANNERS.

I RECOGNIZED MANY SLOGANS ON THE PLACARDS AROUND THE ROOM.

Keep It Simple
Easy Does It
Think
Let It Begin With Me
Let Go and Let God

ALL THE PEOPLE LOOKED LIKE WHITE, MIDDLE-CLASS PROFESSIONALS.
ONE BLACK COUPLE... TWO ASIAN PEOPLE...

IT WAS ALL SO...
CORNY.

THIS IS MY SON DAVID!
WOW! SO NICE TO MEET YOU! I JUST LOOOVE YOUR PARENTS.

PEOPLE FLOCKED TO THEM LIKE ROYALTY. I SQUIRMED WITH EMBARASSMENT.

AT 10:00 AM ON THE DOT, THE CHAIRPERSON STARTED THE MEETING.

LET'S BEGIN WITH THE SERENITY PRAYER.
SEE YOU AT BRUNCH!
THANK GOD!

GOD, GRANT ME THE SERENITY...
WOW!

WE'LL HAVE AN ACOA GIVE A QUALIFICATION* FOR 20 MINUTES, THEN BREAK OFF INTO SMALL-GROUP SHARING.

AND NOW... TO SHARE HIS EXPERIENCE, STRENGTH, AND HOPE... PLEASE HELP ME WELCOME... JAY!
CLAP!
CLAP!
CLAP!
CLAP!

* WHEN ANY 12-STEP MEMBER SHARES HIS OR HER STORY WITH A GROUP.

MY NAME IS JAY AND I'M AN ADULT CHILD.
HI, JAY
HI, JAY

I DIDN'T HEAR ANY OF JAY'S QUALIFICATION. I WAS TOO BUSY CRINGING AT MY MOM'S GRUNTS OF "IDENTIFICATION." *

MMMHH!
UGH!

THE SMALL GROUP WAS BETTER — IF ONLY BECAUSE I GOT AWAY FROM MY PARENTS.
I'LL SHARE FIRST.
WHEW

THE THEMES HIT A LITTLE CLOSER TO HOME THAN AA.

MY DAD WAS JUST SO FUCKING INSANE!

HA
HA HA HA

AND THE FORMAT WAS SOOTHING. EVERYONE GOT EXACTLY THREE MINUTES.

THAT'S TIME.

THANKS!

NO ONE COULD INTERRUPT DURING YOUR SHARE. NO "CROSS TALK."

WHO WOULD LIKE TO SHARE NEXT?

I FOUND THE TONE OF THE SHARES TO BE EERILY FAMILIAR.

SHE TALKS JUST LIKE MOM...

* THE RECOVERY PROCESS HAPPENS WHEN AN ADDICT SEES HIMSELF IN ANOTHER ADDICT'S STORY.

I RISKED EXPOSING SOME PAIN DURING MY SHARE, BUT I ONLY USED ABOUT THIRTY SECONDS OF MY TIME.

≷MMMHH≶

≷SIGH≶ SOMETIMES I JUST WANT TO HIDE FROM EVERYONE.

IT STILL FELT GREAT AND I GOT COMPLIMENTED.

IT TOOK COURAGE TO SHARE THAT.

NICE SHARE. KEEP COMING BACK!

CRAVING MORE POSITIVE FEEDBACK, I WENT TO TWO MORE MEETINGS WITH MY PARENTS. THEN I HIT A BRICK WALL.

THESE PEOPLE ALL SEE OUR FAMILY AS A SUCCESS STORY. I CAN'T BE HONEST WITH ANY OF THEM!

NOW I HAD TO HAVE A DEEPLY UN-COMFORTABLE CONVERSATION.

I THINK YOUR MEETING IS REALLY GREAT. IT'S JUST NOT MY THING.

WELL, YOU DIDN'T GIVE IT A FAIR CHANCE. YOU'RE SUPPOSED TO TRY **SIX MEETINGS.**

I DON'T WANT TO GO TO YOUR MEETING, OKAY?!? YOU SAID I HAD A CHOICE AND I CHOOSE THERAPY!

MY DAD ASKED AROUND CHURCH FOR A THERAPIST RECOMMENDATION. LUCKILY, THERE HAPPENED TO BE A SOCIAL WORKER IN OUR PARISH.

A FEW DAYS LATER, I HAD MY FIRST SESSION WITH JIM.
LEGALLY BLIND
STUDYING TO BE AN EPISCOPAL PRIEST
BLACK BELT IN KARATE

I REALLY LOVED HIS DARK SENSE OF HUMOR.
LOOK, AT LEAST YOU'RE NOT TURNING TRICKS AT THE ENTRANCE TO THE HOLLAND TUNNEL!
HA HA

I FINALLY HAD A PLACE TO LET IT ALL RIP.
I FUCKING HATE HIM!!

PART OF WHY I FELT SAFE WAS THE FACT THAT JIM HATED THE 12 STEPS.*
BUNCH OF WHINERS...

IF YOU NEED TO MAKE YOURSELF INTO A **CRIPPLE** TO GET HELP, I FEEL SORRY FOR YOU!

ALCOHOLISM ISN'T REALLY A DISEASE.

I'M **BLIND!** I HAVE A FUCKING **DISEASE**, OKAY?!?

DAVID, YOU DON'T NEED TO ADMIT YOU'RE POWERLESS OVER ANYTHING!

YOU NEED TO FEEL **POWERFUL** FOR ONCE IN YOUR LIFE!

* IT'S FAIRLY COMMON FOR THERAPISTS TO DISTRUST THE 12 STEPS AND VICE VERSA.

I LOVED HIM LIKE A FATHER.

AND HE LOVED ME BACK.
THANKS, JIM!
HA HA
SEE YA NEXT WEEK.

THERAPY REALLY WORKED! JIM GOT ME TO QUIT SMOKING WEED AND START MEDITATING.

PRACTICING MINDFULNESS

ME AND LAIRD'S BAND GOT A DEAL WITH OUR FAVORITE RECORD LABEL.

SHIMMY DISC

OUR FIRST CD WOUND UP IN TOWER RECORDS.

I HOPE SECURITY DOESN'T RECOGNIZE MY FACE!

WE EVEN CHARTED ON COLLEGE RADIO ACROSS THE COUNTRY.
HOLY SHIT!

I WAS PIECING TOGETHER AN IDENTITY I COULD BE PROUD OF.

THAT ALL SOUNDS WONDERFUL!

AND AFTER YEARS OF SELF-HATRED AND LUSTING AFTER UN-AVAILABLE GIRLS, I SUDDENLY FELL DEEPLY IN LOVE.

REBECCA

SHE GAVE ME THE KIND OF LOVE THAT SAID, "WHOEVER YOU WERE, YOU'RE NOT THAT PERSON ANYMORE. NOW YOU'RE MY BELOVED."

PLUS WE HAD GREAT SEX.

BY THE TIME I GRADUATED HIGH SCHOOL, I HAD FIGURED OUT MY FORMULA FOR A HAPPY LIFE.

THE 12 STEPS WERE MY PARENTS' THING.

THEY HAD NO SWAY OVER ME, AND I PLANNED TO KEEP IT THAT WAY.

VROOM!

1993-95

AFTER SURVIVING A YEAR OF LONG-DISTANCE ROMANCE, I FOLLOWED REBECCA TO OBERLIN COLLEGE. I REALLY DIDN'T CONSIDER ANY OTHER SCHOOLS.

SOB!
MOM
FINALLY FREE!!!

REBECCA AND I HAD A BLISSFUL TWO-MONTH HONEYMOON PHASE.
HI.
YOU REALLY GO TO SCHOOL WITH ME NOW?!?

BUT THEN WE STARTED FIGHTING.
I'M NOT SLEEPING OVER TONIGHT!
FINE!

SHE SOMETIMES FELT LIKE A MOM.
DON'T YOU OWN A BELT?
MY EYE STARTED TO WANDER.
CUTE, ANDROGYNOUS RIOT GRRL PIXIES

TALKING TO MY MOM ONLY CAUSED ME MORE CONFUSION.
YOU SOUND VERY CO-DEPENDENT* TO ME.

I REALLY THINK YOU NEED TO FIND A 12-STEP GROUP THAT DEALS WITH RELATIONSHIPS!

I'LL BE PRAYING FOR YOU.

I DIDN'T HAVE JIM TO STEER ME.
SHIT! WHAT IF SHE'S RIGHT?

I STARTED TO PANIC.

WHAT IF I WAS STUCK IN SOME KIND OF UNHEALTHY, ADDICTIVE TRAP?

WHAT IF IT WOULD NEVER GET BETTER?

MAYBE I COULDN'T STOP ON MY OWN!

* THIS WORD CAME FROM AL-ANON. SHE HAD MOVED AWAY FROM ACOA AND WAS GOING TO THE ORIGINAL PROGRAM FOR FAMILY MEMBERS OF ALCOHOLICS. FOUNDED BY LOIS WILSON, THE WIFE OF AA'S FOUNDER, BILL WILSON, AL-ANON IS JUST AN ABBREVIATED VERSION OF "ALCOHOLICS ANONYMOUS". THE HYPHEN IS MEANT TO DIFFERENTIATE IT FROM AA, WHICH FOCUSES ON SOBRIETY. WHEREAS AL-ANON FOCUSES ON THE COMPULSIVE ENABLING AND CARETAKING TO WHICH FRIENDS AND RELATIVES OF ALCOHOLICS ARE PRONE.

I NEED TO FIND A 12-STEP GROUP! WE SHOULD TAKE A BREAK FROM EACH OTHER FOR A WHILE. WE'RE TOO CO-DEPENDENT.
WHAT DOES THAT EVEN MEAN?!?

THERE WAS A **CO-DEPENDENTS ANONYMOUS** MEETING AT THE STUDENT UNION EVERY TUESDAY. I DECIDED TO TRY IT.

I'M SICK OF FEELING FUCKED UP ALL THE TIME.

I'M TAKING CHARGE OF MY LIFE!!!

AT FIRST I THOUGHT I HAD THE WRONG ROOM.

YOU'RE HERE FOR **CODA**? GREAT!
MIDDLE AGED

LET'S START WITH THE SERENITY PRAYER.

THIS IS SO FUCKING WEIRD.
GOD, GRANT ME THE SERENITY...

MAYBE I SHOULD JUST LEAVE.
OKAY! HAVE A SEAT.

HE CHAIRED THE ENTIRE MEETING AS IF THERE WAS A ROOM FULL OF PEOPLE.
ARE THERE ANY NEWCOMERS WHO'D LIKE TO INTRODUCE THEMSELVES?

UMM... HI, I'M DAVID.
HI, DAVID!

I DIDN'T SPEAK AFTER THAT. I JUST GOT THE HELL OUT OF THERE AS SOON AS THE MEETING WAS OVER.

I'M SORRY I SAID ALL THAT. MY MOM IS CRAZY.

CRAZINESS WAS IN THE AIR THAT YEAR.
WHY CAN'T WE STOP FIGHTING?!?

I WAS GOING CRAZY WITH LUST.
WE CAN GO SKINNY DIPPING...
"JUST FRIENDS"

I THOUGHT REBECCA MIGHT BE UP FOR A NONTRADITIONAL ARRANGEMENT.
MAYBE WE COULD SEE OTHER PEOPLE, BUT STILL STAY TOGETHER?
WHAT? NO WAY!!!
SHE BROKE UP WITH ME ON THE SPOT.

I PLANNED A SPONTANEOUS VISIT HOME TO RALLY MYSELF.
OF COURSE YOU CAN COME, BUT I HAVE TO TELL YOU SOMETHING... YOUR FATHER AND I ARE SEPARATING.

OVER THE NEXT TWO MONTHS, SEVERAL HIGH SCHOOL FRIENDS WENT ON MEDICATION. ONE WAS HOSPITALIZED WITH SCHIZOPHRENIA. ANOTHER ATTEMPTED SUICIDE BY JUMPING IN FRONT OF A TRAIN.

MY BROTHER LUKE HAD STARTED SMOKING WEED IN COLLEGE.

I TRIED ACID, TOO.

IT WAS HORRIBLE! I WAS CONVINCED I HAD BEEN RAPED BY THE DEVIL...
THE ONLY THING THAT STOPPED ME FROM KILLING MYSELF WAS THE THOUGHT OF MOM CRYING AT MY FUNERAL.

VICTOR HAD DROPPED OUT OF COLLEGE TO PURSUE MUSIC. HE WAS LIVING WITH JUNKIES IN THE SAME EAST VILLAGE PERFORMANCE SPACE WHERE LAIRD AND I USED TO PLAY.

CREEPIER THAN I REMEMBER.

C'MON... SMOKE SOME WEED WITH YOUR BIG BROTHER.
OKAY...*

* I HADN'T SMOKED IN TWO YEARS.

WITHOUT REBECCA OR JIM OR ANY STABLE FAMILY SUPPORT, I SPUN OUT.

FUCK IT. I WANT TO STEAL THIS.

I MOVED DORMS FIVE TIMES IN FOUR MONTHS.

MY SONGS AND PAINTINGS LOST THEIR SPARK.

EVERYTHING WAS AS GRAY AS THE SKY IN OHIO.

WHAT'S THE POINT?
HOW DO I EVEN KNOW WHEN IT'S DONE?

WHEN MY MOM TOLD ME SHE WAS MOVING TO MANHATTAN, I DROPPED OUT OF OBERLIN TO MOVE IN WITH HER.

ROOM
MOVING

IN AA, THEY TELL NEWCOMERS TO "STICK WITH THE WINNERS." MAYBE MY MOM'S WINNING STREAK WOULD RUB OFF ON ME.

3
THE MEANING OF EXISTENCE
CAN'T BE DEFINED
BY RELIGION
OR IDEOLOGY

1995-97
I NOW LIVED IN A HIGH RISE ON THE UPPER EAST SIDE.
IT WAS DIZZYING.
LET ME GET THAT FOR YOU, SIR!
WAS I SUDDENLY RICH?
TWENTY-THREE FLOORS?!?
WE'RE ON FOURTEEN.
IT WAS JUST A ONE-BEDROOM WITH NO REAL VIEW TO SPEAK OF.
BUT I WAS IN MANHATTAN!
WOO-HOO!!!
WITH MY MOM... BUT STILL!

DURING THE FIRST WEEK WE WENT SHOPPING TOGETHER EVERY DAY.

COMFY!

FUTON SALE

WE COULD PAINT THESE!

UNFINISHED

?

I ATE EVERY MEAL WITH HER IN BETWEEN ASSEMBLING FURNITURE AND HANGING PICTURES.

PERFECT!

IT WAS MORE TIME THAN I HAD EVER SPENT ALONE WITH HER IN MY LIFE.
I'M PROUD OF YOU, MOM!

OUR BOND WAS STRONG!
THANK YOU, ANGEL!

AS WE ROUNDED THE SECOND WEEK, THINGS DARKENED BETWEEN US.

VICTOR CALLED FROM OUT ON THE ROAD.
RIIIING!

HE WAS BROKE.
OF COURSE YOU CAN STAY HERE!
WHAT?!?

I FELT COMPLETELY BETRAYED. THIS WAS **OUR** TIME TOGETHER!

HER TONE WITH ME CHANGED OVERNIGHT.

INSTEAD OF HER PARTNER IN SURVIVAL, NOW I FELT MORE LIKE DEAD WEIGHT.

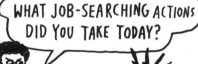

DAVID!

WHAT JOB-SEARCHING ACTIONS DID YOU TAKE TODAY?

SHE EXPECTED ME TO CONTRIBUTE TO THE FOOD AND RENT BILLS.
YOU MAKE $100,000 A YEAR!
THE LUNCHES AND DINNERS STOPPED.
ONE PLAIN SLICE.

ANY MONEY SHE GAVE ME WOULD BE CONSIDERED A LOAN UNLESS SHE DECIDED TO MAKE IT A GIFT.

IT WAS MONEY THAT BROKE MY PARENTS' MARRIAGE APART AND NOW IT WAS BREAKING US APART, TOO.*

HE MAXED OUT ALL OF OUR CREDIT CARDS WHEN HE WAS OUT OF WORK!

WHEN I FOUND THAT OUT, IT FELT AS BAD AS IF HE'D BEEN SLEEPING WITH ANOTHER WOMAN!!!
LATEST DIET: MACROBIOTIC

I HAD A HARD TIME SYMPATHIZING WITH HER POINT OF VIEW.

* THAT'S WHAT I WAS TELLING MYSELF AT LEAST.

I KNEW MOM HAD DISCOVERED **DEBTORS ANONYMOUS** (HER FOURTH PROGRAM) JUST BEFORE LEAVING MY DAD.

OVEREATERS ANONYMOUS

AL-ANON

DEBTORS
ANONYMOU

BUT I HADN'T REALIZED WHAT AN UNSTOPPABLE MISSION SHE WAS ON.

DID YOU SEE MY NEW BAG? NO MORE **DEPRIVATION** FOR ME...

FROM NOW ON, IT'S **ABUNDANCE!**

THE PATH TO ALL OF HER CURRENT SUCCESS STARTED WITH BASIC **SOLVENCY:** NOT DEBTING ONE DAY AT A TIME.

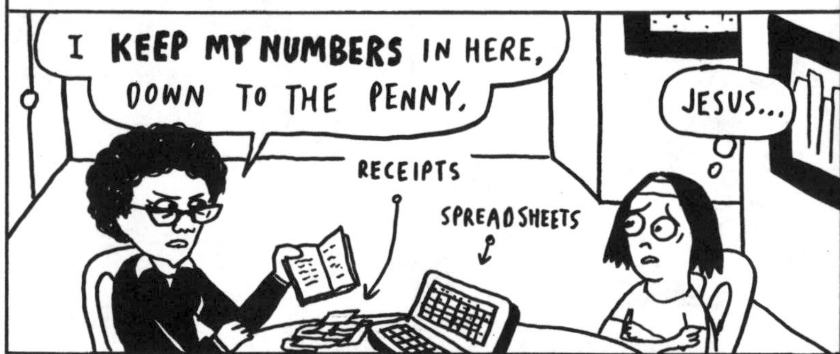
I **KEEP MY NUMBERS** IN HERE, DOWN TO THE PENNY.
RECEIPTS
SPREADSHEETS
JESUS...

THESE DA PRINCIPLES WERE CHARGED WITH DIVINE AUTHORITY FOR HER.

AND THEY REALLY SEEMED TO WORK!

THAT SUMMER, THERE WAS NO TIME FOR GRIEF. IF I COMPLAINED ABOUT BEING HEARTBROKEN OVER REBECCA, SHE COMPARED MY FEELINGS TO DRUG USE OR MASTURBATION.

YOU'RE NOT EVEN TRYING TO GET OVER HER. YOU'RE WALLOWING...

THIS IS WHAT LETTING GO LOOKS LIKE...

YOU **LET... GO!**

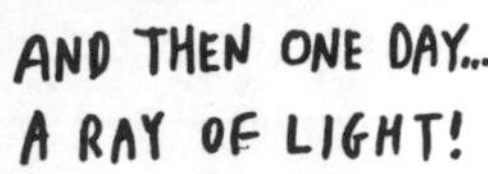
AND THEN ONE DAY... A RAY OF LIGHT!

RIIING

AFTER WEEKS OF CALLING MY MOM'S CORPORATE HEADHUNTER FRIENDS, I FINALLY BOOKED A TEMP GIG.

IT'S CALLED "THE LIGHTHOUSE." THEY'LL GIVE YOU $10 AN HOUR...

!!!

THEY'RE LIKE A NONPROFIT THAT SERVICES THE BLIND!
OH ANGEL, THAT'S GREAT NEWS!

IT TURNED OUT TO BE A CUSTOMER-SERVICE CALL CENTER IN LONG ISLAND CITY, QUEENS.

INDUSTRIAL HELLSCAPE

THE WORK WAS AWFUL.

I HAD TO ANSWER QUESTIONS FROM BLIND PEOPLE HAVING TROUBLE WITH THEIR MAIL-ORDER PRODUCTS.

REFUSED TO WEAR CUSTOMER-SERVICE HEADSET

MOST OF THEM WERE PISSED OFF. ONE GUY TAPPED A BROKEN PIECE OF HIS CANE AGAINST THE PHONE.
IT'S **THIS PIECE** THAT I NEED. RIGHT HERE!!! TAP! TAP! TAP! TAP!
SIR, I CAN'T SEE IT!

BY THE THIRD DAY, I WAS HANGING UP ON PEOPLE WHO ANNOYED ME.
CLICK!

BY THE SECOND WEEK, I STOLE AN EXPENSIVE TAPE RECORDER FROM THE PRODUCT WAREHOUSE* DURING MY LUNCH BREAK.

POUND
POUND
POUND
POUND
♫

BEFORE THE START OF THE THIRD WEEK I WAS FIRED.

WHAT?!?

A WEEK OF UNEMPLOYMENT FOLLOWED.

* YES, I WAS LITERALLY STEALING FROM THE BLIND.

AS MY JOB SEARCH FOUNDERED AND I SANK INTO A LOW-GRADE DEPRESSION, MOM RAMPED UP THE PRESSURE.
YOU KNOW WHO THIS REMINDS ME OF.

THIS IS REALLY A FAMILY DISEASE OF **UNDEREARNING** THAT YOU HAVE.

HONEY, PLEASE, TRY GOING TO A DA MEETING!

I PROMISE THEY CAN HELP YOU!

I STARTED THINKING ABOUT LIVING WITH MY FATHER INSTEAD.

BUT THE ONE TIME I SLEPT OVER CURED ME OF ANY ILLUSIONS ABOUT THAT PLAN.
SORRY, I DON'T HAVE ANY EXTRA SHEETS OR BLANKETS. HERE ARE SOME TOWELS.

I HAD TO SLEEP IN OUR BASEMENT.
IT WAS COLD.

HE HAD RENTED OUT OUR BEDROOMS TO AA NEWCOMERS SO HE COULD AFFORD THE MORTGAGE PAYMENTS.

KNOCK KNOCK
!

SORRY... FORGOT MY KEYS... CAN HE SLEEP HERE, TOO?
NEW TENANT, STUMBLING DRUNK

DAD!!!...

WHEN I GOT BACK TO MY MOM'S, VICTOR HAD ARRIVED.
HEY, BRO...

WITHIN A COUPLE DAYS, HE MADE A DIFFICULT LIVING SITUATION EVEN MORE UNBEARABLE.

DID YOU TOUCH MY BASS?!?

YOU NEED TO UNDERSTAND SOMETHING...

I'M AT A DIFFERENT LEVEL OF PROFESSIONALISM WITH MY MUSIC NOW. IT'S REALLY IMPORTANT THAT YOU DON'T TOUCH ANY OF MY STUFF!

I TRIED TO AVOID MY MOM, BUT WHENEVER I SAW HER...
... IT WAS THE "UNDEREARNER" NARRATIVE.
OVER AND OVER AND OVER.
SHE NEVER GAVE IN.
NO MATTER WHAT I SAID.
LEAVE ME ALONE!
FINALLY, I RELENTED.
FINE! I'LL GO TO ONE MEETING! ARE YOU HAPPY NOW?!?

SHE MUST HAVE THOUGHT SHE WAS SAVING MY LIFE, TERRIFIED I'D TURN INTO A DRUG ADDICT OR A DEADBEAT.

IF YOU'RE HAVING PROBLEMS WITH MONEY AND DEBT AND THINK YOU MAY BE A COMPULSIVE DEBTOR...

...YOU HAVE COME TO THE RIGHT PLACE AND WE CAN HELP YOU.

THE HOUR I SPENT AT MY FIRST **DA** MEETING WAS INTERMINABLE. THE VIBE WAS ANAL RETENTIVE, CONTROLLING, AND CORNY.

HA-HA
NOW KEEPING MY NUMBERS FEELS LIKE BRUSHING MY TEETH!
HA HA HA
HA HA

I HATED EVERYONE IN THE ROOM AND COULDN'T RELATE TO A WORD THEY SAID.

GOD... SHUT UP! ALL OF YOU!!!

WORSE, THE NIGHT I CHOSE HAPPENED TO BE A "BUSINESS MEETING."

THAT'S ALL THE TIME WE HAVE FOR SHARING. WE ENCOURAGE EVERYONE TO STICK AROUND UNTIL THE END OF THE HOUR.

I TRIED TO STICK IT OUT. IT WAS HARD TO FOLLOW THE FORMAT.*
I'LL ENTERTAIN A MOTION TO ACCEPT LAST MEETING'S MINUTES.
SO MOVED.

AFTER A TREASURY REPORT, IT WAS TIME FOR "OLD BUSINESS."
NOW WE'LL OPEN THE FLOOR TO DISCUSSION.

THE GROUP'S PREVIOUS TREASURER HAD STOLEN ALL THEIR MONEY.
WHAT THE FUCK?

I MAKE A MOTION THAT WE INVOLVE THE POLICE!
HOW?!? WE'RE ANONYMOUS!

IN MY OPINION, HE JUST HAS A REALLY BIG AMENDS TO MAKE WHEN HE'S READY.
THAT'S RIDICULOUS!
HE CAN'T JUST GET AWAY WITH STEALING FROM US!

* ROBERT'S RULES OF ORDER, A PARLIAMENTARY PROCEDURE

AS TEMPERS FLARED, THE CHAIRPERSON LOST CONTROL. IT FELT LIKE ONE OF MY PARENTS' LATE-NIGHT SCREAMING MATCHES.

!!!
!!
!!
!!!
!

EVERYONE, PLEASE! RAISE YOUR HAND AND WAIT TO BE RECOGNIZED.

WHAT KIND OF IDIOTS ASK A "COMPULSIVE DEBTOR" TO BE THEIR TREASURER?!?

I COULDN'T TAKE ANOTHER MINUTE!

POUND
POUND
POUND
POUND
POUND
THEY'RE ALL NUTS!

I GAVE MOM MY REPORT.

DAVID, PLEASE! YOU HAVE TO TRY AT LEAST SIX MEETINGS!

IT'S JUST NOT MY THING!

IT'S THE ONLY WAY TO REALLY GIVE THE PROGRAM A CHANCE...

NO WAY!!!

MAYBE THE FEAR OF HAVING TO GO TO THOSE MEETINGS WAS ENOUGH MOTIVATION FOR ME TO FIND WORK.

I'LL FIGURE THIS OUT MYSELF!

THE NEXT DAY, I COLD CALLED EVERY CARPENTRY SHOP IN THE PHONE BOOK, STARTING WITH "A."

BY THE TIME I GOT TO "C," I HAD FOUND SOMEONE TO HIRE ME.

AROUND THE SAME TIME, VICTOR FOUND AN APARTMENT IN BROOKLYN.*

HE AND OUR CAMP FRIEND GERRY HAD ENOUGH FOR THE SECOND DEPOSIT IF I COULD SCRAPE TOGETHER A MONTH'S RENT.

IT'S A HUGE THREE BEDROOM! MY BUDDY LIVES ACROSS THE HALL...

* LUKE WAS LIVING THE COLLEGE LIFE ON A BUCOLIC CAMPUS IN VIRGINIA.

THE NEIGHBORHOOD WAS ROUGH.

THE KITCHEN HAD VISIBLE ROACH AND RAT TRAPS.

AND MY BROTHER WAS AN ASSHOLE.

I WAFFLED FOR A FEW DAYS.

MAYBE I SHOULD STAY HERE A LITTLE LONGER AND SAVE UP FOR MY OWN PLACE...?

OH ANGEL... MAYBE IT WON'T BE SO BAD.

I FEEL LIKE I REALLY NEED TO HAVE THIS PLACE TO MYSELF NOW.

THAT SETTLED IT. I MOVED OUT.

FOR THE NEXT TWO YEARS I WAS VERY POOR.

I MADE ABOUT $200 PER WEEK DOING BACKBREAKING WORK.

I LIVED OFF DOLLAR SLICES OF PIZZA.

SAWDUST

AND THE LEFTOVER SANDWICHES GERRY BROUGHT HOME FROM HIS JOB AT STARBUCKS.

A FRIEND OF MINE GOT MUGGED IN FRONT OF OUR BUILDING ONCE.

FUCK!
I'M SO SORRY!

WE HAD CRACK VIALS IN OUR STAIRWELL.

BUT I LEARNED CARPENTRY.
AND I HAD SPACE TO PAINT.
AND MAKE MUSIC.
AND SMOKE WEED ONCE IN A WHILE.
WHATEVER MY MOM THOUGHT OF THE WAY I CHOSE TO LIVE...
...SHE LEFT ME IN PEACE.

REBECCA GRADUATED FROM OBERLIN IN 1996 AND WE FELL BACK IN LOVE.

THERE'S NOTHING SWEET IN MY LIFE WITHOUT YOU.

WE MADE PLANS TO LIVE TOGETHER.

I HAD COBBLED TOGETHER ENOUGH PAINTINGS, DRAWINGS, AND COMIC STRIPS TO APPLY TO ART SCHOOLS.

MY FIRST CHOICE WAS SAN FRANCISCO ART INSTITUTE.

I GOT ACCEPTED!
YAY!

WE STAYED IN NEW JERSEY FOR A SUMMER.

'BYE!
VROOM!

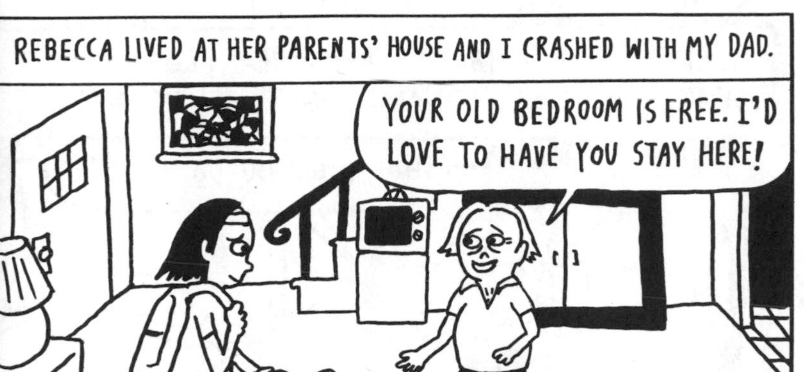
REBECCA LIVED AT HER PARENTS' HOUSE AND I CRASHED WITH MY DAD.
YOUR OLD BEDROOM IS FREE. I'D LOVE TO HAVE YOU STAY HERE!

I TRIED WORKING AT AN ART-SUPPLY STORE.
WHEN WILL THIS DAY BE OVER?

BUT I RESENTED THE CUSTOMERS AND STOLE.
I SHOULD BE SHOPPING HERE, NOT WORKING HERE! I'M AN ARTIST!

JUST THIS ONE RAPIDOGRAPH PEN...

I SWITCHED TO A CARPENTRY SHOP IN SOUTH HACKENSACK THAT I FOUND IN THE PHONE BOOK.

THEY SPECIALIZED IN MAKING COUNTER-TOPS FOR BANKS AND CHURCHES.
YOU KNOW HOW TO USE THE SPRAY GUN?

REBECCA STILL HAD $3,000 SAVED FROM THE SUMMER BEFORE. IT WAS A HUGE SAFETY NET.

HOW DID YOU DO THAT?!?

INSTEAD OF WORKING, SHE VOLUNTEERED AT A NONPROFIT FOR PRISON REFORM. I ENVIED HER FREEDOM.

MOST NIGHTS SHE SLEPT OVER IN MY ROOM.

IN THE MORNING SHE MADE ME A HOT BREAKFAST.

AND SHE DROVE ME TO AND FROM WORK WITHOUT COMPLAINT.

YOU'RE A GOOD WIFEY.
HA.
CHOMP
CHOMP

I FOUND SOME JOY IN CLOCKING IN FOR AN HONEST DAY'S WORK.

CLASSIC ROCK

I ONLY STOLE ONE "PLAYBOY" FROM A CO-WORKER.

HE'S A RACIST ANYWAY.

MY PAY WAS $240 PER WEEK. MY ONLY REAL EXPENSE WAS FOOD.

BUT I STILL HAD TROUBLE SAVING FOR OUR BIG MOVE.

WHICH COMIC BOOK SHOULD I BUY?!? I WORK SO HARD... I DESERVE THEM BOTH!

AT THE END OF THE SUMMER, I WAS SHORT ON MY HALF.

WHAT HAVE YOU BEEN SPENDING IT ON?!?

I DON'T NEED YOU MICROMANAGING ME!!!

AS LUCK WOULD HAVE IT, I GOT AN UN-EXPECTED TAX REFUND IN THE MAIL.

IT BROUGHT ME UP TO THE AMOUNT I HAD PROMISED TO SAVE.
SEE? IT ALL WORKED OUT!

IN EARLY AUGUST, WE SHAVED OUR HEADS. REBECCA'S PARENTS GAVE US ONE OF THEIR CARS.

EEK!
ARE YOU **SURE?!?**
THAN
YOU!

WE LOADED IT UP AND DROVE ACROSS THE COUNTRY.

WE PLANNED TO STAY WITH FRIENDS OR SLEEP IN OUR TENT AT CAMPSITES.

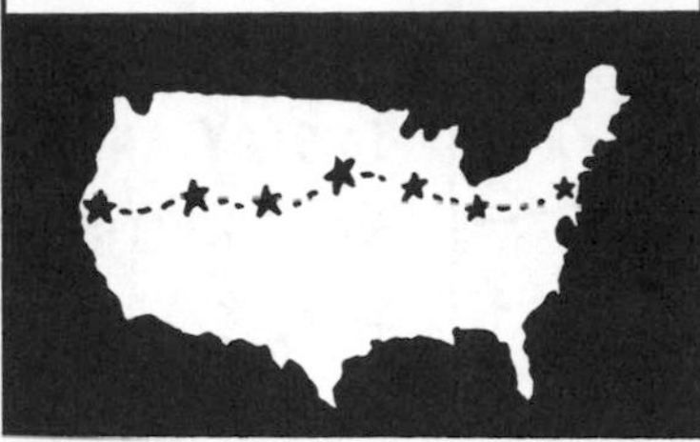

WE ALMOST BROKE UP IN IOWA CITY.

I'M GONNA STAY UP AND TALK WITH MARK...
!

DO YOU STILL HAVE FEELINGS FOR HIM?

MAYBE. I'M NOT SURE.

IF YOU DO, IT'S FINE! I CAN TAKE A BUS THE REST OF THE WAY.

NO PROBLEM!

WE SURVIVED AND KEPT GOING AND THAT'S WHEN THE COUNTRY GOT BEAUTIFUL.

BADLANDS

YELLOWSTONE

WHEN WE GOT TO NEVADA, WE HADN'T YET FOUND A PLACE TO STAY AND IT WAS STARTING TO GET DARK.

THERE WAS A CAMPGROUND ON THE MAP A FEW MILES AWAY FROM US.

BUT THE WHOLE DRIVE WAS HAIRPIN TURNS ON THE SIDE OF A CLIFF.

DAVE, MAYBE WE SHOULD TURN AROUND.

WHERE?!? THE ROAD IS BASICALLY ONE LANE!

I KEPT DRIVING UP.
DAVE, I'M REALLY SCARED!
WE'RE FINE!

AT THE TOP, THERE WAS ONE CAMPSITE LEFT– CLOSE TO THE CLIFF'S EDGE.

IT'S TOO WINDY!

DAVE, I'M SCARED WE'RE GOING TO BLOW OFF THE SIDE OF THE MOUNTAIN.

I WENT TO SLEEP.

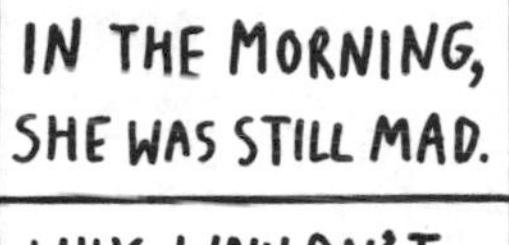
IN THE MORNING, SHE WAS STILL MAD.

WHY WOULDN'T YOU LISTEN TO ME?

BUT WHEN WE STEPPED OUT OF THE TENT, WE SAW ONE OF THE MOST SPECTACULAR VIEWS OF OUR LIVES!
OH MY GOD!

A DAY LATER WE WERE CROSSING INTO CALIFORNIA.
Welcome to California
SIERRA COUNTY

IT WAS STRANGE AND GORGEOUS AND WILD, AND WE BOTH FELT FREE.

THIS WAS WHERE WE WERE GOING TO PLANT OURSELVES

AND REALLY GROW.

HOMER
DAVID
4
NEVER SEEMS TO GET OLD♫
♫ OUR KINDA LOVE
LIMITED
25% OFF

1997-2000

I WAS HUNGRY FOR SCHOOL. FOR THREE YEARS STRAIGHT I WORKED LIKE CRAZY AND GOT ALL A'S.

MY SCHOOL LIFE AND HOME LIFE WERE ALMOST COMPLETELY SEPARATE.

REBECCA AND I HAD SETTLED IN THE EAST BAY. WE HAD OBERLIN FRIENDS NEARBY.

OAKLAND
SCHOOL

MOST WEEKENDS WE COOKED WITH THEM AND WATCHED MOVIES.

SCALLION PANCAKES

BARBARELLA

AND WE SMOKED PLENTY OF BAY AREA WEED.

ANYONE FOR SECONDS?

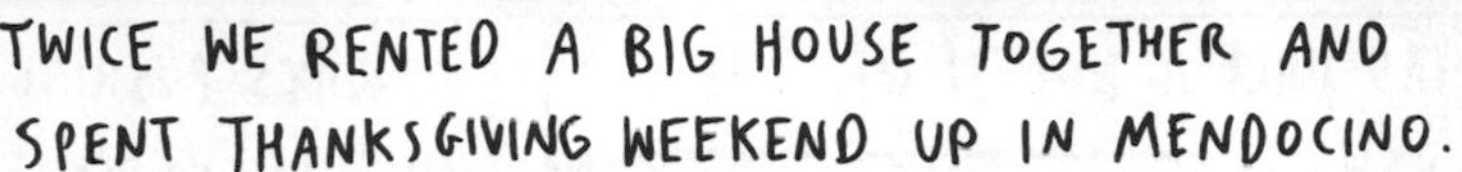
TWICE WE RENTED A BIG HOUSE TOGETHER AND SPENT THANKSGIVING WEEKEND UP IN MENDOCINO.

I NEVER WANT TO GO HOME.

DESPITE THE IDYLLIC BACKDROP, REBECCA AND I HAD A FIGHT THAT ALMOST ENDED US.

THEY SHOULD BE ABLE TO TELL WHICH ONE OF US IS YOUR GIRLFRIEND!

I HAD A WANDERING EYE, BUT IT WAS MORE THAN THAT.

SHE'S SO PERFECT...

I WANTED TO BE **EVERYONE'S** BOYFRIEND.

IT WAS BARELY SEXUAL. I FELT A DESPERATE, COMPULSIVE NEED TO BE A "SAFE" GUY FOR WOMEN TO TRUST.

LIZ'S BOYFRIEND IS GETTING VIOLENT! I TOLD HER SHE COULD SLEEP HERE TONIGHT...

I WANTED TO PROTECT THEM.

I HAD HALF A DOZEN OF THESE CRUSHES.
I FOUND THE PICTURES YOU TOOK WITH JAMIE— MAKING EYES AT EACH OTHER.

ALWAYS PUSHING MYSELF CLOSER TO THE LINE.

YOU'RE IMAGINING THINGS!

I'M SLEEPING AT CATHERINE'S.
WHAT?!?

WE BOTH DID THERAPY, BUT IT WASN'T HELPING US AS A COUPLE.
YOU'RE ALWAYS THWARTING ME!
I ALWAYS FEEL STEAMROLLED!

PART OF THE PROBLEM WAS MONEY. WHENEVER IT WAS TIME TO PAY OUR BILLS, I WAS SHORT.

I GUESS I CAN COVER YOU AGAIN.
I'LL PAY YOU NEXT WEEK.

IT WAS HUMILIATING.

THANKS, HONEY.

THE TRUTH WAS I HAD CHOSEN A SCHOOL I COULDN'T REALLY AFFORD.

MY STUDENT LOAN WAS MASSIVE.
I'M GOING NO MATTER WHAT!
BARELY READING PAPERWORK
PUTTING MYSELF DEEP IN DEBT

MY DAD TOOK OUT A PARENT LOAN TO HELP ME, BUT HE USED IT TO PAY HIS MORTGAGE THEN SENT ME WHAT WAS LEFT OVER.

WHEN ARE YOU SENDING THE CHECK?

IT WAS ALWAYS LATE.

WHY DOES HE SPEND $20 TO OVERNIGHT ME A CHECK I CAN'T CASH?!?

Don't deposit until I tell you.

SCRAWLED QUICKLY ON GARBAGE FOUND AT THE POST OFFICE

MY MOM WOULDN'T SEND ME ANY MONEY ON PRINCIPLE.

RRRING!

SHE HAD COVERED LUKE'S COLLEGE BILL AND MY DAD WAS SUPPOSED TO COVER MINE.

BEYOND THAT, I SENSED SHE WAS PRACTICING TOUGH LOVE BASED ON AL-ANON. SHE WOULDN'T "RESCUE" ME.

ANGEL, I FEEL **SURE** THAT YOU CAN EARN ALL YOU NEED TO TAKE CARE OF YOURSELF.

I **HATE** YOU!

SHE TREATS ME LIKE I'M AN **ADDICT** TRYING TO MOOCH OFF HER!

I CALLED LUKE A LOT THAT YEAR TO COMMISERATE. HE HAD RECENTLY TOLD ME HE WAS GAY.

MAYBE YOU SHOULD MOVE OUT HERE!

IT WAS A MUCH NEEDED DISTRACTION HAVING HIM LIVE WITH US.
WELCOME TO GAY MECCA!
LATE '90s LUKE
BUT ONCE HE GOT HIS OWN PLACE, THE FIGHTING WITH REBECCA RESUMED.
SOB SOB SOB
I DON'T EVEN KNOW WHAT WE'RE FIGHTING ABOUT ANYMORE!
4:00AM
A FEW WEEKS OF DAILY FIGHTS LED UP TO MY WINTER BREAK.
I DON'T THINK I WANT TO GO HOME FOR CHRISTMAS.
I'LL GO BY MYSELF!
WE PLANNED TO CHECK IN EACH DAY BY PHONE.
SAFE FLIGHT.
I STOPPED CALLING AFTER CHRISTMAS AND THEN MADE OUT WITH AN OLD FLAME FROM OBERLIN.
ARE YOU SURE YOU WANT TO DO THIS?
YEAH... REBECCA AND I ARE PROBABLY BREAKING UP.
WE BOTH TOOK MUSCLE RELAXERS

THE LEAD-UP WAS THRILLING.

POUND
POUND
POUND
POUND
POUND

BUT ONCE I CROSSED THE LINE, ALL I WANTED TO DO WAS GO BACK TO THE OTHER SIDE AGAIN.

I FELT HOLLOW AND SAD AND FULL OF REMORSE.
GOOD NIGHT...

CONFESSING AS SOON AS I GOT BACK BROUGHT EVERYTHING TO A HEAD.

REBECCA WAS HURT AND ANGRY, BUT SHE KNEW THINGS HADN'T BEEN RIGHT BETWEEN US FOR A WHILE.

WE NEED HELP.

NEITHER OF US LOVED THE IDEA OF COUPLES THERAPY.

HOW FUCKED UP ARE WE THAT WE BOTH NEED THERAPY TWICE A WEEK?!?
I KNOW!

BUT IT TURNED OUT TO BE THE BEST DECISION WE COULD HAVE MADE.

WE SAW A GRADUATE STUDENT (NAMED REBEKAH) FOR A SLIDING-SCALE FEE.

FIVE YEARS OLDER THAN US

TRUST SLOWLY RETURNED.

"POST-THERAPY HUG"

WITH REBEKAH'S ENCOURAGEMENT WE TOOK THE STEP OF COMBINING OUR BANK ACCOUNTS.

THIS TERRIFIES ME!
IT MAKES ME FEEL SAFE.
ATM

WE PAID ALL OUR BILLS AS A COUPLE. NO MORE DEBT BETWEEN US.

I WORKED AT REINING IN ALL MY CRUSHES AND FANTASIES.

YOU ALREADY HAVE A GIRLFRIEND!

I ALSO TRIED TO BE MORE SUPPORTIVE OF REBECCA'S WRITING.

DURING MY LAST YEAR AT ART SCHOOL...

I WANT TO GO TO GRAD SCHOOL.

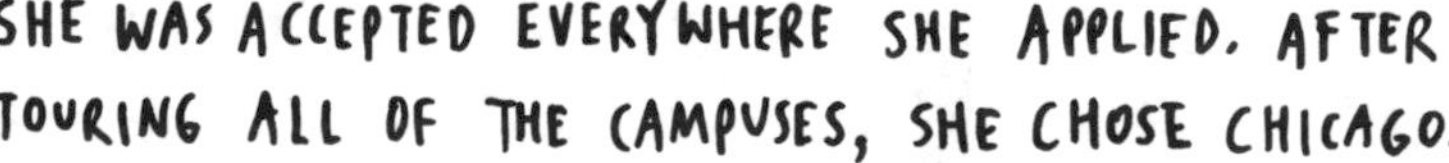
SHE WAS ACCEPTED EVERYWHERE SHE APPLIED. AFTER TOURING ALL OF THE CAMPUSES, SHE CHOSE CHICAGO.

WOW... THIS IS A **CITY!**

WE PLANNED ON ANOTHER CROSS-COUNTRY DRIVE. THIS TIME I NOT ONLY STUCK TO MY SAVINGS GOAL, I SURPASSED IT.
THAT TEMP AGENCY SAYS I CAN MAKE $25 AN HOUR!!!
WOWEE ZOWEE!
TWICE WHAT I WAS CURRENTLY MAKING

I CHEERFULLY DROVE THREE HOURS ROUND TRIP FROM OAKLAND TO SANTA CLARA EACH DAY UNTIL WE MOVED.
I'M THE BREADWINNER NOW!
LASSIC
OCK!
SAN MATEO BRIDGE

WE SAID OUR GOODBYES TO OUR FRIENDS. AND LUKE.

AND WE WENT IN FOR ONE LAST THERAPY SESSION.
YOU GUYS SHOULD REALLY THINK ABOUT GETTING MARRIED!
!
!

2000-2002

SOON AFTER WE MOVED TO CHICAGO, I SCORED AN INTERVIEW AT A TWO-PERSON AD AGENCY.

I NEED SOMEONE TWO DAYS A WEEK.

SHE LIKED MY PORTFOLIO. I ASKED ABOUT THE PAY.

ABOUT $50 OR $60 AN HOUR.
!

I PLAYED IT COOL.

THAT WORKS. SHOULD WE SAY $55?

I WOULD START NEXT WEEK!

I CAN COVER MY HALF OF OUR BILLS WORKING TWO DAYS A WEEK!!!

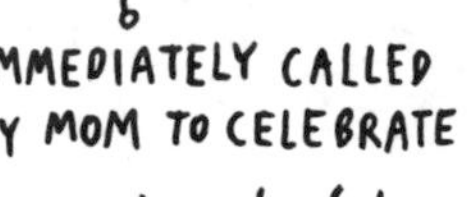
IMMEDIATELY CALLED MY MOM TO CELEBRATE

THAT'S GREAT, ANGEL! AND REMEMBER: AS FAST AS YOU JUMPED FROM $25 TO $55, YOU CAN DO THE SAME JUMP AGAIN... TO $100 OR MORE!

DON'T LIMIT YOURSELF! THE UNIVERSE IS SO ABUNDANT AND WANTS US TO HAVE MORE THAN WE CAN COMPREHEND!

I HUNG UP FEELING COMPLETELY DEFLATED AND REGRETTED CALLING HER AT ALL.

REBECCA WAS SYMPATHETIC.

SHE MADE IT SEEM LIKE I'M SETTLING BUT IT'S SO MUCH MONEY! AND THE POINT IS I'LL HAVE TIME TO MAKE ART!

I KNOW!

WHY DOES SHE ALWAYS HAVE TO COMPETE WITH ME?!?

I TRIED TO SHRUG IT OFF AND ENJOY MY EXCITEMENT.

I WAS SUDDENLY LIVING A CHARMED LIFE IN A NEW CITY.

I HAD A GIRL WHO LOVED ME, A CUSHY, HIGH-PAYING JOB, AND TONS OF FREE TIME.

HAVE YOU EVER DESIGNED A "BUCK SLIP"?

NO...

FOR A SHORT WHILE, I WAS HAPPY AND PRODUCTIVE.

IT'S EASY. I'LL SHOW YOU.
WHEW

AND THEN I SLOWLY GOT MORE AND MORE MISERABLE.

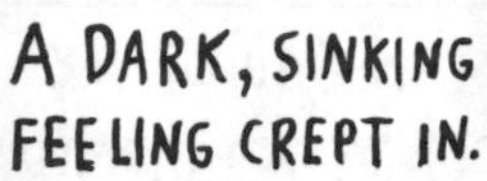
A DARK, SINKING FEELING CREPT IN.

FUCK...

AND IT ROTTED MY ATTITUDE.

WHY DO I HAVE TO GO TO THIS STUPID JOB?!?

LIKE A DISEASE.

GOOD MORNING!
GOD, I HATE YOU.

BEFORE LONG, I COULD FEEL THAT MY BOSS DIDN'T WANT ME AROUND BUT FELT STUCK WITH ME.

I DIDN'T WANT TO BE THERE EITHER, BUT COULDN'T RESIST THE MONEY. I FELT LIKE A SEX WORKER.

WHAT ELSE COULD I DO THAT WOULD PAY THIS WELL?
YOUR CABLE BILL

PART OF THE PROBLEM WAS THAT I SPENT MONEY LIKE I WAS RICH.

I WANT THIS SO BADLY...

I DESERVE IT!

POUND
POUND
POUND

$50 IMPORTED HARDCOVER BOOK

WILL THAT BE ALL, SIR?

CAN I SEE THE DESSERT MENU?

I CLUNG SO TIGHTLY TO THE NARRATIVE IN MY MIND.

I ONLY HAVE TO WORK TWO DAYS A WEEK!

WHAT?!?

BUT OUR BANK ACCOUNT WAS ALMOST ALWAYS AT ZERO OR IN OVERDRAFT. IT JUST DIDN'T ADD UP.

ANY TIME REBECCA TRIED TO GO OVER OUR BILLS, AN ITCHY, IRRITABLE HATRED WOULD RISE UP IN ME—THAT FEELING OF BEING "PUT UPON."

YOU EITHER HAVE TO EARN MORE OR SPEND LESS!

I WOULDN'T DO EITHER. I LOST MYSELF IN DRAWING COMICS.

AND WATCHING PORN.

DIAL-UP MODEM

EVEN THAT WAS FRUSTRATING. I COULD NEVER FIND WHAT I WANTED TO SEE.

UGH...
hot bitch gets her tight cunt fucked
slut wants big cock to fill her wet hole

EVERYTHING WAS SILICONE TITS AND SHAVED PUSSIES AND BAD ACTING.

EVEN THOUGH WE HAD LEFT CALIFORNIA WITH THOUGHTS OF MARRIAGE BEGINNING TO STIR, IT STILL FELT LIKE A DISTANT, ABSTRACT CONCEPT.

BIG ROCK?
TUX?
TRAIN?
HAWAII?

IT HADN'T OCCURRED TO ME THAT REBECCA HAD BEEN WAITING FOR ME TO ASK.

15-HOUR DRIVE HOME

SHE'D BEEN HOPING THAT CHRISTMAS WOULD BE THE DAY.

MY BROTHER VICTOR HAD ASKED HIS GIRLFRIEND IN FRONT OF US THE YEAR BEFORE. NOW THEY WERE IN THEIR FIRST YEAR OF MARRIAGE.

THERE'S ONE MORE PRESENT...

SHOW OFF!

CHOKE

I RESENTED THE UNSPOKEN PRESSURE TO COPY HIM.

HOW LONG WERE THEY DATING AGAIN?

SO INSTEAD OF A RING, I BOUGHT REBECCA A SILKSCREEN POSTER AND CD FOR A BAND SHE DIDN'T LIKE THAT MUCH.

HER DISAPPOINTMENT WAS OBVIOUS TO ALL.

LATER IN THE DAY, I TALKED TO MY MOM ABOUT MY DOUBTS.

I JUST DON'T WANT TO MAKE THE WRONG CHOICE AND WIND UP DIVORCED...
DAVE, YOU AND REBECCA HAVE SOMETHING THAT YOUR FATHER AND I **NEVER** HAD.

SHE'LL MAKE A LOYAL AND LOVING WIFE!
WOW.

IT WAS SO HELPFUL. SOMETIMES MOM REALLY CAME THROUGH FOR ME.

THAT NIGHT, REBECCA AND I WENT FOR A LONG WALK.
I DON'T WANT TO WAIT FOREVER, YOU KNOW...

SHE LOOKED SO SWEET.

WHAT IS WRONG WITH YOU? OF COURSE YOU WANT TO MARRY HER. YOU'RE JUST SCARED!

BACK AT MY MOM'S HOUSE, WITH EVERYONE ASLEEP, WE WENT UP TO THE GUEST BEDROOM.

I GOT DOWN ON ONE KNEE.
REBECCA, WILL YOU MARRY ME?
DO YOU MEAN IT?
LET'S DO IT.
YES! OF COURSE!

WE MADE LOVE LIKE TEEN-AGERS THAT NIGHT. EVERY-THING WAS CHARGED, ALIVE, NEW!

AMID THE RING SHOPPING AND WEDDING PLANNING, I FELT AN URGENT NEED TO MAKE SOMETHING HAPPEN WITH MY ART.

JEWELR

WITH SOME PERSISTENCE AND RIDING A WAVE OF CONFIDENCE, I GOT MYSELF INTO TWO GALLERY SHOWS AND SOLD A COUPLE OF PAINTINGS.

I ALSO LANDED A REGULAR ILLUSTRATION GIG AT A FREE WEEKLY NEWSPAPER, AND I GOT SOME NICE RESPONSES TO MY COMICS FROM A FEW CARTOONISTS I ADMIRED.

REBECCA WAS BUSY CHURNING OUT STORIES, POEMS, AND PHOTOS, CULMINATING IN AN ART INSTALLATION AT HER COLLEGE GALLERY.

SHE MADE A NUMBER OF NEW FRIENDS AT SCHOOL AND OUR SOCIAL LIVES EXPANDED.

BY MIDSUMMER WE FLEW OFF FOR OUR WEDDING IN NYC AND OUR HONEYMOON IN ITALY, PAID FOR BY OUR FAMILY AND FRIENDS.

OUR HEARTS WERE FULL TO BURSTING WHEN WE GOT BACK TO CHICAGO IN THE FALL.

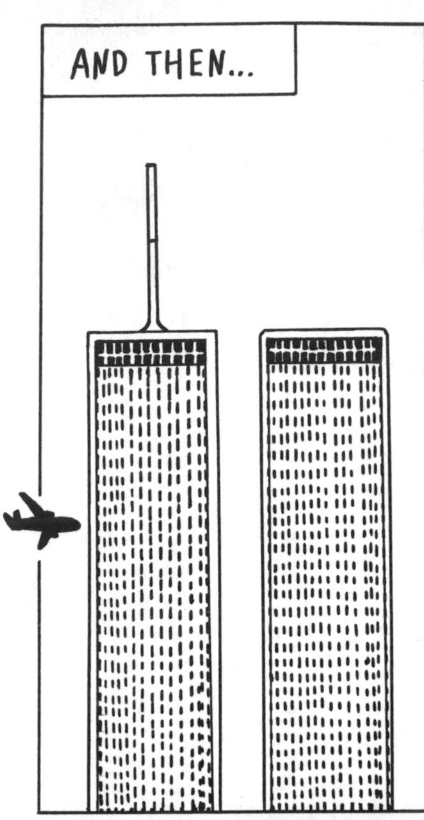
AND THEN...

...SUDDENLY NOTHING MADE ANY SENSE.

'M GONNA FLY... I'M GONNA
REACH MY DESTINATION
NO ONE'S GONNA
STOP ME...
UNTIL...
I REACH THE SKY ♪
5

2002

WE WERE NUMB FOR DAYS, WEEKS. REBECCA HAD CLASSES TO KEEP HER OCCUPIED.
SEE YOU TONIGHT.
BYE.

BUT I HAD RETURNED HOME WITHOUT A JOB.
Monster.com

BEFORE WE LEFT FOR NEW YORK, I HAD TOLD MY BOSS ABOUT OUR WEDDING AND ASKED FOR A MONTH OFF.
I'M SORRY ... I REALLY NEED SOMEONE HERE THAT MONTH. I'LL HAVE TO FIND SOMEONE ELSE.
WHAT?!?

FROM REBECCA'S EXTENDED FAMILY AND CLOSE FRIENDS WE HAULED IN ABOUT $9,000 - A FORTUNE TO ME.
CAN'T WE JUST USE SOME WEDDING MONEY?
PAYING BILLS
WE SHOULD BE SAVING **ALL** OF IT!

I THOUGHT OF IT AS A CUSHION, AN INVESTMENT IN MY FUTURE AS A "PROFESSIONAL" ARTIST.

OVER THE NEXT FOUR MONTHS, WE WENT THROUGH $7,000 TO COVER OUR LIVING EXPENSES.

YOU KNEW YOU WERE MARRYING AN ARTIST! I WANT TO DO THIS FULL-TIME! WHY DON'T YOU SUPPORT ME?!?

REBECCA WAS EXASPERATED!

I JUST WANT YOU TO PUT OUR **BASIC SECURITY** FIRST!

SHE TOOK THE LAST $2,000 AND PUT IT IN AN IRA SO WE WOULDN'T SPEND IT.

I OPENED A CREDIT CARD TO SELF-PUBLISH MY FIRST COMIC BOOK.

WHY AREN'T YOU EXCITED FOR ME?!?

WE CAN BARELY PAY OUR RENT!!!

IT WASN'T LONG BEFORE WE WERE USING IT TO BUY GROCERIES, TOO.

SIR, THIS WAS DECLINED...
TRY THIS ONE...?

OUR FIGHTING GOT BAD AGAIN, AND I COULD SEE IT WAS MY FAULT.

WHAT'S WRONG WITH ME?

I FELT AN UNMOVABLE UNWILLINGNESS IN MY HEART AND IT STARTED TO SCARE ME.

DESPERATE, I CALLED MY DAD FOR ADVICE.
GET OUT A PIECE OF PAPER AND WRITE DOWN FIVE THINGS YOU COULD DO FOR WORK.
THIS IS ACTUALLY PRETTY HELPFUL

BUT THEN HE CAME OUT WITH THIS:
ART IS A WONDERFUL THING, BUT WHEN IT TURNS TO **ADDICTION** YOU NEED TO BE CAREFUL!
SIGH
DROP

UGH! I GUESS BOTH OF MY PARENTS THINK I'M AN ADDICT!

THE NEXT DAY I REMEMBERED THAT THE AGENCY THAT FOUND ME WORK IN SAN FRANCISCO HAD AN OFFICE IN CHICAGO. I MADE AN APPOINTMENT.

WE HAVE A "TEMP-TO-PERM" AT A TEXT-BOOK PUBLISHER IN EVANSTON.

SOUNDS GREAT!

CLACK CLACK CLACK

THE DAYS WERE DREADFULLY LONG. THERE WAS NOTHING TO DO.

GUESS I'LL CHECK MY EMAIL AGAIN.

YAWN

OR MAYBE I'LL CALL LUKE. IT'S BEEN A WHILE.

WE TALKED FOR ALMOST AN HOUR. I TOLD HIM HOW I FELT STUCK IN MY WORK LIFE. HE WAS UPBEAT, ENERGIZED, FULL OF FAITH IN GOD AND "THE UNIVERSE."

CLACK CLACK CLACK CLACK
DAVE, YOU HAVE LIMITLESS POTENTIAL!
CLACK CLACK CLACK

YOUR FISTS ARE SO TIGHTLY CLOSED, READY TO FIGHT.

HOW DID HE GET SO WISE AND CONFIDENT? WHERE WAS THIS COMING FROM?*

JUST OPEN YOUR HANDS UP A TINY BIT AND SEE WHAT STARTS TO FLOW IN...

CLACK CLACK CLACK

CLACK CLACK CLACK CLACK CLACK CLACK CLACK

* HE WAS SAYING THINGS MY MOM ALWAYS SAID BUT I HEARD IT DIFFERENTLY.

YOU'VE FIGURED OUT A LOT IN YOUR 26 YEARS. YOU'RE SMART.

BUT I THINK YOU NEED TO BE OPEN TO THE MYSTERIES OF LIFE.

THE FORCES THAT ARE **UNSEEN!**

I ENVIED THE CLARITY OF HIS MESSAGE AND HIS WHOLEHEARTED BELIEF, SOMETHING I HADN'T FELT SINCE I WAS A CHILD.

I CALLED HIM AGAIN THE NEXT DAY.

I GUESS WHAT I'M SAYING IS RESONATING!

I ALSO CHECKED IN WITH MY DAD.

I'M QUITE INTERESTED IN HIS SPIRITUAL AWAKENING!

BUT MY MOM COULD SENSE SOMETHING WAS OFF.

I'M PRETTY WORRIED...

THE THIRD TIME I CALLED, I STARTED TO WORRY, TOO.
LUKE, WHEN DID YOU START FEELING YOUR NEW-FOUND FAITH?

I DON'T KNOW. IT MIGHT BE ALL THESE FLUORESCENT LIGHTS OUT HERE.

THEY MIGHT HAVE BEAMED THE MESSAGES INTO MY HEAD...

HE WAS SERIOUS.
OH FUCK. WHAT'S HAPPENING TO HIM?!?
POUND
POUND
POUND
POUND

MY MOM TOOK OVER AND CALLED HIM TWICE A DAY.

IT CAME OUT THAT HE HAD BEEN TAKING ECSTASY AND SMOKING LARGE AMOUNTS OF POT EVERY DAY, INCLUDING AT WORK.

WHEN SHE SUGGESTED HE MIGHT NEED TO SEE A DOCTOR, LUKE SCREAMED AT HER.

LUCKILY, HE WOULD BE COMING TO NEW YORK THAT WEEK FOR A TECH CONFERENCE AND WAS STAYING WITH HER.

HE WAS SUPPOSED TO DEMO SOFTWARE AT THE COMPANY BOOTH.

INSTEAD HE GAVE AN IMPROMPTU TALK ABOUT 9/11 AND OSAMA BIN LADEN, INTERWOVEN WITH HIS PERSONAL BRAND OF SPIRITUALITY.

WHEN HIS SUPERVISOR TRIED TO INTERVENE, LUKE YELLED AT THE TOP OF HIS LUNGS IN FRONT OF A CROWD OF PEOPLE.

MY DAD MET MY MOM AT HER PLACE THAT NIGHT.

WHEN LUKE ARRIVED...

THEY TALKED HIM INTO COMMITTING HIMSELF...
AT THE NEARBY PSYCHIATRIC HOSPITAL.

AFTER LUKE WAS BRIEFLY HOSPITALIZED, IT WAS DECIDED THAT HE WOULD LIVE WITH MY MOM FOR A WHILE.

MOM TOLD MY HR LADY, "YOU'RE DEALING WITH **ME** NOW!" SHE GOT ME SIX MONTHS' SEVERANCE!

GIDDY

THAT'S GREAT, LUKE!

AND COMPLETELY AWFUL!

I CAME TO VISIT A MONTH LATER...

WOW. HE'S GAINED A LOT OF WEIGHT!

HE SEEMED MOSTLY NORMAL, BUT STILL SAID A FEW STRANGE THINGS.

I WANT TO WRITE A THESIS ABOUT LORD OF THE RINGS AND TALK ABOUT HOW THE RINGS SYMBOLIZE ME
BUTTHOLES
HA
HA

WE TALKED ABOUT HIS UNFINISHED BUSINESS IN S.F.

I STILL HAVE TO MOVE OUT OF MY APARTMENT AND DEAL WITH MY CAR.

HMMM...

A TRIP TO CALIFORNIA SOUNDED GOOD TO ME. I VOLUNTEERED TO HELP HIM.

LUKE CONVINCED MY MOM THAT HE WAS OKAY TO GO ALONE.
DAVE CAN FLY OUT A FEW DAYS AFTER I GET PACKED AND THEN WE CAN DRIVE ACROSS THE COUNTRY TOGETHER.
SURE!

MAYBE THIS WILL CLEAR MY HEAD, AND I'LL COME HOME READY TO GET A JOB.

WHAT FOLLOWED WAS THE MOST HARROWING WEEK OF MY LIFE.

FROM THE MOMENT I SAW LUKE AT THE AIRPORT, I KNEW SOMETHING WAS OFF.
LET ME GET THAT BAG FOR YOU!
SHAVED
HE LOOKED LIKE HE HAD AGED TEN YEARS.

HE HAD EITHER STOPPED TAKING HIS MEDS OR STARTED DOING DRUGS OR BOTH.
I LOVE THIS SONG!
♫ I'M GONNA FLY. I'M GONNA REACH MY DESTI
INCREDIBLY LOUD, NONDESCRIPT DANCE MUSIC

CHOKE SOB
SOB SOB SOB SOB
?

INSTEAD OF GOING TO HIS HOUSE, LUKE INSISTED ON GETTING A CAR WASH AND SHOPPING FOR A GOODBYE PARTY HE WAS THROWING HIMSELF.
IT'S CALLED ABUNDANCE!
INSANE AMOUNT OF FOOD
WHEN WE GOT BACK TO LUKE'S PLACE, I FELT SPOOKED. IT WAS A DARK, CREEPY BASEMENT APARTMENT.
YOU CAN SLEEP IN HERE. MY ROOMMATE'S AWAY.
I NOTICED LUKE HADN'T EVEN STARTED PACKING.
I'M BUSY SAYING GOODBYE TO FRIENDS.
OVER THE COURSE OF THE DAY, THINGS WORSENED BETWEEN US.
LUKE HEARD VOICES, SCREAMED AND CURSED TO HIMSELF IN THE SHOWER. IT WAS TERRIFYING.
NO! YOU ARE, YOU GODDAMN PIECE OF SHIT
HE SOUNDS JUST LIKE DAD...

I FELT WEIRD SLEEPING IN A STRANGER'S BED. THE SHEETS DIDN'T FEEL CLEAN. I BARELY SLEPT.
GIANT BOTTLE OF LUBE

LUKE WAS UP ALL NIGHT, TOO.
I THINK I'M BEING POSSESSED BY MY ROOMMATE'S DEAD LITTLE SISTER.

THE MORE I WORRIED, THE ANGRIER HE GOT.

I'M HAVING SECOND THOUGHTS ABOUT LEAVING YOU HERE AND STAYING AT MELA'S TONIGHT...

DAVE, I'M **FIIIINE!!!** IMAGINE ME IN A LITTLE BOX... PUT THE BOX IN GOD'S HANDS AND **LET GO!**

HE GAVE ME A HARRY POTTER BALLOON.
HP

IF YOU DON'T BELIEVE IN GOD, **THIS** CAN BE YOUR HIGHER POWER!
HP

SPENDING TIME WITH MY FRIEND MELA DID ME GOOD.

TALKING EVERYTHING OUT RESTORED ME TO SANITY.
JESUS! THAT'S A LOT FOR YOU TO HAVE TO DEAL WITH.

UP UNTIL THIS MOMENT, I HAD DOWNPLAYED HOW AWFUL THINGS WERE WHENEVER MY PARENTS CALLED, BUT THE SCENE I RETURNED TO JOGGED ME OUT OF MY DENIAL.

HI, DAVE.

I WISH I COULD DO THIS WORK OF ART JUSTICE.

WHAT'S ALL THIS?!?

HIS ROOMMATE HAD COME BACK TO GET A FEW THINGS, AND LUKE CONFRONTED HIM ABOUT HIS DEAD SISTER POSSESSING HIM.

RATHER THAN GET VIOLENT WITH HIM I PUT MY FIST THROUGH A WINDOW.

BUT NOW I FEEL BAD, SO I USED ALL THE GLASS TO MAKE A SHRINE FOR HIS SISTER.

IT'S BEAUTIFUL.

IT REALLY WAS. AND IT WAS ALSO SHOCKINGLY INSANE.

LUKE'S GOODBYE BRUNCH WOULD BE HAPPENING IN AN HOUR. AFTER TWO FULL DAYS IN CALIFORNIA, WE HADN'T PACKED.
CAN YOU HELP ME PUT OUT THE FOOD?
OKAY...

TURNOUT WAS LOW— FOUR FRIENDS WHEN HE WAS EXPECTING AT LEAST TWENTY. NONE OF THEM SEEMED TO NOTICE ANYTHING WAS WRONG WITH LUKE.

I'VE BEEN COMMUNICATING WITH THE DALAI LAMA...

MAYBE THEY'RE **ALL** CRAZY!

MMMM...

AFTER AN HOUR, THEY LEFT AND LUKE CRIED ON MY SHOULDER, EXHAUSTED.

SOB
IT'S OKAY...

I GOT HIM TO TAKE A NAP.

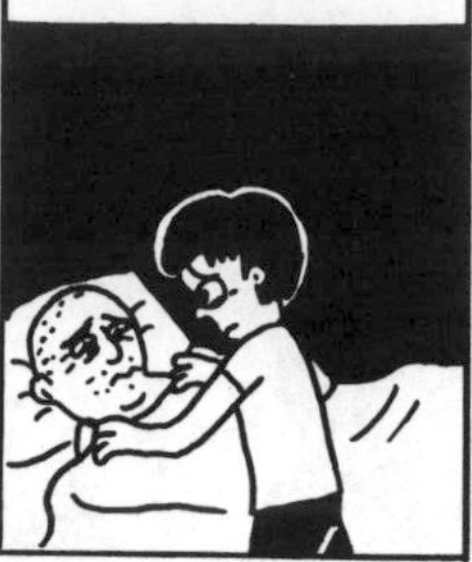

AND THEN I CALLED MY MOM.

I NEED HELP. THIS IS TOO HARD!

SHE TOLD ME ABOUT A BOOK SHE WAS READING ABOUT MENTAL ILLNESS.

YOU'RE SUPPOSED TO JUST AGREE WITH EVERYTHING HE SAYS.

I NEED YOU TO COME OUT HERE!

WHEN LUKE WOKE UP, I IGNORED HER ADVICE AND TRIED BEING TOUGH ON HIM ABOUT PACKING.

NO! I'M GOING OUT TONIGHT. I NEED SOME SPACE FROM YOU!

HE PLANNED TO GO SEE A BARTENDER WHO HAD BEEN LEADING HIM ON AND THEN DECLINING HIS ADVANCES FOR YEARS.

LUKE, THIS IS MORE CRAZY SHIT! **I FORBID YOU TO GO!**
HA
HA

DAVE, I'LL FLY OUT THAT WINDOW AND YOU'LL NEVER SEE ME AGAIN!

HE GOT IN THE SHOWER AND I CALLED MY MOM AGAIN.
!!!
DAVE, I THINK YOU NEED TO CALL THE POLICE.

WHEN THE POLICE ARRIVED, I LED THEM TO THE BACK PATIO WHERE HE WAS ON THE PHONE WITH A FRIEND.

I HAVE TO GO.

HE SHOOK HIS HEAD AND STARED AT ME WITH HATRED.

THEN, SICKENINGLY, HE SMILED AND SPOKE CALMLY AND POLITELY TO THE COPS, MAKING IT SEEM LIKE **I** WAS THE CRAZY ONE!

HE DOES HAVE A POINT. IT'S A BASEMENT APARTMENT... "FLY OUT THE WINDOW" DOESN'T MEAN HE'S JUMPING TO HIS DEATH.
IT'S A METAPHOR!

I HAVE TO GET DRESSED. EXCUSE ME, OFFICERS...
!
THIS IS IT. I'M GOING TO LOSE HIM.
LOOK, WE CAN SEE SOMETHING'S A LITTLE OFF HERE, BUT WE CAN'T HAVE HIM COMMITTED AGAINST HIS WILL.

NOT UNLESS HE HARMS HIMSELF OR ANOTHER PERSON.
HE'S GOING TO DIE TONIGHT.
POUND
POUND
POUND

DURING ANOTHER FRANTIC CALL TO MY MOM WHILE THE COPS WAITED, SHE TOLD ME TO TRY PRAYING.

I WAS DESPERATE, OPEN TO ANYTHING THAT MIGHT WORK.

GOD, IF YOU EXIST, PLEASE SEND ME SOME HELP. I CAN'T DO THIS ALONE... PLEASE!!!
GODDAMN MOTHERFUCKER!

IT SEEMED LIKE MY PRAYER WAS ANSWERED INSTANTLY.

RING!

MY MOM REMEMBERED OUR OLD CHURCH FRIENDS LIVED NEARBY.

I JUST TOLD JAMES WHAT'S HAPPENING. HE HASN'T LEFT WORK YET AND CAN BE THERE IN TEN MINUTES. SEE IF THE COPS CAN STALL LUKE UNTIL THEN!
THANK YOU!

IT WAS TAKING LUKE A WHILE TO GET READY, AND THE COPS DIDN'T MIND STAYING LONGER.

DO YOU WANT ANY FOOD? THERE'S PLENTY!

I WAS OVERJOYED TO SEE JAMES WHEN HE ARRIVED.

HE LISTENED TO ME DESCRIBE EVERYTHING IN A PANIC AND GENTLY INSISTED WE PRAY.

HEAVENLY FATHER... THANK YOU FOR BRINGING US TOGETHER.

WHEN LUKE EMERGED FROM HIS ROOM, HE LOOKED TRULY MAD.

I'M READY!
YANKEES CAP
CANDY FLOWER
RUMPLED SUIT
SNEAKERS

JAMES TOOK CHARGE.

HI, OLD FRIEND! **WO**
THAT IS SOME OUTFIT
JAMES?!?

WHERE I HAD BEEN ANGRY AND CONTROLLING, JAMES WAS CALM AND GENTLY PERSUASIVE.

WHAT DO YOU SAY TO DINNER? MY TREAT!
YAY!

THE COPS MADE SURE LUKE GOT IN JAMES'S CAR AND WE SPED OFF.

LUKE KNEW ON SOME LEVEL HE WOULDN'T BE GOING BACK TO HIS APARTMENT.

WHY ARE YOU BRINGING YOUR SUIT-CASE?

AND HE'D HAVE TO LET GO OF HIS PLANS TO SEE THE BARTENDER.

JUST IN CASE I NEED IT.

AS WE PASSED THE NIGHTCLUB, I WATCHED LUKE BLOW A KISS OUT THE WINDOW.

HE HAD TEARS IN HIS EYES.

DRIVING ACROSS THE BAY BRIDGE TOWARD JAMES'S HOUSE IN THE SUBURBS, I FELT MY BODY RELAX.
WE WERE SAFE IN HIS HANDS NOW.
THANK GOD.

LUKE AND I SPENT A BEAUTIFUL COUPLE OF DAYS WITH LISA AND JAMES AND THEIR CHILDREN.

WE JUMPED ON THEIR TRAMPOLINE.
HA HA
LUKE IN HIS UNDERWEAR

AND WE SANG CAMPFIRE SONGS IN TWO-PART HARMONY WHILE PLAYING LEGOS AND EATING LOTS OF CANDY.

♫ ROCKABYE SWEET BABY JAMES ♫

ON THE THIRD DAY, JAMES INVITED A MAN NAMED BILL FROM HIS CHURCH TO COME TALK TO LUKE. JAMES TOLD ME HE RESPECTED BILL'S FAITH.

HOWDY!

WE PACKED SNACKS AND WATER FOR A HIKE IN A NEARBY CANYON.

LUKE TOLD ME LATER HE HAD BEEN TERRIFIED THAT WHEN WE GOT TO THE TOP OF THE HILL, JAMES'S FRIEND WAS GOING TO KILL HIM.

BUT IT WOUND UP BEING A POSITIVE CONVERSATION AMID A BREATHTAKING VIEW THAT WENT ON FOR MILES.

BILL ALLUDED TO JESUS SEVERAL TIMES.

GOOD TO KNOW YOU ALWAYS HAVE A FRIEND.

IT SEEMED TO REMIND LUKE OF THE CHRISTIAN VALUES HE LEARNED AT CHURCH WHEN WE WERE LITTLE.

IT GROUNDED HIM.
CAREFUL UP AHEAD, DAVE.

HE TALKED REALISTICALLY ABOUT WHAT IT WOULD TAKE TO MOVE OUT OF HIS APARTMENT.
I ONLY NEED WHAT'S IN MY ROOM. EVERYTHING ELSE I CAN LET GO.

AND THERE WERE FLASHES OF INSIGHT INTO HIS CONDITION.
I'M SORRY THIS HAS BEEN SUCH A CRAZY TRIP FOR YOU...

NOW AS A TEAM, WE CALLED MY MOM AND FORMULATED A PLAN OF ACTION.

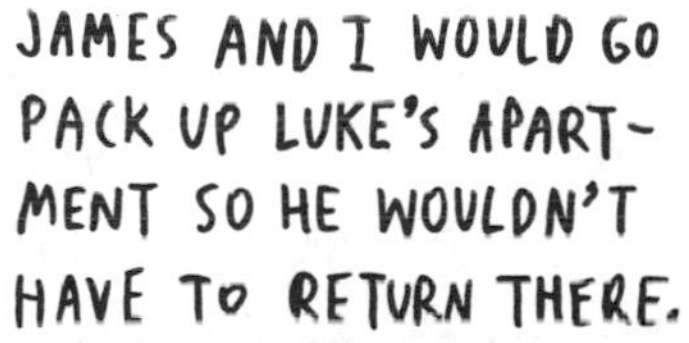
JAMES AND I WOULD GO PACK UP LUKE'S APARTMENT SO HE WOULDN'T HAVE TO RETURN THERE.

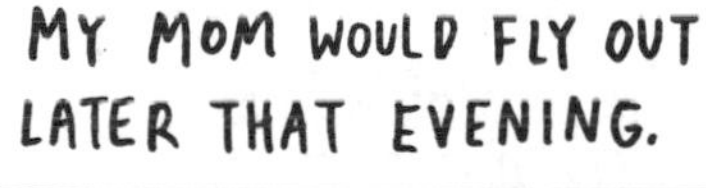
MY MOM WOULD FLY OUT LATER THAT EVENING.

TWO DAYS AFTER THAT, SHE AND LUKE WOULD DRIVE ACROSS THE COUNTRY. I HAD HAD ENOUGH AND WAS READY TO FLY BACK HOME. *

LUKE INSISTED ON PICKING UP MY MOM FROM THE AIRPORT, AND RATHER THAN FIGHT, WE LET HIM GO.

GOD, GIVE ME STRENGTH...
TRYING IT OUT ON MY OWN
!!!

STARVED AND EXHAUSTED AFTER PACKING, JAMES AND I WENT OUT TO DINNER.

SUSHI?

JAMES ASKED ME TO SAY GRACE WHEN OUR FOOD ARRIVED.

GOD... THANK YOU... UMM...

I COULDN'T DO IT.

WHAT IF LUKE RUNS AWAY OR GETS INTO AN ACCIDENT?

* WE DIDN'T THINK IT WAS SAFE FOR LUKE TO FLY IN THE POST-9/11 CLIMATE. IF HE HAD AN OUTBURST AND TALKED ABOUT TERRORISTS, HE COULD EASILY HAVE BEEN DETAINED.

I'LL CALL HIM...
WHOOPS! MY PHONE JUST DIED.

SIGH I JUST WISH WE COULD HAVE A SIGN THAT HE'S OKAY.

SUDDENLY JAMES'S PHONE CAME BACK FROM THE DEAD AND RANG. IT WAS MY MOM. THEY WERE FINE.

RIIIING

IT WAS A MIRACLE. THERE WAS NO OTHER WORD FOR IT.

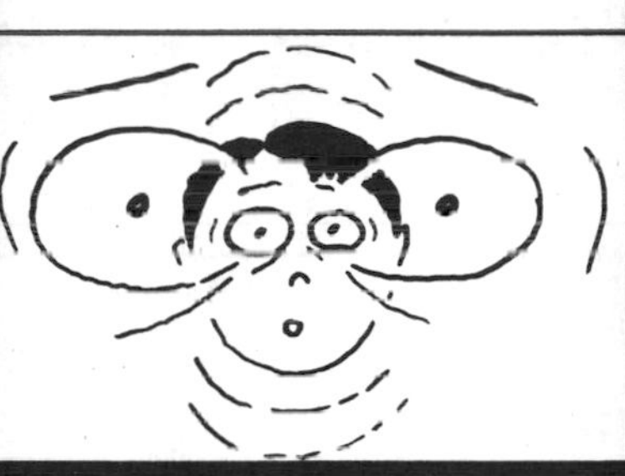

NOW WE COULD RELAX AND ENJOY OUR MEAL.

WHEN WE LIVED IN PARIS, I HEARD EVERY DAY HOW "AMER-EE-CANS ARE STUUUPEDE!"
HA HA

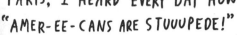

AFTER A FEW MINUTES, JAMES SWITCHED GEARS.

I WANT TO ASK YOU ABOUT SOMETHING.

HOW DO YOU FEEL ABOUT YOUR BROTHER'S HOMOSEXUALITY?
GULP
WELL, TO BE HONEST, I HAD TO COME TO TERMS WITH THE PART OF ME THAT'S GAY, TOO.
BUT ONCE I DID THAT, IT WAS EASY TO ACCEPT HIM.
I'VE KNOWN ON SOME LEVEL THAT HE WAS GAY SINCE PRE-K.
REALLY? BECAUSE I'VE ALWAYS THOUGHT, "GUYS? YUCK!" WHO WOULD WANT TO DO THAT?!?
I USED TO FEEL THAT WAY, TOO. BUT THEN I OUTGREW IT.
HMM...
WELL, THE BIBLE'S PRETTY CLEAR ON THIS POINT: IT'S A SIN.

I DON'T TAKE THE BIBLE LITERALLY, JAMES.

I WAS HAPPY WHEN WE FINISHED EATING AND WENT BACK TO HIS HOUSE. MY MOM AND LUKE WERE THERE.

OH, ANGEL... YOU'VE BEEN THROUGH A LOT, I KNOW.

MY FLIGHT WAS THE NEXT DAY, SUNDAY. JAMES INVITED US ALL TO CHURCH WITH THEIR FAMILY BEFORE I HAD TO LEAVE.

THERE'S A YOUTH SERVICE OR YOU CAN JOIN LISA AND I IN THE MAIN CHAPEL.

LET'S GO WITH THE KIDS!

SOME PART OF ME FANTASIZED THAT I WOULD FINALLY FEEL AT HOME AT CHURCH. THIS WOULD BE THE PERFECT END TO MY CALIFORNIA TRIP.

♫ ♪ PRAISE HIM FROM WHOM ALL BLESSINGS FLOW... ♫ ♪

A LOST SHEEP RETURNING TO THE FOLD.

BUT FIVE MINUTES INTO THE SERVICE, I REALIZED THAT EVEN THOUGH I WAS EXPERIENCING A NEWFOUND FAITH IN GOD, MY FEELINGS ABOUT CHURCH HADN'T CHANGED.

I HATE THIS!

BEING "FORCED" TO LISTEN TO THE SERVICE MADE ME ANGRY AND JUDGMENTAL.

SMUG WHITE ELITES PREACHING RADICAL LOVE AND FORGIVENESS TO SPOILED, COMFORTABLE BRATS.

FUCK THIS.
WHERE ARE YOU GOING?!?

JAMES HAPPENED TO BE COMING TO CHECK ON US AND FOUND ME SITTING ON A BENCH IN THE COURTYARD, MISERABLE.
I SHOULD HAVE KNOWN THAT WOULD BE HARD FOR YOU.
WHY DON'T YOU JOIN US IN THE OTHER CHAPEL?
IT WAS MUCH WORSE.
THE PASTOR WAS IN A GLEAMING WHITE SUIT, HIS VOICE BOOMING THROUGH A STATE-OF-THE-ART SOUND SYSTEM.
THE CHOIR WAS WHITE AND SOULLESS.
THEY WERE SURROUNDED BY FLOWERS AND LIT UP LIKE A TACKY BROADWAY PRODUCTION.*
THEY BELONG TO A "MEGACHURCH"?
SORRY, I CAN'T DO THIS.

* MORE JUDGMENT

WHEN I GOT BACK TO THE COURTYARD, LUKE WAS THERE.
WANNA HACK?
HACKY SACK

I SUDDENLY FELT HAPPY.

BEFORE LONG, WE HAD A CROWD OF 15 OR 20 KIDS SURROUNDING US.
LOOK AT THE JUGGLERS!
WOW! THEY'RE SO GOOD!
CAN WE TRY?!?

LUKE WAS FUNNY AND CHARMING.

ALRIGHT. SHOW ME WHATCHA GOT, KID!

HA HA

HE TAUGHT THEM ALL ONE AT A TIME– A NATURAL CAMP COUNSELOR.
THEY LOVE HIM.
I FELT CONNECTED TO GOD AGAIN.

SOON IT WAS TIME TO SAY MY GOODBYES, FIRST TO MOM AND LUKE.

"I'LL MISS YOU THE MOST, SCARECROW!"
HA HA

AND THEN TO JAMES.

I DON'T KNOW HOW TO THANK YOU FOR ALL YOU DID.

HE ASKED IF WE COULD HAVE A REGULAR BIBLE STUDY PHONE CALL. I POLITELY DECLINED.

I DOUBT THAT GOD BROUGHT US TOGETHER JUST TO HELP YOUR BROTHER MOVE OUT OF HIS APARTMENT!
ACTUALLY, I THINK THAT'S EXACTLY WHAT HE DID.

AT THE AIRPORT, MY FLIGHT WAS DELAYED. SECURITY WAS OVERWHELMED. IT WAS A MESS. NORMALLY I WOULD HAVE BEEN BESIDE MYSELF WITH WORRY AND IRRITATION.

BUT I COULD FEEL THAT A CHANGE HAD TAKEN PLACE IN ME. I HAD PEACE IN MY HEART.
AS I LOOKED AROUND, I FELT SURE I COULD TELL WHO HAD GOD IN THEIR LIFE.
I WAS ONE OF THEM.

LUKE AND MY MOM MADE IT HOME TO NEW YORK BY THE SKIN OF THEIR TEETH.

WHEN LUKE TURNED IN HIS LEASED CAR, THEY TOLD HIM IT HAD FOUR COMPLETELY BALD TIRES.
YOU COULD HAVE CRASHED AT ANY MOMENT ON THAT TRIP!

MY DAD HAD REFUSED TO COME OUT AND HELP WHILE I WAS IN CALIFORNIA.
I'M HAVING CHEST PAINS JUST THINKING ABOUT IT!

BUT HE TOOK CREDIT FOR THEIR SAFE RETURN BECAUSE HE HAD BEEN PRAYING FOR THEM THE WHOLE TIME.*

* THIS STILL IRRITATES ME TO NO END!

WHEN I GOT HOME TO REBECCA SHE WAS A BIT FREAKED OUT.

I DON'T KNOW WHAT TO MAKE OF ALL THIS.

I HAD A HARD TIME DESCRIBING WHAT HAD HAPPENED TO ME.

IT WAS LIKE A STATE OF GRACE. I WANT TO LIVE LIKE THAT ALL THE TIME!

ONE THING WAS CERTAIN: OUR MONEY TROUBLE VANISHED OVERNIGHT.

HI, I'M CALLING TO SEE WHAT OPPORTUNITIES YOU HAVE FOR ME.

TEMP AGENCY

CLAC
CLAC
CLAC
CLAC

I IMMEDIATELY BOOKED A $60-AN-HOUR DESIGN GIG AT OGILVY AND MATHER, A HUGE AD AGENCY. THEY PAID TIME AND A HALF FOR OVERTIME.

CAN YOU STAY LATE AGAIN?
SURE!

IT WAS HARD TO ARGUE WITH ALL THAT MONEY COMING IN.

BECOMES HELLO
GOODBYE
WATCHING OVER YOU UNTIL
♫ I'LL BE UP ABOVE

2002-2004

LUKE AGREED TO LIVE WITH MY MOM FOR A YEAR.

HE TOOK HIS MEDS DAILY AND WAS RESTORED TO SANITY.

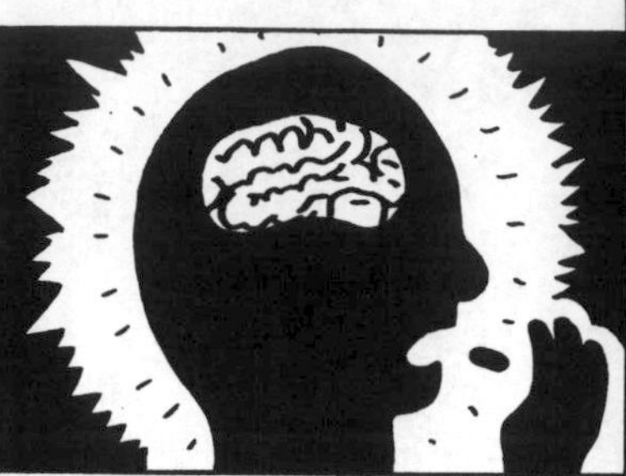

AT MY MOM'S URGING, HE JOINED SEVERAL 12-STEP GROUPS.

I IDENTIFY WITH THE LABEL "ADDICT." I HAVE A PROBLEM, BUT I'M HOPEFUL.

AFTER A YEAR, LUKE HAD A MIRACULOUS TURNAROUND.

I'VE GIVEN UP DRUGS AND ALCOHOL.
YOU LOOK GREAT!
I'VE ALSO BEEN SWIMMING EVERY DAY.

AFTER HE GOT HIS OWN PLACE, HE DRIFTED AWAY FROM THE TWELVE STEPS.

THE PEOPLE IN THOSE MEETINGS ARE CRAZY!

HA
HA

REBECCA AND I MOVED BACK TO NEW YORK AFTER SHE FINISHED GRAD SCHOOL.

GOD WAS SMILING ON US.
SAY CHEESE!
UGH! I'M HUGE!
PREGGERS
LIFE WAS GOOD.

I WAS STILL HOLDING ON TO MY NEWFOUND FAITH. I'D PRAY VAGUELY AND SOMETIMES CONSULT THE I-CHING.

STILL IN PJs

HAVE A GOOD DAY, HONEY.

SHAKE SHAKE

'BYE... LOVE YOU!

BUT MY PROBLEMS WERE STARTING TO OVERWHELM ME.

SHIT. I'M GONNA BE LATE AGAIN.

TUMS

I HAD USED MY CHICAGO CONTACTS TO GET A JOB AT OGILVY'S NEW YORK OFFICE.
WORLDWIDE PLAZA
XXX GIRLS
I WORKED IN THE TYPOGRAPHY STUDIO, FIXING KERNING AND LETTERSPACING ON IBM PRINT ADS.
THEY PAID ME $55,000 A YEAR PLUS VACATION AND BENEFITS.
FUCK.
HUF

IT WAS MY FIRST "REAL JOB" AND FOR A FEW MONTHS I WAS EXCITED.

BEST FRIEND JACOB

MY BOSS'S NAME IS **NICK**. HE'S LIKE THIS TOP DESIGNER FROM LONDON. I'M SO LUCKY TO BE WORKING FOR HIM!

BUT SOON MY OPTIMISM CURDLED INTO FAMILIAR RESENTMENT AND BITTER DISAPPOINTMENT.

HE'S AN ARROGANT, PRIMA DONNA PRICK! I FUCKING **HATE** HIM.

HMM...

HI, NICK! SORRY I'M LATE!

'MORNING. JOHN'S BEEN LOOKING FOR YOU.

OKAY, THANKS!

HE WAS ALWAYS PROMISING ME EXCITING PROJECTS AND THEN TAKING THEM AWAY AT THE LAST MINUTE.

I FINISHED THAT PITCH LAST NIGHT, BUT HERE'S SOMETHING YOU CAN WORK ON...

PLUS ALL THE CUTE GIRLS LOVED HIM.

♪ HI, NICK! ♫
OH HELLO, LOVE!
INTRODU ME!

A MONKEY COULD DO THIS WORK!
HA HA HA HA

I'D BLOW OFF STEAM IN THE BATHROOM.

OH! YES! FUCK ME, DAVE! UNNNH!

I HAD NO WORK FRIENDS SO I OFTEN SPENT MY LUNCH HOUR SITTING IN A NEARBY CATHEDRAL, TRYING TO CONNECT TO SOMETHING.

THE "STATE OF GRACE" I FELT IN CALIFORNIA WAS FAR AWAY, LIKE A FAINT RADIO SIGNAL.

PORN MADE THE SIGNAL DISAPPEAR ALTOGETHER.
I'M GOING TO BED, HONEY.
I'M JUST GONNA FINISH COLORING THIS PAGE.

I OFTEN WATCHED THE SAME TWO-MINUTE LOOP.

Q
MOV
4way.mov

AN EASTERN EUROPEAN WOMAN WITH SHORT HAIR LETS THREE MEN INTO HER HOME. THEY FUCK HER ALL AT ONCE.

AS IT BUILDS, SHE LOOKS LOST IN ORGASM – CHEEKS FLUSHED, MOANING AS THE GUYS FILL HER FROM EVERY ANGLE.

UNNNH!

IT NEVER FAILED TO GET ME OFF.

FOR THE ENTIRE DAY AFTER WATCHING, I'D FEEL DIRTY INSIDE.

AND I COULDN'T TURN OFF MY LUST.

HA HA HA

THEY CAN TELL I'M REALLY A CREEPY LOSER.

OGILVY POOL TABLE

GOD, I WANT TO FUCK HER SO BAD.

HA HA

IN MY SPARE TIME I WAS DRAWING A COMIC STRIP ABOUT EVERY SEXUAL ENCOUNTER I'D HAD SINCE PRE-K.

WANNA WATCH SOMETHING TOGETHER?

NAH, I GOTTA WORK ON THIS...

I PAINTED EACH INCH-SIZED PANEL LIKE A MONK WORKING ON AN ILLUMINATED MANUSCRIPT.

WHEN I COULDN'T STAND ANOTHER MINUTE OF LOOKING AT SQUIRMING LITTLE BODIES FUCKING AND SUCKING, I'D GO JERK OFF.

MONEY TROUBLE STILL PLAGUED ME.

HOW CAN WE HAVE **ZERO** IN THE BANK?!? I MAKE $55,000 A YEAR!

WE LIVE IN NEW YORK NOW!

MANY NIGHTS I WOKE UP AT 3AM WITH TERRIBLE ACID REFLUX.

OWWW!

I'D GET UP AND WORK ON MY COMICS.

OWWW

THIS PATTERN WAS STARTING TO FEEL BEYOND MY CONTROL. I WAS LOCKED IN.

THE TERROR I WAS FEELING ABOUT BECOMING A DAD HAD ME IN KNOTS.

UNNNH!
NEW MORTGAGE
STUDENT LOAN
LESS TIME FOR ART
SHITTY CORPORATE JOB

I WAS AT A LOSS.

OWWW!
UNNNH!

BY THE SUMMER OF 2004, REBECCA QUIT HER FULL-TIME TEACHING JOB AND GOT READY FOR THE BIRTH.

I WENT INTO WORK ONE MORNING AND GOT THE NEWS I WAS BEING LAID OFF.
CAN WE HAVE A MOMENT, DAVID?
?
BOSS'S BOSS

INSTEAD OF FEELING DEVASTATED, I WAS ODDLY ECSTATIC.

WE CAN GIVE YOU TWO MONTHS' SEVERANCE AND BLAH BLAH BLAH BLAH BLAH...

THIS IS GOD'S WILL FOR ME!

I'LL HAVE TIME WITH THE BABY AND I'LL GET MY ILLUSTRATION CAREER UP AND RUNNING!

I'LL NEVER HAVE TO WORK IN ADVERTISING AGAIN!!!

WITH MY COMICS HAVING APPEARED IN A HIGH-PROFILE ANTHOLOGY A MONTH EARLIER, MY NAME GOT AROUND.

WHAT AM I DOING IN THIS THING?

WOWWIE ZOWWIE!

I LANDED A FEW ASSIGNMENTS FOR THE NEW YORK TIMES.

FLIP
FLIP
FLIP
FLIP
STEVE HELLER

AS A PARTING GIFT AND A SHOW OF SUPPORT, MY ONE EXECUTIVE-LEVEL FRIEND AT OGILVY HIRED ME AS AN ILLUSTRATOR FOR A NEW YORK PUBLIC LIBRARY CAMPAIGN.

HE'S PAYING ME $10,000 AND MY ART WILL HANG ON A GIANT BANNER IN FRONT OF THE MAIN BRANCH!

THIS WAS IT! I HAD MADE IT ALL HAPPEN. I HAD ARRIVED.

AND THEN MAYA DROPPED INTO MY LIFE.

BEAUTIFUL LITTLE FUNNY LITTLE MAYA.

WITH PIERCING BLUE EYES, UNQUENCHABLE CURIOSITY...

...AND A VOICE LIKE A TRAIN WHISTLE!

SHE BLEW AWAY EVERY-THING I THOUGHT I KNEW...

...BECOMING A NEW CENTER OF GRAVITY.

FOR DAYS ON END, ALL I WANTED TO DO WAS HOLD HER.

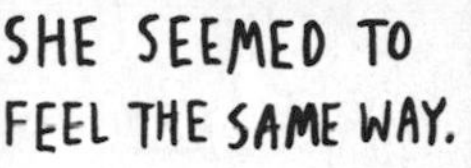
SHE SEEMED TO FEEL THE SAME WAY.

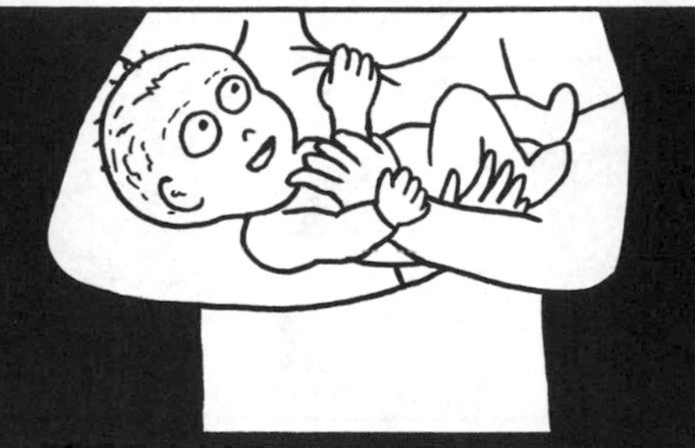

WAAAAAA!!!

AT FIRST MY BRAIN COULDN'T COMPREHEND A FEELING OF LOVE THIS STRONG.

FOR THE PREVIOUS FIFTEEN YEARS, I HAD ALWAYS LINKED LOVE WITH SEX AND LONGING.

BUT HERE, FINALLY, WAS SOMETHING PURE.

SOMEHOW THROUGH THE HAZE OF COOING AND CRYING AND SCREAMING AND SHUSHING, CLEANING, WIPING, SLEEPING, AND WAKING UP, MY ARTWORK STILL CALLED TO ME.

I PUT HUNDREDS OF SLEEP-DEPRIVED HOURS INTO MY COMICS.

BUT PAID WORK WAS A FAR-OFF DISTANT THOUGHT.

GOTTA WORK ON THIS STRIP!

I STRUGGLED TO FINISH THE LIBRARY JOB THAT HAD EXCITED ME WEEKS EARLIER.

UGH! MORE REVISIONS?!?

THE LIBRARY MONEY, WHEN IT FINALLY ARRIVED, WASN'T THE WINDFALL I'D BEEN EXPECTING.

AFTER TAXES, IT COVERED ABOUT A MONTH OF OUR EXPENSES.

OKAY, WE'RE ALL CAUGHT UP WITH OUR BILLS!

I THOUGHT THERE'D BE SOME EXTRA!

AS MAYA APPROACHED THREE MONTHS, OUR BANK ACCOUNTS ONCE AGAIN APPROACHED ZERO.

DAVE, YOU NEED A FULL-TIME JOB!
I DON'T WANT TO GO BACK TO ADVERTISING! IT'S LIKE PROSTITUTION!

WHY CAN'T YOU JUST SUPPORT WHAT I'M DOING NOW?

BECAUSE IT DOESN'T PAY ENOUGH!

I DON'T CARE WHAT YOU HAVE TO DO! GO GET SOME CARPENTRY WORK!

THAT STUNG. I TOOK IT TO MEAN, "I DON'T CARE ABOUT YOU OR YOUR ART OR YOUR HAPPINESS."

BUT ON SOME LEVEL I KNEW SHE WAS RIGHT.
WAAAAAAAAAAH
UCK!

HERE WAS THAT SAME STUBBORN UNWILLINGNESS FROM CHICAGO REARING ITS UGLY HEAD AGAIN.

LEAVE ME THE FUCK ALONE!

IT MADE NO SENSE.

I **HAVE** TO FINISH THIS!!!

I LOVED THESE TWO PEOPLE MORE THAN ANYONE ELSE IN MY LIFE. AND YET, I WOULDN'T— OR COULDN'T— GO GET A JOB.

WHAT'S WRONG WITH ME?

TO RELIEVE SOME OF THE BURDEN, MY MOM CAME EVERY OTHER DAY DURING THOSE EARLY MONTHS.

HELLO, MY DEARS!

SOMETIMES SHE WASHED ALL OF OUR DISHES.

OR CLEANED OUR BATHROOM.

SCRUB
SCRUB

OR STOCKED UP OUR FRIDGE.

SOMETIMES SHE'D SPEND A FEW HOURS WITH MAYA WHILE WE SLEPT.

I WAS GRATEFUL FOR THE HELP, BUT COULD BARELY STAND TO BE IN THE SAME ROOM WITH HER.

BLAH
BLAH
BLAH
TALKING TO A SPONSEE

THE DISCOMFORT I USUALLY FELT WAS NOW FULL-BLOWN IRRITATION, BORDERING ON HATRED. I DIDN'T UNDERSTAND IT.

IT MIGHT HAVE BEEN THAT SHE'D FALLEN OFF THE WAGON AND GAINED A LOT OF WEIGHT.

DOES SHE THINK I DON'T NOTICE?

ON ONE VISIT, SHE TOLD ME SHE WAS BACK IN OA.

THAT'S GOOD.

FOR THE NEXT FEW WEEKS SHE WOULD ARRIVE WITH A ROLLING COOLER FULL OF FOOD OKAYED BY HER SPONSOR.

HI, ANGEL!
HI, MOM... WHAT'S ALL THAT?
WAAAAAH!

IT SEEMED LIKE EVERY WEEK THERE WERE NEW RULES ABOUT WHICH FOODS SHE COULD OR COULDN'T EAT. IT WAS HARD TO KEEP UP.

I KNEW IT HAD WORKED FOR HER IN THE PAST, BUT NOW IT WAS STARTING TO SEEM CRAZY.

I'M NOT EATING ANY STARCHES AT ALL RIGHT NOW.

OOOKAY...

DURING HER NEXT VISIT, THINGS WERE AT AN ALL-TIME LOW WITH REBECCA. WE WERE TWO MONTHS BEHIND ON ALL OUR BILLS.

I WAS WORKING ON TWO BOOK PROPOSALS INSTEAD OF JOB HUNTING.

WHAT IS IT, ANGEL? I CAN SEE YOU'RE IN PAIN.

IT'S JUST... I CAN'T SEEM TO FIND THE MOTIVATION TO FIND A JOB. I'M STUCK.

OH, DAVID...

IT FEELS LIKE THERE ARE SOME BIG TEARS AROUND THIS ONE... IT'S LIKE I CAN ALMOST TASTE YOUR TEARS.

UCK! MOM, STOP!

≡CHOKE≡

YOU'RE ALWAYS TRYING TO FIX ME!

AND **YOU** WON'T LET ME COMFORT YOUR "LITTLE BOY..." *

IT'S LIKE... YOU LET ME IN A LITTLE AND THEN SLAM A STEEL DOOR IN MY FACE! ≡SOB≡

I'M DONE TALKING ABOUT THIS!

≡WAAAAAH≡

RRRRGHH!!!

AS SHE WAS SAYING GOODBYE...
ANGEL, I KNOW YOU ALREADY KNOW ABOUT THIS, BUT MAYBE YOU CAN READ IT AGAIN WITH AN OPEN MIND.
MORE 12-STEP BULLS
FUCK YOU!

* SHE WAS ALWAYS TRYING TO GET ME TO CONNECT WITH MY "INNER CHILD," TOO.

AN HOUR AFTER SHE LEFT, MY RAGE TURNED TO REMORSE. I HAD MADE MY MOTHER CRY.

AND I HAD MADE REBECCA FEEL SCARED AND UNPROTECTED WHEN SHE WAS VULNERABLE.
I'M A HORRIBLE PERSON.
SHE'S ASLEEP.

SIGH

I THOUGHT I KNEW THIS PAMPHLET BY NOW. I FELT SURE ITS HAM-FISTED LANGUAGE WOULDN'T REACH ME.

"SIGNPOSTS ON THE ROAD TO BECOMING A COMPULSIVE DEBTOR"

INSTEAD IT PIERCED MY HEART.

DIFFICULTY MEETING PERSONAL FINANCIAL OBLIGATIONS

T KNOWING ACCOUNT BALANCES

OVERWORKING OR UNDEREARNING

"BORROWING" ITEMS SUCH AS PENS AND BOOKS AND NOT RETURNING THEM

LIVING IN CHAOS AND DRAMA AROUND MONEY

IVING IN SELF-MPOSED DEPRIVATION

A FEELING OR HOPE THAT SOMEONE WILL TAKE CARE OF YOU

CHOKE THIS IS LIKE MY LIFE STORY!

SOB SOB
SOB SOB SOB

I MADE A DECISION TO TRY THE PROGRAM IN EARNEST, TRULY WITH AN OPEN MIND FOR THE FIRST TIME.

IF THAT'S WHAT YOU THINK YOU NEED.

THERE WAS A DEBTORS ANONYMOUS MEETING THAT VERY NIGHT.

I'M TAKING CHARGE OF MY LIFE!

THE MEETING WAS IN THE BASEMENT OF A CHURCH ON THE UPPER WEST SIDE.
IS THIS REALLY IT?

HOMELESS PEOPLE SWARMED THE RAILING AND STEPS.

SOME OF THEM WERE INSIDE, TOO.

THE WALLS WERE YELLOW, THE LIGHTING WAS FLUORESCENT, THE FLOOR HAD BEEN MOPPED, BUT THERE WAS STILL A PERMANENT LAYER OF GRIME.

SHOULD I SIT IN ONE OF THE ROWS OR AT A TABLE?

I CHOSE A TABLE WHERE THE PEOPLE LOOKED RELATABLE.
"STICK WITH THE WINNERS..."

THE MEETING STARTED.
HI, JOHN
HI, I'M JOHN. I'M A DEBTOR.
HI, JOHN.
HI, JOHN

HE FELT FAMILIAR TO ME. HE HAD THAT SAME SOOTHING, GOD-CENTERED WAY OF TALKING AS JAMES DID IN CALIFORNIA.

HE READ THE PREAMBLE.

DEBTORS ANONYMOUS IS A FELLOWSHIP OF MEN AND WOMEN WHO BLAH BLAH

I FOUND MYSELF JUDGING EVERYONE EXCEPT JOHN.

NOW LET'S EACH READ A STEP.

IT WAS HARDER THAN I THOUGHT IT WOULD BE TO KEEP AN OPEN MIND.

WHO'S THIS WEIRDO?

"STEP ONE: ADMITTED WE WERE POWERLESS OVER DEBT THAT OUR LIVES HAD BECOME UNMANAGEABLE."

PFFT YOU'RE SO COOL FOR MEMORIZING THAT!

IT CAME AROUND TO ME AND I READ, TOO.

"STEP 11: SOUGHT THROUGH PRAYER AND MEDITATION TO IMPROVE OUR CONSCIOUS CONTACT WITH GOD AS WE UNDERSTOOD HIM, PRAYING ONLY FOR KNOWLEDGE OF HIS WILL FOR US AND THE POWER TO CARRY THAT OUT."

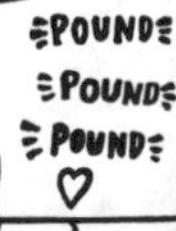
POUND
POUND
POUND

SCARED

I HATE THAT... WHY **ONLY** HIS WILL FOR US? CAN'T WE ASK FOR THINGS WHEN WE PRAY?!?
"STEP 12: HAVING HAD A SPIRITUAL AWAKENING AS A RESULT OF THESE STEPS BLAH BLAH BLAH BLAH..."

THE NIGHT I HAD CHOSEN HAPPENED TO BE A BIG BOOK MEETING.* THERE WAS ANOTHER HALF HOUR OF READING BEFORE ANYONE COULD SHARE.

THE BIG BOOK'S LANGUAGE WAS ARCANE AND POMPOUS TO MY EARS. WE WERE SUPPOSED TO REPLACE **ALCOHOL** AND **ALCOHOLIC** WITH **DEBTING** AND **DEBTOR**.
THIS IS EXCRUCIATING!
"ALC—" I MEAN... "DEBTING WAS LIKE A RAPACIOUS CREDITOR..." WAIT, THAT DOESN'T MAKE ANY SENSE!
HA
HA HA HA HA

FINALLY, WE REACHED THE PART OF THE MEETING WHEN WE COULD SHARE.

PLEASE KEEP YOUR EYE ON OUR SPIRITUAL TIMEKEEPER FOR YOUR ONE-MINUTE WARNING.

"SPIRITUAL TIMEKEEPER"?

I HAD HOPED THAT HEARING PEOPLE'S STORIES WOULD HELP ME "IDENTIFY," BUT I FELT EVEN MORE IRRITATION. LUKE WAS RIGHT. THESE PEOPLE WERE CRAZY.

* MOST 12-STEP GROUPS TREAT THE BIG BOOK OF AA AS A SACRED TEXT.

ONE PERSON WAS BEING TOO REVERENTIAL TOWARD THE FOUNDERS OF AA.

ANOTHER WAS TALKING ABOUT HER DEAD CAT.

THE THIRD HAD SIX-FIGURE CREDIT-CARD DEBT FROM SHOPPING TOO MUCH.

SOB

I WAS DYING TO SHARE.

THEY'LL BE BLOWN AWAY BY MY SHARE! THEY'LL SAY "I CAN'T BELIEVE YOU'RE JUST A NEWCOMER... YOU'RE SO WISE!"

EACH PERSON WHO SHARED CHOSE THE NEXT PERSON.

LET'S SEE... SOMEONE IN THE BACK.
PICK ME!

FINALLY...

NOW IS THE TIME FOR NEWCOMER SHARES.
YES, YOU!
WHEW!

AS SOON AS I OPENED MY MOUTH, I SOUNDED JUST AS LOST AS EVERYONE ELSE. NO ONE WAS BLOWN AWAY.

HI... UMM... I'M A CARTOONIST AND I GUE AN UNDEREARNER... MY PARENTS ARE IN THE 12 STEPS, BUT I'M STILL A NEWCOMER I GUESS...
SHUT UP, YOU IDIOT!

DURING THE TREASURY BREAK, JOHN ASKED FOR ANNOUNCEMENTS. A FEW PEOPLE SPOKE ABOUT DA RETREATS AND SERVICE OPPORTUNITIES.

AS JOHN WAS WRAPPING UP, A HOMELESS WOMAN FROM THE BACK ROW STOOD UP.

YES... WELL, I WANT TO THANK YOU FOR YOUR SERVICE TO THE POSTMASTER GENERAL.
ZZZZ
SNICKER

SHE WENT INTO AN INCOMPREHENSIBLE RANT THEN LUMBERED OFF TO THE BATHROOM.

OKAY, WE'LL NOW RETURN TO SHARING.

POUND
POUND
POUND
POUND

IT WAS SCARY HOW MUCH SHE SOUNDED LIKE LUKE.

HI, I'M DIDI. I'M A DETTUH.

BEFORE DIDI COULD SHARE, THERE WAS AN INTERRUPTION.

EXCUSE ME. I'M SORRY, BUT THAT WOMAN IS SHITTING WITH THE DOOR WIDE OPEN.

I NEED TO GET THE FUCK OUT OF HERE!
HMM...

IT SAYS HERE IF THERE'S A DIS-RUPTION IN THE MEETING, WE NEED TO TAKE A GROUP CONSCIENCE.
POUND
POUND
POUND
POUND
POUND

I MAKE A MOTION THAT WE CALL THE POLICE.

I MAKE A MOTION THAT WE ASK HER TO LEAVE.

JOHN CALMLY TALLIED OUR VOTES AND THEN CONFRONTED HER.

EXCUSE ME, WE'VE TAKEN A GROUP CONSCIENCE AND I'M AFRAID I NEED TO ASK YOU TO LEAVE.

A FEW LONG MOMENTS PASSED.
MUMBLE MUMBLE
MOTHER FUCKING WHITE BABBOON...

I CAN'T BELIEVE THAT WORKED!
SORRY, EVERYONE...

THERE WAS STILL TIME FOR A FEW SHARES.
I JUST FEEL SO MUCH COMPASSION FOR HER. I MEAN, THAT COULD SO EASILY BE ME.

I'VE GOT A DISEASE JUST LIKE HER. I'M A DEBTOR.
MMM...

FINALLY, THE LAST SHARE...
HI, I'M TERRY. I'M A DEBTOR.
PRETTY SMILE.
HI, TERRY

THANKS, JOHN, FOR YOUR SERVICE AND WELCOME TO THE NEWCOMERS. I HOPE YOU KEEP COMING BACK. THERE'S A LOT OF OTHER MEETINGS IF YOU DIDN'T LIKE THIS ONE!
HA HA
HA
HA

I'M JUST FEELING GRATEFUL TO BE ALIVE TODAY. I'VE GOT SHELTER AND FOOD.

MY DEBT IS ALL PAID OFF AND MY BILLS ARE IN ON TIME THANKS TO THIS PROGRAM.

ON TOP OF ALL THAT, I HAVE MY ART. I FEEL LIKE I'M EXACTLY WHERE I'M SUPPOSED TO BE.

AFTER THE MEETING, I WALKED TO THE TRAIN WITH TERRY.
IT WAS BRAVE OF YOU TO SHARE, DAVID.

SHE TOLD ME ABOUT 12-STEP MEETINGS WITH AN ARTIST FOCUS.

I HOPE I SEE YOU AGAIN.

AS I RODE HOME, I THOUGHT ABOUT THE SHIFT IN MY THINKING OVER THE COURSE OF THE MEETING.
MAYBE I WAS "EXACTLY WHERE I WAS SUPPOSED TO BE," TOO.
WASN'T THE MEETING ALMOST TAILOR-MADE FOR ME? WITNESSING JOHN HANDLE THAT MENTALLY ILL WOMAN WITH SUCH POISE AND GRACE?

GOD, IS THIS YOUR WILL FOR
JOINING DA?

way

MAYBE IT IS!

THIS IS A
PARTNERSHIP AND THROUGH THIS WE ARE
STRONGER THAN THE SUN

2004-2005

AS SOON AS I ENTERED THE **DA WRITERS MEETING** IN THE WEST VILLAGE THAT FOLLOWING SATURDAY, I FELT A HUGE EXPLOSION OF GOD ENERGY.

IT WAS A BIG GROUP, MAYBE SIXTY PEOPLE OR MORE.

I DON'T REMEMBER THE QUALIFICATION, BUT THE SHARES WERE ALL HEARTFELT, ARTICULATE, AND WISE, WITH THE RIGHT MIX OF SINCERITY AND DOWNTOWN NEW YORK SARCASM

I'M A WORTHLESS PIECE OF SHIT IN THE CENTER OF THE UNIVERS
HA HA
HA HA
HA
HA HA HA HA HA HA

I GOT CALLED ON TO SHARE BEFORE THE TREASURY BREAK. I HAD PLACED MYSELF DIRECTLY ACROSS FROM THE CHAIRPERSON.

YES, YOU.

HI, I'M DAVID AND I'M AN UNDEREARNER AND A DEBTOR.
HI, DAVID
HI, DAVID

I FELT MOTIVATED TO HAVE A "GOOD" SHARE. TAKING A CUE FROM TERRY, I THANKED THE CHAIRPERSON AND SPEAKER AND STUCK WITH THE THEME SHE HAD INTRODUCED.

IT WAS SUCH A RUSH TO BE SEEN AND HEARD BY TALENTED ARTISTS AND WRITERS.
I WAS LITERALLY STEALING FROM THE BLIND.
HA HA HA HA
HA HA

ALL THAT UNDIVIDED ATTENTION.

THANKS FOR LETTING ME SHARE.

KEEP COMING BACK

KEEP COMING BACK

IT MADE ME HIGH.

THIS TIME I HAD NO TROUBLE LISTENING TO ALL THE SHARES. THERE WAS SOMETHING TO IDENTIFY WITH IN EVERYONE'S STORY.

I TOLD HIM, "THIS IS WHAT I'M WORTH—NOT A PENNY LESS!"

I HAD THE UNCANNY SENSE THAT I WAS HEARING EXACTLY WHAT I NEEDED TO HEAR—THAT GOD WAS SPEAKING TO ME THROUGH OTHER PEOPLE.

WALKING HOME, I LOOKED AROUND AT THE FLOWERS, TREES, EVEN THE COLORS AND TEXTURES OF THE GARBAGE ON THE SIDEWALK. IT WAS ALL PERFECTLY IN PLACE IN A GOD-CENTERED UNIVERSE!

I TRIED SHARING MY ENTHUSIASM WITH REBECCA.

!

HONEY, YOU SOUND LIKE YOU'RE LOSING YOUR MIND.
HA
HA

THE FOLLOWING WEEK, I TRIED TO SHARE IT WITH SOMEONE AT THE MEETING.

OH!
YOU'RE ON THE PINK CLOUD. JUST ENJOY IT. IT WON'T LAST.
POP!

HER REACTION IRRITATED ME.

MAYBE I'M DIFFERENT FROM YOU AND IT **WILL** LAST!

IN THOSE FIRST FEW WEEKS, I MADE A COUPLE OF ROOKIE MISTAKES.

AFTER HEARING A WISE, MIDDLE-AGED MAN SHARE, I IMPULSIVELY ASKED HIM TO BE MY SPONSOR.

I JUST REALLY IDENTIFIED WITH YOU.
THANKS.

HE GAVE ME HIS NUMBER, BUT NEVER ANSWERED THE PHONE OR RETURNED MY CALLS.

HI, THIS IS LAWRENCE... PLEASE LEAVE YOUR NAME AND NUMBER AT THE TONE.
BEEEEEEEEEEEEEEEP

THE NEXT WEEK, A WOMAN NAMED CLARA SAT NEXT TO ME BEFORE THE MEETING BEGAN.

ANYONE SITTING HERE?

I DIDN'T FEEL MUCH OF A CONNECTION WITH HER, BUT SHE SEEMED TO LIKE ME.

HA HA
YOU'RE FUNNY!

SOMEHOW SHE TALKED ME INTO BEING HER "ACTION PARTNER", WHICH ENTAILED HAVING DAILY CHECK-IN CALLS.

AFTER A WEEK I FELT TRAPPED.

BLAH BLAH BLAH BLAH BLAH BLAH BLAH BLAH

ACTION LIST

SHE SHOWED FLASHES OF INTENSE NEEDINESS AND OFTEN GAVE ME CONTROLLING ADVICE I HADN'T ASKED FOR.

LET'S SKIP THE FEEDBACK PART OF THE CALL TODAY IF YOU DON'T MIND.

WHY, IS SOMETHING WRO

I FOUND MYSELF WATCHING A LOT OF PORN TO BLOW OFF STEAM. FINALLY, I FACED WHAT I HAD TO DO AND CALLED HER TO BREAK OFF OUR "PARTNERSHIP."

SHE CRIED AS IF I WAS A BOYFRIEND ABANDONING HER.

I WAS JUST ABOUT TO TELL YOU THAT I NEED **MORE** COMMITMENT FROM YOU... CHOKE

SOB

THIS IS NUTS!

POUN
POUND
POUND
POUND
POUND

ASIDE FROM THESE MISSTEPS, I STARTED SEEING RESULTS RIGHT AWAY FROM WORKING THE PROGRAM.

KEEPING MY NUMBERS DOWN TO THE PENNY
CANDY .50¢

HONEY, DO YOU WANT TO SEE MY SPENDING PLAN*?
SURE!

I TRACKED MY INCOME AND SPENDING AND UPCOMING BILLS IN AN EXCEL DOCUMENT.

WITH A LITTLE SUPPORT AND FRIENDLY COMPETITION IN THE ROOM, I WAS ABLE TO DO THIS ACCOUNTING EASILY.

THIS IS **DAY 25** OF SOLVENCY FOR ME!

CLAP! CLAP! CLAP!

CLAP! CLAP!

WOO!

AND, MIRACULOUSLY, MY JOB SITUATION RIGHTED ITSELF WITHIN THAT FIRST MONTH.

SOMEONE AT OGILVY WANTS TO HIRE ME IN A DIFFERENT
!

IT PAID $20,000 MORE THAN MY PREVIOUS ROLE, AND I'D BE MANAGED BY SOMEONE WHO UNDERSTOOD AND APPRECIATED ME.

* NOT A "BUDGET," A DIRTY WORD IN DA

MY RESENTMENT TOWARD OGILVY EVAPORATED. DA WAS WORKING!

I'M SO GRATEFUL TO HAVE THIS JOB!
WORKING IN THE HALLWAY
NO CUBICLE AVAILABLE

REBECCA APPRE-CIATED THE CHANGE.

HAVE A GOOD DAY AT WORK. HERE'S YOUR LUNCH.

BUT TENSION STARTED BREW-ING OVER MY LEAVING EVERY SATURDAY MORNING TO GO TO THE WRITERS MEETING.

IT'S MY HOME GROUP.
I FEEL LIKE YOU DON'T WANT TO SPEND ANY TIME WITH US.
BA!
BA!

I COULDN'T EXPLAIN TO HER HOW IT BLISSED ME OUT.

I HAD BECOME AN EXPERT AT GETTING CHOSEN TO SHARE. IT WAS INCREDIBLY VALIDATING.

DAVID!

THE FEW TIMES I LEFT WITHOUT GETTING TO SHARE, I FELT DEVASTATED.

POUND
POUND
POUND
POUND
AAAND... LAST SHARE... LIZ!

PEOPLE OFFERED A RANGE OF ADVICE.

I COME HERE TO PICK UP MY MESSAGES FROM GOD. I'M HERE TO **LISTEN**.

WHILE YOU'RE WAITING TO BE CALLED ON, PRAY TO BE OF SERVICE TO THE MEETING WITH YOUR SHARE. IT'S GOD'S WILL WHO GETS PICKED!

"DON'T THINK LESS OF YOURSELF. JUST THINK OF YOURSELF LESS!"

I KNEW I HAD THE "WRONG" SPIRITUAL ATTITUDE, BUT MY HEART KEPT CALLING OUT.

I **NEED** TO SHARE!!!

EVENTUALLY I GOT SOME ADVICE THAT I WAS HAPPY TO TRY.

DO A **90-IN-90.*** YOU'LL GET PLENTY OF CHANCES TO SHARE.

I TOLD MY MOM.

GREAT, ANGEL! WHEN I STARTED I THINK I DID THREE 90-IN-90s IN A ROW! **HAHA**

*90 MEETINGS IN 90 DAYS

REBECCA WASN'T AT ALL HAPPY.

WHY ARE YOU SO AGAINST MY RECOVERY?!?

IT SEEMS LIKE YOU NEED MORE AND MORE MEETINGS! THAT'S FOUR HOURS OUT OF BOTH SATURDAY AND SUNDAY! THAT SHOULD BE FAMILY TIME!!!

I DIDN'T HAVE A GOOD RESPONSE. I TOLD HER IT WAS PAINFUL FOR ME TO BE HOME WITH THEM DOING "NOTHING."

AFTER ABOUT AN HOUR OF FOCUSED ATTENTION WITH MAYA, I'D START TO LOSE PATIENCE. I'D FEEL LIKE I SHOULD BE DOING SOME WORK OR AT LEAST READING SOMETHING USEFUL.

SHE JUST WANTS TO DUMP IT OUT AGAIN. THIS IS TORTURE.
zzZZZ
BA!
RAFFI

WHY CAN'T I JUST SIT HERE AND ENJOY SOME TIME WITH MY DAUGHTER?

IT WAS MY DISEASE! WITH A MEETING, AT LEAST I HAD A "DAILY REPRIEVE" FROM MY INSANITY.
I GOTTA HEAD OUT.
BA!
OKAY.

I DISCOVERED SEVERAL NEW MEETINGS DURING MY 90-IN-90.
HI, I'M DAVID AND I'M A DEBTOR.
HI, DAVID
HI, DAVID
"PROSPERITY GROUP"
"DA STEPS AND TOOLS"
HI, DAVID
HI, DAVID
"A PATH TO SOLVENCY"
"OVERCOMING UNDEREARNING"
HI, DAVID
"DA EAST SIDE LUNCH MEETING"
"DA WRITERS MEETING"
HI, DAVID
HI, DAVID
HI, DAVID
"VISION MEETING"
"ENOUGH"
ONE MEETING CALLED "CAME TO BELIEVE" WAS JUST A FEW BLOCKS FROM OGILVY.
IT BECAME MY OTHER HOME GROUP.
HUY, AH'M IRA AN' AH'M A DETTUH.
HI, IRA
HI, IRA
I'LL DEFINITELY BE ABLE TO SHARE.
HI, IRA
HI, IRA.

IRA BECAME ONE OF MY FAVORITE PEOPLE IN DA.

HE WAS A TENDER, DISHEVELED, OLD-SCHOOL NEW YORKER WITH A DISFIGURED HAND THAT FLAPPED WHEN HE SPOKE.

I REALLY HATE THIS THING.

HE HAD INJURED IT ON A FACTORY JOB AND GOT A FEW HUNDRED THOUSAND DOLLARS SETTLEMENT.

I STILL LIVE WITH A LOTTA DEPRUHVASHUN.

HE WENT TO SEVERAL MEETINGS PER DAY ALL YEAR ROUND.

IF THEY HAD A MEETING FOR PEOPLE WHO GO TO TOO MANY MEETINGS, I'D GO TO THAT, TOO!
HA
HA
HA
HA

STACY WAS A FIERY, MIDDLE-AGED ACTRESS AND DOG WALKER.

SHE COULD BE INTENSE.

I WAS A LOW-DOWN DIRTY DEBTOR.

SHE ONCE TOLD ME SHE HAD A VISION OF ME ACCEPTING AN AWARD IN HOLLYWOOD.

I'M PSYCHIC. I CAN SEE THESE THINGS!

CAREY WAS A TALL, BABY-FACED ACTOR WITH WHITE HAIR.

HE SHARED WITH RUTHLESS HONESTY.

I'M SO FULL OF RESENTMENTS TODAY. I DON'T LIKE ANYONE IN THIS ROOM!
HA HA
HA
HA HA
HA
IDENTIFYING

MY MOTHER HAD MY TEETH PULLED UNNECESSARILY WHEN I WAS LITTLE. THESE FALSE TEETH AREN'T WHITE! THEY DON'T LOOK RIGHT!

I DON'T CARE WHAT ANYONE THINKS. I'M GOING TO HAVE THEM REPLACED EVEN IF I HAVE TO **DEBT!!!**

PATTY WAS A BEAUTIFUL ACTRESS AND PERSONAL TRAINER.

WE CLICKED RIGHT AWAY, LIKE WE'D ALREADY BEEN FRIENDS FOR YEARS.

DAVID! I LOVED YOUR SHARE! WHICH WAY ARE YOU WALKING?

WE GOT INTO A ROUTINE OF WALKING TOGETHER AFTER THE MEETING.

YOU'RE SO SPIRITUALLY CENTERED. AND FUNNY!

BLAH BLAH BLAH BLAH BLAH BLAH BLAH

HA HA

SHE'D HUG ME GOOD-BYE LIKE A LOVER.

YOU'RE A GOOD MAN, DAVID...

ONE TIME A WOMAN AT THE MEETING THOUGHT PATTY WAS MY WIFE. I WAS MORTIFIED.

SORRY. IT'S NONE OF MY BUSINESS!

ONE DAY PATTY ASKED ME IF I HAD TIME TO SIT AND TALK.

I JUST WANT TO TELL YOU THAT COUPLE YEARS AGO, I WAS RAPED RIGHT AFTER ESCAPING FROM A CULT.

WHY DID SHE TELL ME ALL THAT?

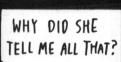

THINGS COOLED OFF FOR BOTH OF US AFTER THAT.

I'M GONNA RUN. I HAVE TO GET BACK TO WORK.

OKAY.

A FEW WEEKS LATER, SHE STOPPED COMING TO THE MEETING AND DIDN'T RETURN MY CALLS.

AFTER MY 90-IN-90 WAS OVER, I FELT COMPELLED TO GO DEEPER INTO THE PROGRAM. THE THREE-MINUTE SHARES WEREN'T DOING IT FOR ME ANYMORE.

?
ORNING RITUAL
I WANTED TO FIND A SPONSOR.
I WANTED TO DO SERVICE AT MEETINGS.
MORE THAN ANYTHING, I WANTED TO QUALIFY.

I HAD THE REQUIRED 90 DAYS OF SOLVENCY, BUT NOW I NEEDED TWO **PRESSURE RELIEF GROUPS.***

I'M JUST PUTTING IT OUT TO THE MEETING THAT I NEED PRG PEOPLE!

A SUGGESTION THAT NEVER WORKED

I MET A GUY NAMED JACK AT A NEW MEETING ACROSS TOWN.

GREAT SHARE!

I ASKED HIM SPONTANEOUSLY.

SURE, I'D LOVE TO HELP YOU.

FINDING A WOMAN PROVED TRICKIER. I WAS AFRAID TO APPROACH ANYONE I FOUND ATTRACTIVE.

SIGH THERE'S NO WAY!

POUND
POUND
POUND
POUND

HA HA HA

AND A LOT OF THE OLDER WOMEN PUSHED MY BUTTONS.

I CAN'T BE-LIEVE YOU HAVE A KID. YOU LOOK LIKE A BABY YOURSELF!

THE REALLY SPIRITUALLY CENTERED ONES WERE ALL FULL UP WITH SERVICE COMMITMENTS. IT WAS IMPOSSIBLE!

* SHARING ALL MY FINANCIAL RECORDS AND ANY FEARS OR BLOCKS WITH A SOLVENT MAN AND WOMAN IN THE PROGRAM

ONE WEEK AT THE WRITERS MEETING, I LISTENED TO A WOMAN NAMED STEPH QUALIFY.

BEFORE I START—JUST SO YOU ALL KNOW—I REALLY CAN'T DO ANY MORE SERVICE RIGHT NOW. I'M A BIT OVERCOMMITTED.

I LIKED HER SHARE WELL ENOUGH BUT WASN'T AMAZED. THERE WAS SOME OTHER HOOK THAT COMPELLED ME TO APPROACH HER AFTERWARD.

I KNOW YOU SAID YOU CAN'T DO ANY SERVICE, BUT I REALLY NEED A PRG. IT WOULD JUST BE LIKE A ONE-OFF.

SIGH

SHE RELUCTANTLY AGREED. I WAS ELATED.
JUST DON'T TELL ANYONE, OK?

I MADE A PLAN WITH JACK AND STEPH FOR THE FOLLOWING WEEK.

BRING TWO MONTHS' WORTH OF NUMBERS AND YOUR SPENDING PLAN.

WE MET AT AN UPSTAIRS SEATING AREA OF A KOREAN DELI, CLOSE TO THE WRITERS MEETING.
OTHER DA MEMBERS GETTING PRGS

I ARRIVED WITH MY COLOR-CODED EXCEL SPREADSHEET PRINTED ON A GLEAMING WHITE SHEET OF 11×17 PAPER.

WHAT'S NEXT? WILL YOU SHOW UP WITH YOUR NUMBERS FRAMED?
HA HA HA

THEY DIAGNOSED ME AS A PERFECTIONIST AND THOUGHT I SHOULD GO EASIER ON MYSELF.

DAVID, WE'RE NOT AIMING FOR SELF-IMPROVEMENT. THIS IS A PROGRAM OF **SELF-ACCEPTANCE.**

OH...!

JACK GOT EXCITED ABOUT MY COMICS. HE GAVE ME GREAT ENCOURAGEMENT.

YOU GOTTA KEEP PURSUING THIS!!! I WANT TO SEE YOU GO TO THAT CONVENTION!
YEAH?!?

STEPH DIDN'T SAY MUCH. AT ONE POINT SHE HINTED THAT I SHOULD GET HER SOME WORK AT OGILVY.

I DO PROOFREADING FOR AGENCIES AS A SIDE JOB...

AS WE WERE WRAPPING UP, SHE SAID BITTERLY:

MAYBE YOU SHOULD BE HELPING ME. YOU SEEM TO HAVE EVERYTHING FIGURED OUT!

JACK AND STEPH AGREED TO A SECOND PRG A MONTH LATER. I ENDURED STEPH'S PASSIVE AGGRESSION AGAIN SINCE IT MEANT I COULD QUALIFY.

TWO DAYS LATER, I WAS ASKED TO QUALIFY AT THE WRITERS MEETING. IT WAS ONLY A FEW DAYS AWAY.
FRANCINE
WOW! I'M TERRIFIED, BUT YES! THANK YOU!

SHE SOOTHED MY FEARS.
"TRUE BELIEVER" EYES
JUST ASK GOD TO GUIDE YOU IN SHARING YOUR EXPERIENCE, STRENGTH, AND HOPE.

TELL US "WHAT IT WAS LIKE, WHAT HAPPENED, AND WHAT IT'S LIKE NOW."*
OKAY!

I PREPARED MY SPEECH ALL WEEK, WRITING AND REVISING MY NOTES ON THE COMPUTER.

I WANTED TO MAKE SURE I INCLUDED ALL THE RIGHT DETAILS.

- STEALING AND LYING AS A TEENAGER
- DRUG USE AS A TEENAGER
- UNWILLINGNESS TO WORK
- RESENTFUL FEELING OF BEING "PUT UPON"
- FALLING BEHIND ON BILLS, UNDEREARNING
- INABILITY TO FIND JOY WITH MY FAMILY

* BIG BOOK OF AA AGAIN

IT WAS CLEAR TO ME THAT I HAD A SPIRITUAL DISEASE.

NOW, THANKS TO DA, I WAS TAKING CARE OF MY FAMILY AND NURTURING MY ART.

I WAS GOING TO BE AS BIG AS I COULD POSSIBLY BE AND NO ONE WOULD HOLD ME BACK!

I ENDED MY SPEECH WITH A MARIANNE WILLIAMSON QUOTE THAT I HAD HEARD AROUND THE ROOMS.*

ASK OURSELVES, "WHO AM I TO BE BRILLIANT, GORGEOUS, TALENTED, AND FABULOUS?"

"ACTUALLY, WHO ARE YOU NOT

YOU ARE A CHILD OF GOD! YOU

PLAYING SMALL DOES NOT

SERVE THE

*IT'S OFTEN ERRONEOUSLY ATTRIBUTED TO NELSON MANDELA, A MISTAKE I MADE, TOO

WHEN THE MOMENT TO SPEAK FINALLY ARRIVED, I WAS READY.

HI, I'M DAVID AND I'M AN UNDEREARNER AND DEBTOR.
HI, DAVID

I FELT THE IMPACT OF MY WORDS RIPPLING THROUGH THE COMPLETELY FULL ROOM.

SOME PEOPLE WERE CLEARLY IN AWE OF ME.

AP CLAP CLAP CLAP CLAP CLAP CLAP CLAP

I BASKED IN THE APPLAUSE AND COMPLIMENTS AND HUGS AFTERWARD.

THANK YOU SO MUCH!
LINE OF PEOPLE WAITING TO TALK TO ME

I LEFT THE MEETING FEELING LIKE I HAD GRADUATED.

TO MY SURPRISE AND REBECCA'S RELIEF, I NEVER WENT BACK TO THE MEETING AGAIN.

♫ OOH BABY THAT'S
HARD TO CHANGE... I CAN'T
TELL 'EM HOW TO FEEL,
SOME GET
STONED... SOME GET STRANGE... SOONER OR LATER IT ALL GETS K

05-2006

DA HAD BEEN WORKING FOR ME AND NOW THAT I WAS ONLY GOING DURING THE WEEK, IT WASN'T AFFECTING REBECCA AS MUCH.

WHAT SHOULD WE DO TODAY?

BUT SHE STILL DIDN'T LIKE TALKING ABOUT IT.

IT WAS AN AMAZING QUALIFICATION!
HOLD ON, HONEY...

WHEN I TOLD MY DAD ABOUT ATTENDING DA, HE WAS UNENTHUSIASTIC.

HMM... OKAY... THAT'S INTERESTING.

YEAH, IT'S BEEN REALLY HELPFUL!

GETTING ANGRY

HE WAS GOING THROUGH HIS OWN FINANCIAL HELL—FACING FORECLOSURE BECAUSE HE COULDN'T KEEP UP WITH THE MORTGAGE.

KNOW HE STILL FEELS ABANDONED BY MY MOM FOR JOINING DA
HEN LEAVING HIM, BUT I THOUGHT HE'D BE MORE SUPPORTIVE OF ME!
BUT WHEN HAS HE EVER BEEN LIKE THAT?!?

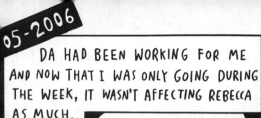

IT WAS GETTING TO THE POINT WHERE ANY CONTACT WITH HIM UPSET ME FOR DAYS.

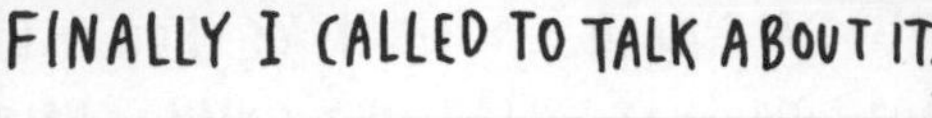
FINALLY I CALLED TO TALK ABOUT IT.

I NEED TO TAKE A BREAK FROM YOU FOR A WHILE. I'M WORKING THINGS OUT IN DA. WAIT FOR ME TO GET BACK IN TOUCH.
OKAY, DAVE. I'LL TRY.
POUND
POUND
POUND
POUND
POUND

LESS THAN TWO WEEKS LATER, HE BARRAGED ME WITH CALLS UNTIL I ANSWERED.

I'M DONE WITH YOU NOT SPEAKING TO ME!

AAAAARGGH!

I HAD BEEN HEARING A PHRASE IN THE ROOMS: "IT'S AN INSIDE JOB." I WAS STARTING TO UNDERSTAND WHAT IT MEANT.

MY OUTER CIRCUMSTANCES HAD CHANGED QUICKLY. I LOVED GOING TO WORK AND WAS MAKING MORE THAN ENOUGH MONEY FOR ONCE IN MY LIFE.

SEE? WE HAVE $5,000 IN THE SAVINGS NOW!
AMAZING!

BUT IT TURNED OUT MY MONEY ISSUES WERE JUST THE TIP OF THE ICEBERG. MY TRUE PROBLEMS RAN MUCH DEEPER.

MAYBE A VOLCANO IS A BETTER METAPHOR
HOT LAVA

ONE DAY IT HIT ME THAT I'D BEEN GOING TO A 12-STEP PROGRAM FOR HALF A YEAR WITHOUT DOING THE STEPS.

THE MEETINGS ARE GREAT, BUT THE STEPS ARE WHAT CHANGED MY LIFE.

I TRIED "WORKING" THEM ON MY OWN, FILLING 50 PAGES IN MY JOURNAL ABOUT HOW **POWERLESS** I WAS OVER DEBTING.*

BUT WHEN I SHARED ABOUT IT AT A MEETING, SOMEONE SAID AFTERWARD:

YOU CAN'T BE YOUR OWN SPONSOR.
OH, RIGHT.

FOR A FEW WEEKS, I LOOKED HARD FOR A SPONSOR, BUT THE ONES THAT INTERESTED ME WEREN'T AVAILABLE.

SORRY. I'M NOT TAKING ON ANY MORE SERVICE COMMITMENTS RIGHT NOW...

* STEP ONE

AND THEN SOME LONGTIME MEMBERS HAD LOST THEIR SOLVENCY FOR PAYING A BILL ONE DAY LATE OR FORGETTING TO RETURN A LIBRARY BOOK ON TIME. THEY COULDN'T DO ANY SERVICE.*

TODAY IS DAY ONE FOR ME.
GASP
CLAP
CLAP
CLAP
CLAP
CLAP
?

STILL DETERMINED TO FIND A SPONSOR, I TRIED A MEETING I'D NEVER ATTENDED.
MAYBE HE COULD BE MY SPONSOR...?

I GOT TO SHARE SINCE I WAS A NEW FACE AND SAT RIGHT UP FRONT.

YES, YOU!

THE MEETING WAS ALMOST OVER.
NO ONE SEEMS LIKE THE RIGHT FIT.
YES, YOU.
ONE MORE PERSON WAS CHOSEN TO SHARE.

* THERE IS NO SET RULE ABOUT WHAT CONSTITUTES SOLVENCY BESIDES "NOT INCURRING NEW UNSECURED DEBT." THIS LEAVES A LOT OF GRAY AREAS THAT MEMBERS TRY TO RESOLVE INDIVIDUALLY OR WITH A SPONSOR OR PRG PERSON.

HIS NAME WAS DARYL.

I WAS BOWLED OVER BY HIS WISDOM, SPIRITUALITY, AND WICKED SENSE OF HUMOR. I SOUGHT HIM OUT AFTERWARD.

I REALLY ENJOYED YOUR SHARE, TOO! I DON'T HAVE A SPONSOR IN DA, EITHER.
DAMN.

BUT I'M LOOKING TO PUT TOGETHER AN ACTION GROUP IF YOU MIGHT BE INTERESTED IN JOINING.

I SHELVED MY SPONSOR SEARCH AND GOT EXCITED ABOUT JOINING DARYL'S GROUP.

I JUST MET THIS AMAZING GUY NAMED DARYL. HE'S SO FUNNY! AND WISE, TOO!

MM-HMM?

YOU'D REALLY LIKE HIM!

DADA!

IN THE MEANTIME, DARYL AND I TOOK TO LEAVING INCREASINGLY LONG "SHARES" ON EACH OTHER'S VOICEMAILS.

HI, IT'S DAVID. JUST WANTED TO TURN OVER THAT TODAY WAS STRESSFUL AT WORK AND I WANT TO COMMIT TO BEING PRESENT WITH REBECCA AND MAYA WHEN I GET HOME.

IT QUICKLY BECAME A DAILY CHECK-IN. I FOUND HIS MESSAGES TO BE PROFOUNDLY INSIGHTFUL AND HILARIOUS, TOO.

I NOTICE A PALPABLE SHIFT IN MY CONSCIOUSNESS AT AROUND THE 40-MINUTE MARK OF EVERY 12-STEP MEETING.
HA HA
GUESS I'M STILL SEEKI
FOR MY "OKAY-NESS."
DON'T MEAN A WOODE
INDIAN'S ASSHOLE. TH
WOULD BE "OAK ANUS

AFTER A FEW WEEKS, DARYL FOUND TWO WOMEN TO JOIN THE GROUP AND WE ARRANGED OUR FIRST MEETING.

WHAT?!? I'M SURE I TOLD YOU ABOUT IT! IT'S AN HOUR AND A HALF. I'LL BE HOME AT 9.
SIGH
REBECCA

WE MET AT AN UPSTAIRS SECTION OF A STARBUCKS.

DARYL HAD RESERVED US ALL COZY LIVING ROOM CHAIRS.

WE ALL TOOK TURNS SHARING OUR FEARS AND GOALS. I FELT ESPECIALLY ENCOURAGED BY DARYL'S FEEDBACK.

MOST PEOPLE AS SENSITIVE AS YOU DON'T SURVIVE INTO ADULTHOOD.

I LIKED ANGELA RIGHT AWAY, BUT SOMETHING ABOUT MARGARET BUGGED ME.

SIGH! I'LL GO NEXT.

I DID MY BEST TO BE SUPPORTIVE.

WOW, THAT SOUNDS REALLY HEAVY...

WE ENDED THE MEETING SOON AFTER.

SILENT SERENITY PRAYER

YOU GUYS ARE LIKE A NEW FAMILY TO ME!

I WALKED HOME BLISSED OUT.

THANK YOU, GOD!

AT HOME, REBECCA WAS ANNOYED. MAYA WAS WIDE AWAKE.

WAAAAAAH!

AFTER I PUT MAYA TO BED, I SAW AN EMAIL FROM MARGARET. IT SAID SHE WAS DROPPING OUT OF THE GROUP.

I was put off by your comment, David. Yeah, it gets "heavy" with me sometimes, okay? I won't be continuing.

DARYL AND I CONTINUED OUR EMAIL THREAD WITH ANGELA FOR A WEEK, BUT THEN SHE DROPPED OUT, TOO.

I'm not feeling supported. You guys should just support each other.

SO MUCH FOR MY "NEW FAMILY"!
ARE YOU COMING TO BED?

VALENTINE'S DAY ROLLED AROUND. INSTEAD OF MAKING PLANS WITH REBECCA, I EXCHANGED LONG, PERSONAL EMAILS WITH DARYL.

I MISS YOU, HONEY! SPEND TIME WITH ME!

THE FAST INTIMACY BETWEEN US KEPT RAMPING UP. I FELT A LITTLE BURST WHENEVER HE SENT A NEW MESSAGE.

IT BECAME ADDICTIVE.

EACH DISCLOSURE INSPIRED A DEEPER ONE IN RETURN.

ON AND ON IT WENT UNTIL THINGS FINALLY REACHED A FEVER PITCH.

Reply

THEN THE FEVER BROKE.

I INTERPRETED SOMETHING DARYL SHARED WITH ME AS HOSTILE, WHICH TRIGGERED A VOLLEY OF EMAILS— EACH OF US CLARIFYING AND RECLARIFYING OUR POINTS.

AFTER A FEW DAYS OF THIS, WE GAVE UP AND AGREED TO HAVE NO MORE CONTACT.

People come into our lives for a Reason, a Season, or a Lifetime. Thanks for a rich Season.

SEVERAL OF MY DA FRIENDS SAID I WAS SHARING A LOT ABOUT PEOPLE WHO WERE DRIVING ME CRAZY.

Y'KNOW I'M NOT JUST POWERLESS OVER MONEY, I'M POWERLESS OVER OTHER PEOPLE, TOO!

IT WAS OFTEN MY MOM AND DAD, SOMETIMES REBECCA, OR A CO-WORKER OR EVEN A PROGRAM MEMBER WITH A POOR SENSE OF BOUNDARIES.

MY DA FRIENDS SUGGESTED I TRY AL-ANON. AFTER A YEAR OF SPIRITUAL PROGRESS, I WAS STILL STRUGGLING WITH STEP 1.

IT MADE SOME SENSE TO ME SINCE I WAS THE SON OF TWO ADDICTS.

AL-ANON

BUT I WAS REALLY SCARED OF BEING SOMEONE WHO NEEDED MULTIPLE 12-STEP PROGRAMS.

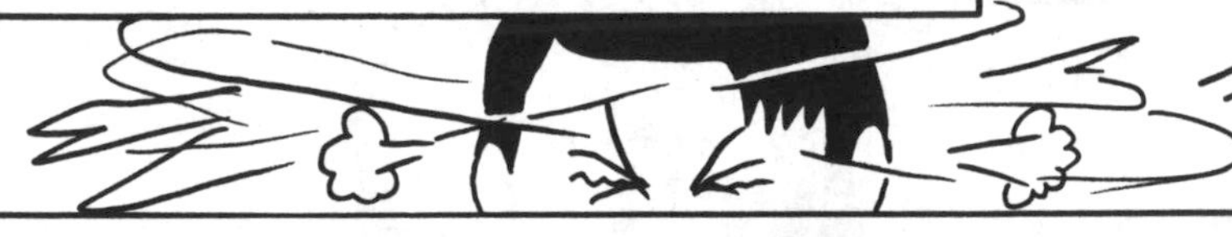

EVENTUALLY THE PAIN BECAME "UNMANAGEABLE" AND I FOUND AN AL-ANON MEN'S MEETING TO ATTEND.

THE THOUGHT OF BEING IN A ROOM FULL OF ONLY MEN WAS INTIMIDATING AS HELL AT FIRST.

POUND
POUND
POUND
POUND
POUND

BUT I NOTICED A LOT OF THE SAME FACES FROM MY DA MEETINGS.

STEVE WAS THERE.

HE ONCE SHARED WITH ME ABOUT ANOTHER PROGRAM HE ATTENDED.

THEY SAY WE'RE POWERLESS OVER OUR CONSCIOUSNESS.

THEY SAY WE NEED TO ASK FOR "CHRIST CONSCIOUSNESS" TO RESTORE US TO SANITY.

I TELL YOU... IT'S AMAZING. AND I'M SOMEONE WHO GREW UP JEWISH!
HMMM...

ANOTHER PERSON I RECOGNIZED WAS ANDREW.

HE WAS AN ALPHA MALE, REAL ESTATE BROKER WITH A SLIGHT SPEECH IMPEDIMENT. HIS SHARES WERE ALMOST ALWAYS THE SAME, BUT INCREDIBLY POWERFUL.

I'M HERE TO RE-WIRE MY BRAIN SO I DON'T LIVE OUT MY PARENTS' LEGACY.

I COME HERE AND CLEAR OUT THE CHANNEL TO GOD AND THEN GO HAVE A GREAT DAY. MY LIFE IS SO ABUNDANT THANKS TO DA, AL-ANON...

ALSO MEN'S SLAA AND THE EMOTIONAL-RELEASE RETREAT WORK I'M DOING.
?

I WOULD SOMETIMES WALK WITH HIM ACROSS TOWN AFTER DA MEETINGS.

I DON'T TAKE BULLSHIT FROM EMOTIONALLY UNAVAILABLE WOMEN.
HEE HEE
GIGGLING AT HIS CONFIDENCE AND MASCULINITY

IF I TRIED TALKING, HE'D INTERRUPT ME AND KEEP TALKING HIMSELF. I DIDN'T MIND AT ALL.

MY PRESSURE RELIEF MAN JACK WAS THERE, TOO. I SAT NEXT TO HIM.

IT'S SO GOOD TO SEE YOU HERE!

IN THE FOLLOWING WEEKS, I GOT CALLED ON TO SHARE A FEW TIMES.

!
YOU.

UNLIKE THE 3-MINUTE TIMED SHARES IN DA, THIS MEETING DIDN'T KEEP TIME.

BLAH BLAH
WOW... 10 MINUTES!

USUALLY THAT MEANT THE SAME 5 OR 6 PEOPLE OUT OF 30 SHARED EACH WEEK. THEY CALLED ON EACH OTHER.

GREGORY.
THANKS, WILLIAM.

WHEN I WAS ONE OF THE CHOSEN FEW, IT FELT LIKE I HAD WON THE LOTTERY.

DAVID.

THE FEEDBACK AFTER THE MEETING WAS ESPECIALLY WARM.

IT WAS WONDERFUL LISTENING TO YOU!

MONTHS WENT BY. I DIDN'T HAVE TO COUNT DAYS OR MEET ANY REQUIREMENTS.

THANKS TO THIS GROUP, I'M LEARNING TO KEEP THE FOCUS ON ME—TO LOVE AND ACCEPT MYSELF **EXACTLY** AS I AM TODAY.

I WASN'T DAVID, A DEBTOR. I WAS JUST DAVID.

"EASY DOES IT..."

GOING EACH WEEK WAS LIKE TAKING A SOOTHING BATH.

THANKS FOR LETTING ME SHARE.

THESE MEN KNEW HOW MUCH I WANTED TO BE PERFECT, HOW EXHAUSTED I WAS, HOW TO TALK ME DOWN WHEN I GOT INTO OVERDRIVE.

YOU SOUND GREAT! KEEP IT UP!

MOST IMPORTANTLY, I GOT TO PRACTICE AND SHARE ABOUT "DETACHING WITH LOVE" FROM THE INSANITY AROUND ME AND TO STOP BEING ATTRACTED TO IT.

AL-ANON SHIELD

ONE DAY AT A TIME IN A -ANON
Courage to Change

THE LANGUAGE IN THE MEETING FORMAT AND THE DAILY READERS I BOUGHT NO LONGER SOUNDED CORNY TO ME.

THESE WORDS WERE A BALM ON MY WOUNDED SOUL.

"IT IS EASIER TO ACCEPT LIMITATIONS IN OTHERS WHEN I ACCEPT MYSELF."
EXHALE

THE CLOSING PARAGRAPH IN EACH MEETING NEVER FAILED TO MOVE ME, ESPECIALLY WHEN VOICED BY WILLIAM.

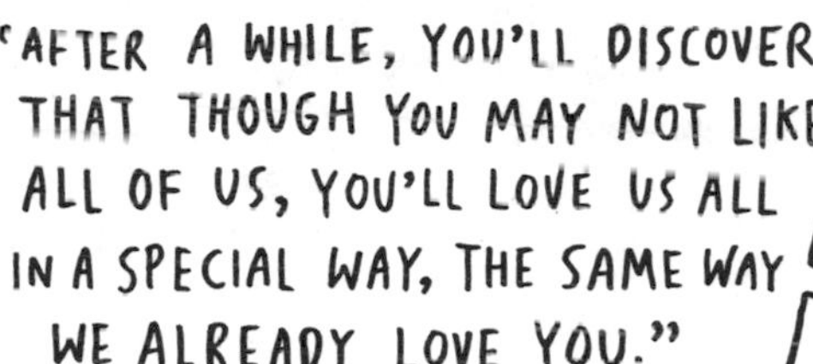
"AFTER A WHILE, YOU'LL DISCOVER THAT THOUGH YOU MAY NOT LIKE ALL OF US, YOU'LL LOVE US ALL IN A SPECIAL WAY, THE SAME WAY WE ALREADY LOVE YOU."

SOOTHING AND GENTLE

WE BECAME CLOSE. I CALLED HIM REGULARLY.*

THAT'S MY WEEK-END NUMBER.

DURING ONE CALL, I SHARED ABOUT THE HEARTBREAK I OFTEN FELT WHEN I TRIED TO SHARE MY SUCCESSES WITH MY MOM.

I'VE LEARNED TO BE VERY CAREFUL WITH WHOM I SHARE MY "GOLD," THE MOST PRECIOUS PARTS OF MYSELF.

WOW.

* I NEVER WORKED UP THE COURAGE TO ASK HIM TO BE MY SPONSOR.

I LOVED GREGORY, TOO.
I HAVE SOME THOUGHTS ABOUT WHAT YOU WERE SHARING IF YOU'D LIKE TO HEAR.
SURE!

OUR PARENTS ARE SUPPOSED TO PREPARE US FOR THE WORLD, TO STRENGTHEN US.

IN OUR CASE, IT'S LIKE THEY SHAKE US AROUND AND FUCK US UP AND THEN PUSH US OUT...

"THERE YOU GO! GOOD LUCK!"
EXACTLY!
HA
HA

FINALLY THERE WAS TED, THE PATRIARCH OF THE GROUP.

HE WAS WEALTHY AND CONFIDENT. HIS SHARES WERE PIERCINGLY HONEST, IF A BIT LONG-WINDED.

I HAD SUCH AN ACUTE SENSE OF PLEASURE SEEING MY DAUGHTER THIS WEEK.

HE REALLY RESPONDED TO MY FIRST AL-ANON QUALIFICATION. I HAD OPENED MYSELF UP WIDE.

I USED TO REALLY WORRY ABOUT MY SEXUALITY, BUT NOW I REALIZE I'M ONLY ABOUT 5% GAY.

HE APPROACHED ME AFTERWARD.

I'M SORRY, BUT I JUST **LOVE** YOU!

HE HUGGED ME AS TIGHTLY AS HE COULD. I WAS FLOODED WITH EMOTION.

HE'S LIKE MY LONG-LOST SPIRITUAL FATHER.

MAYBE HE COULD BE MY SPONSOR!

WE TALKED BY PHONE A FEW TIMES.

HI, TED.

DAVID! IT'S SO GOOD TO HEAR YOUR VOICE!

RIGHT AWAY SOMETHING DIDN'T FEEL RIGHT. HE SEEMED TO NEED SOMETHING FROM ME, BUT I WAS CALLING BECAUSE I NEEDED SOMETHING FROM HIM.

AFTER 10 MINUTES I WANTED TO GET OFF THE PHONE.

ONE MORE THING...

YOU HAVE TO FORGIVE ME FOR SAYING THIS, BUT I'M A BIT OLDER THAN YOU...

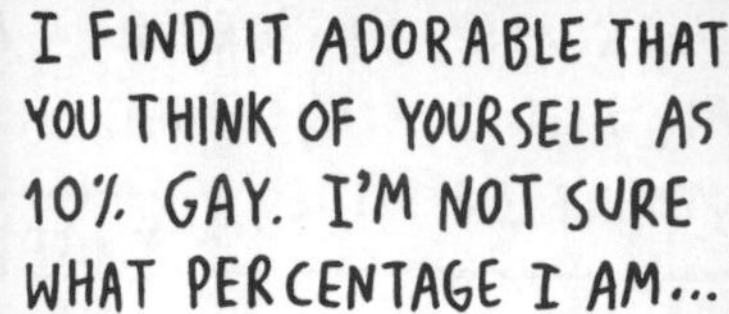
I FIND IT ADORABLE THAT YOU THINK OF YOURSELF AS 10% GAY. I'M NOT SURE WHAT PERCENTAGE I AM...

I SAID 5%

WHEN I SAW HIM AT THE NEXT MEETING, HIS HUG FELT VIOLENT.

HE PULLED ME TO HIM WITH EXTREME FORCE, THEN PUSHED ME AWAY WHEN HE WAS DONE.

I FELT LIKE A RAG DOLL.

AFTER A FEW MORE MONTHS, THE NOVELTY OF BEING WITH THIS GROUP OF MEN STARTED WEARING OFF.

EVERYONE SEEMS SO SAD, LONELY, AND DIRECTIONLESS.*

*I MIGHT HAVE BEEN PROJECTING

I DRIFTED AWAY FOR A MONTH, BUT THEN I WORRIED IT WAS MY DISEASE KEEPING ME AWAY.

WHEN I RETURNED, TED SAW ME IN THE MEN'S ROOM BEFORE THE MEETING.

HEY, STRANGER...

HE TRIED TO PAT MY CHEEK AFFECTIONATELY. IT WAS TOO HARD.

SLAP

I BURNED WITH SILENT RAGE FOR THE WHOLE MEETING.

AND I DIDN'T STAY TO CHAT AFTERWARD.

I GOTTA RUN!

THAT WAS IT FOR ME.

FUCKING ASSHOLE!

I NEVER WENT BACK.

I STILL DIDN'T HAVE A SPONSOR AND HADN'T WORKED THE STEPS, BUT I HAD RECENTLY FOUND ANOTHER PROGRAM TOOL TO TRY. AFFIRMATIONS HELPED COMBAT THE "NEGATIVE CHATTER" OF MY DISEASE:
WHENEVER A NEGATIVE THOUGHT AROSE, I'D REPLACE IT WITH A STATEMENT I WANTED TO BE TRUE.
I AM A POWERFUL EARNER I AM A POWERFUL EARNER I AM A POWERFUL EARNER
DAVID, YOU ARE A POWERFUL EARNER DAVID, YOU ARE A POWERFUL EARNER DAVID, YOU ARE A POWERFUL EARNER
AFTER REPEATING IT IN THE FIRST PERSON FOR A FEW MINUTES, I'D SWITCH IT.
I ENVISIONED THIS AS GOD LOVINGLY TELLING ME THE MESSAGE.
LASTLY I REPEATED IT IN THE THIRD PERSON. BY THEN IT HAD BECOME LIKE A STATEMENT OF FACT. IT SEEMED TO WORK!
DAVID IS A POWERFUL EARNER DAVID IS A POWERFUL EARNER DAVID IS A POWERFUL EARNER
EXCEPT AT HOME.
WHERE WERE YOU? YOU'R AN HOUR LATE!

NOW THAT OUR MONEY TROUBLE HAD VANISHED, OUR FIGHTS WERE ABOUT THE PROGRAM.

THIS IS **EXACTLY** WHAT I WAS AFRAID OF! NOW YOU NEED **TWO** PROGRAMS?!? WHERE DOES THIS END?

YOU SHOULD TRY AN AL-ANON MEETING. IT COULD HELP YOU!
NO WAY.
WHY?!?

IT WOULD HELP YOU DETACH FROM MY INSANITY!

DO YOU EVEN HEAR YOURSELF?!?

ON A DEEPER LEVEL, WE WERE REALLY FIGHTING ABOUT GOD.

YOU NEED TO LET GO AND TRUST MORE.
STOP PROSELYTIZING! WHY DO YOU ALWAYS ACT SO SUPERIOR TO ME?!?

I BELIEVED I WAS FURTHER DOWN THE ROAD THAN HER. I WAS AFRAID SHE'D NEVER CATCH UP AND I'D HAVE TO LEAVE HER BEHIND LIKE MY MOM DID TO MY DAD.

IT WAS FRUSTRATING THAT SHE DIDN'T WANT THE WISDOM I TRIED TO IMPART.

WE SHOULD STOP TALKING ABOUT THIS!

THE SAME WISDOM THAT EVERYONE IN THE ROOM WAS LAPPING UP.

I'M POWERLESS OVER MY WIFE'S WORRYING.
MMMM.

I HAD LEARNED THE "CORRECT" SPIRITUAL ATTITUDE TOWARD MY PROBLEMS WHEN I WAS IN A MEETING.

I'M TRYING TO DETACH WITH LOVE.

BUT IT ALL FELL APART ONCE I GOT HOME. I ALWAYS FELT THWARTED BY REBECCA.

IT'S LIKE YOU'RE TRYING TO **BLOCK** MY SPIRITUAL PROGRESS!

SOMETIMES WE'D STAY UP UNTIL 2AM ARGUING IN CIRCLES ABOUT GOD KNOWS WHAT.

EVERYTHING IN MY LIFE IS GOING GREAT, EXCEPT WITH YOU!

THAT'S WHEN I'D TURN TO PORN.

I'M NOT GOING TO BED YET.

THE WOMAN IN THE VIDEO CLIP FUCKING THREE STRANGERS WAS ALWAYS THERE FOR ME, ALWAYS EXACTLY THE SAME.

BUT THAT DIRTY FEELING THE NEXT MORNING WAS UNBEARABLE.

I NEED A MEETING.
GOWIWWA!

MY STOMACH WAS ALSO STILL IN ROUGH SHAPE.

OWW!

BUT AT LEAST I WAS USING THAT 3AM TIME TO GET WORK DONE ON WHAT WAS BECOMING MY FIRST BOOK.

I DID A LOT OF SCHMOOZING AT COMICS EVENTS AND PARTIES.
CAN I SHOW YOU WHAT I'M WORKING ON?
SURE.

THROUGH A SERIES OF EVENTS THAT I FELT SURE WAS GOD'S HANDIWORK, A LITERARY AGENT CONTACTED ME AT RANDOM.

GET WHATEVER YOU WANT.
STEAK TARTARE?

BEFORE I KNEW IT, HE HAD HELPED ME PITCH AND LAND A TWO-BOOK DEAL WITH MY DREAM PUBLISHER.

WHAT ON EARTH IS HAPPENING?!?

WE SHOULD CELEBRATE!

I SHARED THE NEWS AT MEETINGS AND GAVE ALL THE CREDIT TO THE WORK I'D DONE IN DA. THESE WERE THE PEOPLE I COULD SHARE MY SUCCESS WITH.

CLAP
CLAP
A TWO-BOOK DEAL!

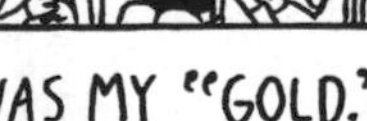
CLAP

THIS WAS MY "GOLD."

I PUT OFF TELLING MY MOM THE NEWS FOR A COUPLE WEEKS. BEFORE FINALLY CALLING HER, I TRIED USING SOME AFFIRMATIONS.

MOM, THERE'S SOME GOOD NEWS I WANT TO SHARE AND I REALLY WANT TO FEEL SUPPORTED BY YOU.
POUND
POUND
POUND
POUND
POUND

I TOLD HER.
WOW, ANGEL... I'M GOING TO PUT INTO WORDS ALL THE DIFFERENT FEELINGS I'M HAVING... READY?
OOKAY...
I'M FUCKING JEALOUS!!!

AND ALSO... I'M SO HAPPY FOR YOU! HOORAY FOR DAVID!

I GOT OFF THE PHONE IMMEDIATELY.
WHAT KIND OF MOTHER SAYS THAT TO HER SON? THE FIRST THING OUT OF HER MOUTH!!!

I WENT STRAIGHT TO WATCHING PORN.
THIS TIME IT WAS A BIGGER, ROUGHER, MORE DEGRADING GANG BANG VIDEO. I CAME INSTANTLY.

CLEANING UP, I HEARD A VOICE RING THROUGH MY HEAD.
THIS ISN'T IN LINE WITH THE SPIRITUAL LIFE YOU'RE TRYING TO LEAD.

I WENT TO WRITE IN MY JOURNAL AND INSTEAD WOUND UP READING SOME OLDER ENTRIES.

TO MY HORROR, IT SEEMED LIKE EVERY PAGE HAD A MENTION OF SOME RO-MANTIC OR SEXUAL FANTASY. IT WAS A STAIN ACROSS MY WHOLE LIFE STORY.

AS A YOUNG TEEN, I WROTE JOURNAL ENTRIES PLEADING WITH MYSELF TO STOP MASTURBATING, BUT IT NEVER WORKED.

"THINK ABOUT HOW YOU'LL FEEL FOR THE WHOLE NEXT DAY..."
JESUS... I COULD HAVE WRITTEN THIS YESTERDA

I WROTE ABOUT JERKING OFF WHILE DRIVING, AT THE NURSE'S OFFICE AT SCHOOL, THAT TIME AT THE PUBLIC LIBRARY, AND IN THE BATHROOMS OF EVERY PLACE I EVER WORKED.

AM I A SEX ADDICT?
MAYBE THAT'S MY **REAL** DISEASE!

I REMEMBERED RICHARD MENTIONING "SLAA." THE "S" MUST STAND FOR "SEX."

I CAN'T JOIN A THIRD PROGRAM!

MAYBE WITH MY SPIRITUAL STRENGTH FROM DA AND AL-ANON, I COULD STOP JERKING OFF ON MY OWN.

I'M SO SICK OF THIS! TOMORROW WILL BE DAY 1 OF SEXUAL SOBRIETY.*

* STILL SOMEHOW ON STEP ONE!

THE NEXT DAY WAS A SATURDAY. WE WERE SUPPOSED TO ATTEND THE 2ND BIRTHDAY PARTY OF MAYA'S FRIEND.

I TOOK A BATH INSTEAD, SOMETHING I HADN'T DONE IN YEARS.

I'M GONNA TAKE A SHOWER.
IT'S STILL BROKEN.

LAYING IN THE HOT WATER, I WAS FLOODED WITH IMAGES OF SEX AND MEMORIES OF JERKING OFF IN THE TUB AS A TEENAGER.

IT WAS TOO MUCH FOR ME.

FUCK IT.

UNNNNNH

I GOT OUT AND REALIZED THE TUB WAS BROKEN, TOO. IT WOULDN'T DRAIN.

OH NO!

I WAS A MISERABLE PIECE OF SHIT FOR DIRTYING UP THE TUB WHERE MY WIFE BATHED MY DAUGHTER EVERY NIGHT.
POUND
POUND
POUND
POUND
COME
YOU CAN'T EVEN GO ONE DAY WITHOUT MASTURBATING!
I EMPTIED THE WHOLE TUB USING THE GARBAGE CAN, THEN I SCRUBBED IT CLEAN WITH PAPER TOWELS.
SCRUB
SCRUB
SCRUB
SCRUB
EXHAUSTED FROM THAT WHOLE ORDEAL, I TRIED TO BACK OUT OF THE PARTY.
I DON'T THINK I'M UP FOR IT...
JUST COME FOR AN HOUR AT LEAST.
DADDY!
AS SOON AS WE ARRIVED, I WAS A BASKET CASE.

THAT GUY WANTS TO FUCK REBECCA.

I WAS TORMENTED BY MY THOUGHTS.

THEY ALL THINK I'M A PERVERT. I REALLY MUST BE A SEX ADDICT. I CAN'T DO THIS ON MY OWN ANYMORE.

AFTER EXACTLY ONE HOUR, I LEFT. REBECCA WAS ANGRY AND HURT.

I NEED TO MAKE A PROGRAM CALL.

I CALLED ANDREW AND TOLD HIM I WANTED SEXUAL SOBRIETY.

I HEAR YOU, BUDDY.

LOOK, NO ONE WANTS TO GO TO A PROGRAM CALLED "SEX AND LOVE ADDICTS ANONYMOUS," BUT THIS IS MY FAVORITE 12-STEP GROUP IN THE CITY. IT'S A BUNCH OF GUYS WHO CAN STILL GET LAID TRYING TO LIVE A SPIRITUAL LIFE. I'M GOING THIS WEDNESDAY. WILL I SEE YOU THERE?

I COULD HARDLY WAIT.

♫ THERE ARE TIMES THAT I WANT YOU... I WANT YOU SO MUCH I COULD
BUST... I KNOW A THING ABOUT LOVERS... LOVERS LIE DOWN IN
TRUST...
BA-DA-BA-BA-BA-DA-DA-BA... LOVE GOES ON ANYWAY
9

AS SOON AS I ENTERED THE UPTOWN SLAA MEN'S MEETING, I FELT A HUGE BURST OF GOD ENERGY. THERE HAD TO HAVE BEEN OVER 100 PEOPLE IN ATTENDANCE.

THE AL-ANON MEN'S MEETING NOW SEEMED LIKE A TEPID WARM-UP IN COMPARISON.

I SAW A NUMBER OF FAMILIAR FACES FROM DA AND AL-ANON, INCLUDING THE MAN QUALIFYING.

HI, I'M CAL AND I'M A SEX AND LOVE ADDICT.
HI, CAL!

HE TOLD HIS STORY MOVINGLY, PAINTING THE SCENE OF HIS UNAVAILABLE MOTHER SMOKING ALONE IN HER ROOM.

IT WAS COMPLETELY DARK. ALL YOU SAW WAS THE CHERRY ON THE CIGARETTE LIGHTING UP HER FACE...

IT WAS ONE OF HIS EARLIEST MEMORIES.

MY MOM BASICALLY TOLD ME TO LEAVE HER THE FUCK ALONE.

HE TALKED ABOUT BEING SEXUALLY ABUSED AS A CHILD.

HE SUCKED MY DICK.

DISCOVERING PORN AND MASTURBATION.

THEY WERE MY FIRST DRUGS.

LATER IT WAS DRINKING, SLEEPING AROUND, ROMANTIC OBSESSIONS.

MY LOVE ADDICT COULDN'T GET ENOUGH OF THIS ONE CHICK.

THE SINCERITY WAS OVERPOWERING. ANY JUDGMENTAL THOUGHTS I MIGHT HAVE HAD WERE GONE. MY HEART WAS OPEN.

I FINALLY REALIZED, "CAL, YOU DON'T HAVE TO LIVE THIS WAY ANYMORE..."

WHEN CAL FINISHED HIS STORY, THE ROOM ERUPTED IN APPLAUSE FOR A FULL MINUTE. I CHEERED RIGHT ALONG WITH THEM.

THEN CAME THE SHARES: THE MOST REVEALING, HEARTFELT, PAIN-FILLED SHARES I'D HEARD IN ANY ROOMS.

SHE WAS SO WOUNDED... I HAD TO SAVE HER... HEAL HER.

EXHALE

A FEW TALKED ABOUT RECOVERING FROM COMPULSIVELY SLEEPING WITH PROSTITUTES.

IT FREAKED ME OUT, BUT ALSO GAVE THE MEETING AN AIR OF EDGY DANGER THAT APPEALED TO ME. I JUST COULDN'T BELIEVE HOW MUCH THESE MEN TOLD EACH OTHER.

THANKS TO THIS ROOM, I CAN FINALLY ADMIT MY ADDICTION TO **TRANSEXUAL** PROSTITUTES!
MMMMH

DURING THE TIME FOR NEWCOMER SHARES I TOLD MY STORY AS BEST I COULD IN THREE MINUTES.

I'M DAVID AND I'M NEW TO THIS PROGRAM.

HI, DAVID

I GOT A BIG LAUGH WITHOUT MEANING TO.

IT'S LIKE... I ALWAYS WANT TO TAKE CARE OF ALL MY FEMALE FRIENDS... AND ALSO FUCK THEM.

HA HA HA

HA HA HA HA HA

AFTER A FEW MORE SHARES, THE CHAIRPERSON WRAPPED UP THE MEETING.

"WHAT YOU HEAR HERE, LET IT REMAIN HERE."

HEAR, HEAR

I WAS WARMLY EMBRACED BY ANDREW, CAL, AND ANOTHER DA FRIEND. THEY INVITED ME OUT TO DINNER.

I HAD FINALLY FOUND MY SPIRITUAL HOME. THESE WERE THE TRUE BROTHER AND FATHER FIGURES I'D BEEN SEARCHING FOR ALL MY LIFE.

MAYBE ONE OF THEM WILL SPONSOR ME AND TAKE ME THROUGH THE STEPS!

THEY HAD BEEN THROUGH DEGRADING, HELLISH SCANDALS.

NOW THEY WERE TRYING SO HARD TO DO THE RIGHT THING - TO TELL THE TRUTH, TO SURVIVE.

THESE MEN WERE WARRIORS, HEROES! I DESPERATELY WANTED WHAT THEY ALL HAD: SEXUAL SOBRIETY.

SOME HAD GOTTEN ANNIVERSARY COINS FOR 10 OR 15 YEARS OF "NO SEX OUTSIDE OF MARRIAGE, INCLUDING PORN AND MASTURBATION."

THAT'S WHAT I WOULD ATTEMPT MYSELF.

I COULD ALREADY FEEL A CHANGE. WITH THEIR SUPPORT, I'D BE ABLE TO DO IT!

WHEN I GOT HOME, I DECIDED NOT TO SHARE ANYTHING I'D EXPERIENCED WITH REBECCA.

JUST THAT IT WAS A NEW MEN'S MEETING AND IT WAS GOOD.

OKAY...

MY FIRST WEEK OF SOBRIEY WAS INTENSE. I ROUNDED UP ALL THE PORN I HAD.

SUPER 8 FILMS BOUGHT AT FLEA MARKETS DURING ART SCHOOL

3 DVDs

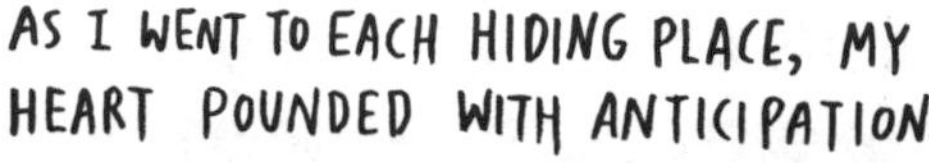
AS I WENT TO EACH HIDING PLACE, MY HEART POUNDED WITH ANTICIPATION.

"ART" MAGAZINES

DIRTY FOUND

POUND
POUND
POUND
POUND

I'M SUCH AN ADDICT!

IT ALL WENT DOWN THE GARBAGE CHUTE.

I FELT A PURITY WASH OVER ME WHEN I WAS DONE.

THAT FIRST NIGHT, I COULD BARELY SLEEP. MY BODY WAS ITCHY AND RESTLESS.

I MUST BE GOING THROUGH WITHDRAWAL.

I PRAYED INCESSANTLY, ESPECIALLY IN THE SHOWER, WHICH USUALLY TRIGGERED A CASCADE OF SEXUAL IMAGES IN MY HEAD.

GOD, PLEASE TURN MY THOUGHTS TO WHAT YOU WOULD HAVE ME DO.
STEEL ROD
TRYING TO PUSH IT DOWN

THERE WERE A SURPRISING NUMBER OF TESTS FOR ME OUTSIDE THE HOUSE, TOO.

GOD, PLEASE TURN MY THOUGHTS...
XXX
LIVE GIRLS!

NOW THAT I HAD AN SLAA LENS ON MY LIFE, I COULD SEE I WAS ADDICTED TO "INTRIGUE."

♫ HI, DAVID! ♫
HEY.

WHAT I'D ALWAYS CONSIDERED HARMLESS FLIRTING WAS REALLY WARMING UP THE PROSPECTS FOR FUTURE AFFAIRS.*

PLEASE TURN MY THOUGHTS

THE POTENTIAL OF SEX WITH CO-WORKERS GAVE ME A HIT.

I LIKE YOUR SHIRT!
THANKS.

NOW THAT I COULD SEE THE "TRUTH," I SUDDENLY TURNED COLD WITH ALL OF THEM. THEY SEEMED CONFUSED AND DISAPPOINTED, BUT MY SOBRIETY CAME BEFORE ANYONE ELSE'S FEELINGS!

* OR SO I'D BEEN TOLD BY OTHER SLAA MEMBERS.

LATER THAT WEEK...
WE'VE BEEN WORKING HARD ON THESE SITE DESIGNS.
CREATIVE DIRECTOR
COOL!

I CAN'T REMEMBER WHAT TRIGGERED IT, BUT MY COPYWRITER PARTNER SAID SOMETHING THAT SOUNDED LIKE THE NAME OF A PORN SITE.

HA HA! WAIT... I GOTTA SHOW YOU GUYS SOMETHING!

DID YOU KNOW THAT IF YOU COPY AND PASTE ANY PORN SITE URL INTO GOOGLE AND THEN DO THIS LITTLE TRICK, YOU CAN GET IN FREE...?

CLACK
CLACK

?

HAHAHA

AAAAAND, THERE YOU HAVE IT... "TUG JOBS"!
HA
HA

WHAT'S THE MATTER, DAVID? YOU LOOK UNCOMFORTABLE.
I AM!

DON'T TELL ON ME, OKAY...?!?

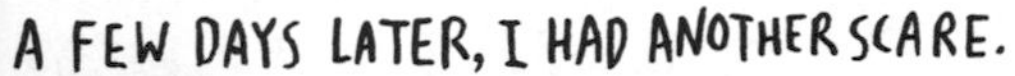
A FEW DAYS LATER, I HAD ANOTHER SCARE.

chinese massage
1 hr $48
call for appointment
212-333-7979

AS PART OF MY DA "SELF-CARE," I HAD BEEN GETTING A FULL-BODY MASSAGE AT LEAST ONCE A MONTH.

DARYL HAD INSPIRED ME WITH HIS PHILOSOPHY ON MASSAGE.

WHENEVER I'VE BEEN IN THE HANDS OF A TRUE HEALER, IT'S LIKE THEY'RE TAKING MY MONEY AND RUBBING IT BACK INTO MY BODY, INCREASING MY EARNING POTENTIAL THREE-FOLD.
WOW.

WITH OUR MOUNTING FAMILY EXPENSES, IT WAS HARD FOR ME TO JUSTIFY GOING TO A FANCY DOWNTOWN SPA.

HI, CAN I COME IN TONIGHT FOR A ONE-HOUR MASSAGE?

THIS NEW PLACE WAS LESS THAN HALF AS MUCH AND I COULD WALK THERE FROM WORK.

I DIDN'T LIKE TO ADMIT IT TO MYSELF, BUT I GOT A PLEASURABLE "HIT" WHENEVER A MASSEUSE AT MY USUAL SPA PULLED DOWN MY UNDERWEAR, EXPOSING MY BUTT.

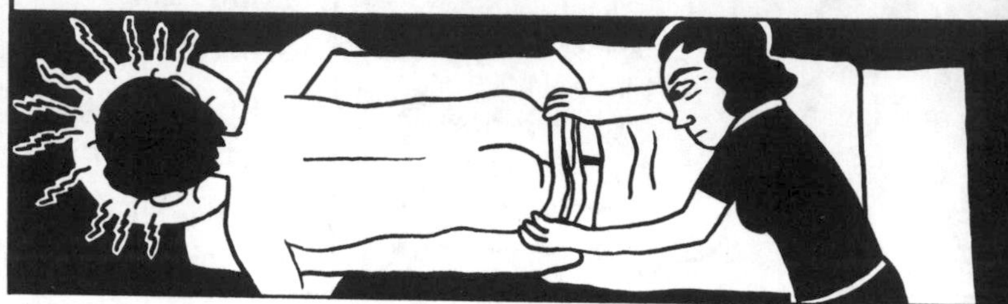

I THOUGHT I COULD DETECT IF THEY WERE ATTRACTED TO ME.

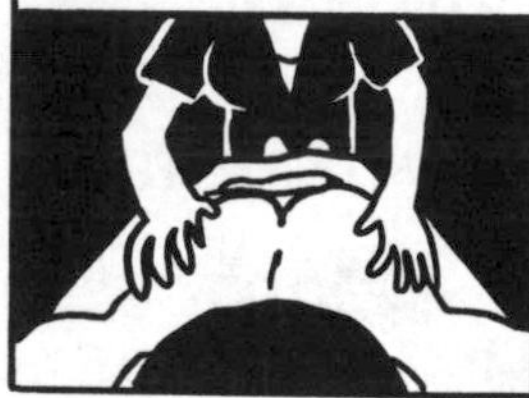

ONE SEEMED OVERLY FOCUSED ON MY INNER THIGHS.

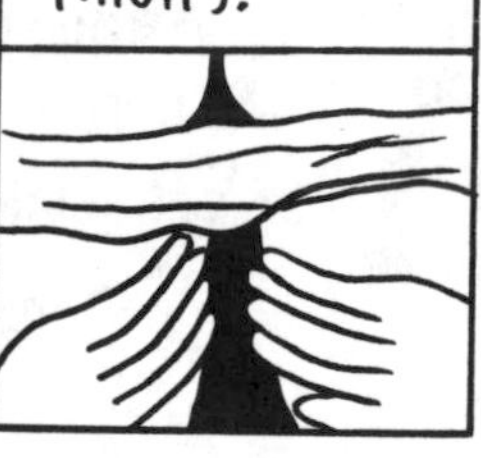

ANOTHER SEEMED TO LINGER ON MY ASS MORE THAN OTHERS.

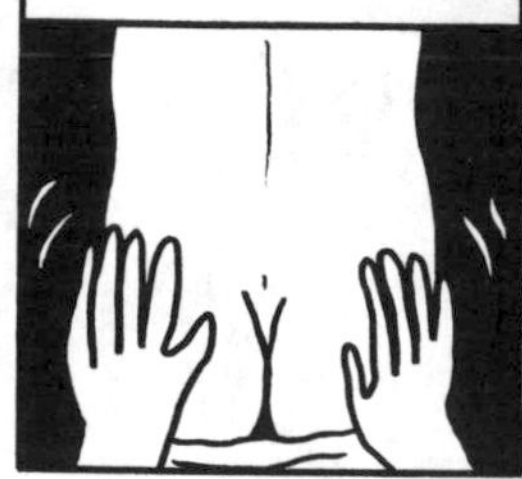

I WOULD CATCH MYSELF FANTASIZING.

IF SHE TRIES TO JERK ME OFF, I'M GONNA LET HER.*

THIS WAS ALL BEFORE SLAA.

GOD, PLEASE PUT ME IN THE HANDS OF A "TRUE HEALER..."

* SHE NEVER DID.

THIS NEW PLACE LOOKED PRETTY SEEDY. IT SHOULD HAVE GIVEN ME PAUSE.

OPEN
NEON SIGN

I WAS BEING HYPER VIGILANT IN EVERY OTHER MOMENT OF MY LIFE, BUT THIS SLIPPED RIGHT BY ME SOMEHOW.

I CHANGED INTO A ROBE IN THE DRESSING AREA, THEN HEADED TO MY ROOM.

BEFORE I COULD LAY ON THE TABLE, MY MASSEUSE WALKED IN WITHOUT KNOCKING.

REMOVE ALL CLOTHING
I-I'M NOT READY!

SHE TRIED REMOVING MY ROBE FOR ME.

UMM... NO, THANK YOU!

SHE LOOKED AT ME COLDLY AND LAUGHED BEFORE CLOSING THE DOOR.

HA HA
???

SHOULD I JUST LEAVE? WHAT AM I DOING?!?

SHE RETURNED AND RIPPED AWAY THE SHEET AGGRESSIVELY.

SHE GAVE ME A HALF-ASSED FULL-BODY RUB DOWN THEN TOLD ME TO TURN OVER.

NO, THANK YOU.
STILL COMPLETELY TENSE

WHAT YOU MEAN "NO"?
I'M DONE. THANKS!

JESUS CHRIST!

AN OLDER SLAA MEMBER WAS SURPRISED BY MY STORY, BUT DIDN'T THINK I'D LOST MY SOBRIETY.

IT'S PART OF MY BOTTOM LINE* TO ALWAYS LEAVE MY UNDERWEAR ON DURING A MASSAGE.

OH... OKAY.

* BOTTOM LINE MEANS A BEHAVIOR WHICH KEEPS AN ADDICT SOBER. IN SLAA, MEMBERS DECIDE ON THEIR OWN WHAT CONSTITUTES SOBRIET

I SHARED WITH ANOTHER SLAA MEMBER.

AS SOON AS I GOT SEXUAL SOBRIETY, THE SAME THING HAPPENED TO ME! ALL THESE CRAZY TESTS STARTED POPPING UP...

MY INSANE EX-GIRLFRIEND SHOWED UP AT MY DOOR, DROPPED TO HER KNEES, AND TRIED TO GIVE ME A BLOW JOB. I HAD TO STOP HER.

"THE WOLF IS ALWAYS AT THE DOOR."

MY SPONSOR SAYS "I HAVE A DISEASE THAT LIVES IN MY NERVOUS SYSTEM AND WANTS ME DEAD!"

ALRIGHT, ALREADY. JESUS!

I DIDN'T SAY ANYTHING TO REBECCA. SHE STILL DIDN'T KNOW ABOUT SLAA.

I'LL GO TO MY USUAL SPA EVERY TWO MONTHS AND I'LL INSIST ON LEAVING MY UNDERWEAR ON!

I SURVIVED THESE TESTS AND STAYED SOBER AND, AS PROMISED, ON THE OTHER SIDE OF THE HURDLES WAS "ABUNDANCE BEYOND MY WILDEST DREAMS."

REBECCA SURPRISED ME WITH SOME NEWS.
I HAVE A PRESENT FOR YOU.
REALLY?
MAYA NAPPING

I STARED AT THE PAPER STORKS AND STROLLERS FOR A LONG TIME.

SUDDENLY IT CLICKED.
YOU'RE PREGNANT?!?
UH-HUH!

WE HADN'T BEEN PLANNING THIS, BUT I WAS ECSTATIC. WE GOT CLOSE AGAIN.

WE SOON FOUND OUT WE WERE HAV-ING A SON.
A BOY! A BOY!!!

RIGHT AWAY REBECCA WAS NAUSEATED. SHE BECAME COMPLETELY DISINTERESTED IN SEX.
BLECCHHH!

STILL, I STAYED SOBER. NO PORN OR MASTURBATION.
GOD, PLEASE TURN MY THOUGHTS TO WHAT YOU WOULD HAVE ME DO...

NO INTRIGUE OR FANTASIES ABOUT OTHER WOMEN.
HAHA HA

I WAS GOING TO DO THIS NO MATTER WHAT.
TODAY IS DAY 15 OFF PORN, MASTURBATION, INTRIGUE, AND FANTASY.
CLAP
CLAP
CLAP

SOON I HAD MY FIRST SLAA COIN.
CLAP CLAP CLAP CLAP CLAP
30 DAYS!

NEXT WAS 60 DAYS.

CLAP CLAP CLAP

BY DAY 89, I FELT LIKE I WOULD GO INSANE FROM SEXUAL FRUSTRATION.

GOD, PLEASE TURN MY THOUGHTS!

ON THE MORNING OF MY 90TH DAY, I HAD A WET DREAM ABOUT REBECCA.

UNNNH

I FELT SO GRATEFUL TO GOD FOR RELIEVING THE TENSION IN A WAY THAT DIDN'T FEEL LIKE CHEATING OUTSIDE OF MY MARRIAGE.

IT MADE ME FEEL HIGH ALL DAY.

THANK YOU!!!

AT THE MEETING THAT NIGHT, I SHARED IN ALL EARNESTNESS...

THIS MORNING I HAD A BLESSED RELEASE.*

SOON AFTER MY 90TH DAY, I WAS ASKED TO QUALIFY. EVEN THOUGH I FELT LIKE A SEASONED PRO IN DA, THIS QUALIFICATION MADE ME NERVOUS.

DON'T WORRY. YOU'RE READY!

OKAY.

100 MEN LOOKING AT ME...

I DIDN'T KNOW HOW TO TELL MY STORY IN SLAA YET. IT KICKED UP DOUBTS.

AM I REALLY A SEX ADDICT?!?

*OF ALL THE THINGS I'VE SHARED IN THIS BOOK SO FAR, THIS SENTENCE MAKES ME CRINGE THE MOST.

AS THE DAY OF MY BIG SPEECH APPROACHED, I TWISTED MYSELF INTO KNOTS TRYING TO GET MY STORY STRAIGHT, JUSTIFYING TO MYSELF WHY I BELONGED IN THE GROUP.

FANTASY
MASTURBATION
PORN
CRUSHES
DIRTY FEELING INSIDE
FEMALE FRIENDS
HATE
SELF-LOATHING
DOZENS OF JOURNAL PAGES

TWO DAYS BEFORE I WAS PLAGUED WITH FEARS THAT NO ONE WOULD SHOW UP.

I HAD NIGHTMARES ABOUT PEOPLE TALKING LOUDLY DURING MY QUALIFICATION.

EVERYBODY SHUT UP AND LISTEN TO ME!!!

FINALLY, THE MOMENT ARRIVED. THE ROOM WAS FULL AND ALL EYES WERE ON ME.

HI, I'M DAVID AND I'M A SEX, LOVE, AND FANTASY ADDICT.

HI, DAVID

HI, DAVID

HI, DAVID

HI, DAVID

I STARED AT MY FEET FOR THE ENTIRE 15 MINUTES.

I'M FEELING REALLY NERVOUS TONIGHT.

POUN
POUN
POU
POU
POU

I RAMBLED.

I'M POWERLESS OVER SEX, LOVE, FANTASY, MONEY, AND DEBTING, WORK, RELATIONSHIPS, AND MORE. I FEEL LIKE I HIT A FAIRLY "HIGH BOTTOM" WHEN IT COMES TO THIS PROGRAM, BUT I BELIEVE I COULD HAVE GONE MUCH FURTHER DOWN IF NOT FOR DISCOVERING SLAA...

POUND

POUND

POUND

POUND

I TALKED ABOUT MASTURBATION AND PORN AND ALSO TRIED TO WEAVE IN WHAT I'D LEARNED IN DA AND AL-ANON. I HAD TO CRAM IT ALL IN.

IT WAS TORTUROUS BECAUSE I KNEW I WASN'T BEING "FULLY PRESENT," WHICH MADE ME FEEL LIKE MORE OF A FRAUD.

IF I GET SEXUAL THOUGHTS IN THE SHOWER, THERE'S A PRAYER I SAY...
FIVE MINUTES LEFT.
THANKS.

I FINISHED UNSATISFIED AND DISAPPOINTED.

THANKS FOR LETTING ME SHARE.

CLAP CLAP CLAP

UGH!

CLAP CLAP CLAP

I DIDN'T HIT IT OUT OF THE PARK. THIS WAS MORE LIKE A FOUL TIP.

ONE MEMBER SPOKE TO ME DURING THE BREAK.

YEAH, THIS ONE DA QUALIFICATION I GAVE, I JUST LEFT A BIG SPACE OF SILENCE. IT WAS POWERFUL.

FUCK YOU!

IT SET OFF MY WORST FEARS ABOUT HOW MY TALK HAD BEEN RECEIVED.

WHY DID HE SAY THAT?

BUT EVERYONE ELSE GAVE ME BEAR HUGS AND WORDS OF ENCOURAGEMENT.

GREAT JOB, MAN! I'M PROUD'A YOU!

AND AT THE END OF THE MEETING, I GOT SHOWERED WITH SOOTHING APPLAUSE.

LET'S THANK OUR SPEAKER, DAVID!
WOO!
WHISTLE!
CLAP! CLAP! CLAP!
CLAP! CLAP!

OVER THE NEXT 3 MONTHS, I STAYED SOBER AND ATTENDED THE MEETING WEEKLY. MOST NIGHTS I GOT TO SHARE, WHICH WAS GOOD BECAUSE I WAS STARTING TO DEPEND ON BEING HEARD.

DAVID.

I WAS STILL ON THE HUNT FOR A SPONSOR WHO COULD TAKE ME THROUGH THE STEPS. NO ONE I ASKED WAS AVAILABLE.

I GOT A 6-MONTH AND THEN A 9-MONTH COIN. IT GOT EASIER TO STAY SOBER.

MY SEX DRIVE HAD SETTLED DOWN.

I NOW REALIZED THAT WHAT I'D ALWAYS ASSUMED TO BE MY NATURE...

I NEED SEX EVERY DAY!

...WAS SOMETHING I'D IMPOSED ON MY BODY.

I'LL JERK OFF ABOUT HER LATER.

IT WAS LIKE A MACHINE I WAS CRANKING UP AND SETTING IN MOTION EVERY DAY.

UNNNH!

THE TRUTH WAS I ONLY REALLY "NEEDED" TO ORGASM ONCE EVERY TWO MONTHS.

UNNNH!

OTHERWISE THIS SEXUAL ENERGY COULD BE CHANNELED INTO WORKING ON MY BOOK.

ANOTHER PAGE DONE!

I WORKED AS MUCH AS I POSSIBLY COULD, DAY AND NIGHT. AND THEN... THE LONG, COLD WINTER GAVE WAY TO SPRING.

THAT'S WHEN SAM DROPPED INTO MY LIFE.

HANDSOME, SOLID LITTLE SAM.

HE WAS A SMILING, PEACEFUL BUDDHA BABY...

... WITH A POWERFULLY, MAGNETIC ENERGY EVERYONE NOTICED.

MAYA'S BIRTH CHALLENGED ME WITH THE QUESTION "WHAT KIND OF **EARNER** DO YOU WANT TO BE?"

SAM SEEMED TO BE ASKING, "NOW THAT YOU HAVE A SON, WHAT KIND OF A **MAN** DO YOU WANT TO BE?"

WHEN HE WAS A MONTH OLD, WE HAD A "BABY WELCOMING" CEREMONY AT OUR APARTMENT, JUST AS WE'D DONE FOR MAYA.

WE ASKED OUR FAMILY TO WRITE MESSAGES TO HIM IN A SPECIAL BOOK.

I WROTE A QUOTE FROM MARILYNNE ROBINSON'S <u>GILEAD</u>.

"If you ever wonder what you've done in your life, and everyone does wonder sooner or later, know that you have been God's grace to me... a miracle. Something more than a miracle."

-Marilynne R.
Gilead

OFTEN WHEN I WAS HOLDING SAM, I'D BE DISTRACTED, LOOKING AWAY AT SOMETHING ELSE.

THEN I'D FEEL HIM GET COMPLETELY STILL. I'D LOOK DOWN AND SEE HIM QUIETLY STARING UP AT ME.

I WANTED TO BE WORTHY OF THAT GAZE OF HIS.

AT THE ONE-YEAR MARK IN SLAA, I RECEIVED A GOLD COIN. I VOLUNTEERED TO DO A 3-MONTH TERM AS CO-CHAIR, BUT I HAD TO BE VOTED IN BY A MAJORITY.

ALL THOSE IN FAVOR OF DAVID, PLEASE RAISE YOUR HAND.
PLEASE...

I GOT ELECTED!
THANK YOU, GOD!

THIS SIMPLE JOB DID MORE FOR MY CONFIDENCE, SELF-ESTEEM, AND SENSE OF MANHOOD THAN ANYTHING I'D EVER DONE BEFORE.

THIS IS A CLOSED MEETING OF SLAA.
PROJECTING AUTHORITY TO 100 MEN

IT WAS DEEPLY SATISFYING TO DO SERVICE FOR THE GROUP THAT HAD ALREADY GIVEN ME SO MUCH.

THE ONLY QUALIFICATION FOR SLAA MEMBERSHIP IS THE DESIRE TO STOP LIVING OUT A PATTERN OF SEX AND LOVE ADDICTION.

ONE NIGHT WHEN I WAS CHAIRING THE MEETING, A MAN NAMED LOU SHOWED UP.

HI, LOU

LOU HAD A DEEP, EARNEST MIDWESTERN VOICE WITH THE CAREFUL CADENCES OF A DEACON OR A PRIEST.

WHY IS HE SMILING AT ME?

SOMETHING ABOUT HIM CREEPED ME OUT.

NOW WE'LL GO TO DAY COUNTS AND ANNIVERSAR

WHEN I GOT TO FIVE YEARS, HE RAISED HIS HAND.

TODAY IS FIVE YEARS OF NO LONGER OBSESSIVELY FALLING IN LOVE WITH TRANSSEXUAL PROSTITUTES.
CLAP CLAP
CLAP CLAP CLAP CLAP

IT WAS STRANGE THAT I HADN'T SEEN HIM ONCE OVER MY YEAR IN SLAA, BUT THE LANGUAGE HE USED WAS CURIOUS, TOO.

OKAY, LET'S GO BACK TO SHARING FOR TEN MORE MINUTES.

WAS HE STILL SEEING THESE PROSTITUTES, BUT NOT FALLING IN LOVE WITH THEM? WAS THAT REALLY HIS BOTTOM LINE IN SOBRIETY?

I SHARED THAT NIGHT ABOUT WHAT IT MEANT TO BE THE FATHER OF A BOY.

I'M FINALLY STARTING TO FEEL LIKE A MAN. I'M HIS PROTECTOR.
MMMH!

AFTER THE MEETING, I COULD SENSE LOU WANTING TO TALK TO ME.

I STAYED BUSY WITH OTHER PEOPLE AND WALKED OUT WITH THEM TO DINNER.

WE GOT OUR MENUS AND I STARTED TO RELAX. I HAD ESCAPED HIM.

SUDDENLY HE BURST THROUGH THE DOOR AND WALKED RIGHT TO OUR TABLE.

!

HE LEANED OVER AND SPOKE IN MY EAR.

WILL YOU BE MY DADDY?

WHAT?!? WHY DID YOU ASK ME THAT?!?
OH... UMM, YOU SHARED SO BEAUTIFULLY ABOUT YOUR SON. I THOUGHT I'D GIVE YOU A COMPLIMENT ABOUT HOW WELL YOU'RE DOING. I NEVER HAD A FATHER LIKE YOU.

WELL IT WAS A STRANG
WAY YOU CHOSE TO
SAY ALL THAT!

OH....

HE LOOKED STRICKEN—LIKE I'D JUST PUNCHED HIM IN THE STOMACH—THEN HE SHUFFLED BACK OUT INTO THE NIGHT.

GOOD!

I NEVER SAW HIM AT OUR MEETING AGAIN AFTER THAT.

WHEW!

IT WASN'T A CONSCIOUS DECISION, BUT I STOPPED GOING OUT TO DINNER, TOO.

JUST A QUICK BITE!
I GOTTA GET HOME...

NOW THAT I WAS NO LONGER A NEW-COMER, I WASN'T GETTING CALLED ON CONSISTENTLY TO SHARE.

ARRIVED EARLY, SITTING ACROSS FROM THE SPEAKER
JERRY.

EVEN IF I WAS THE CHAIRPERSON!

JUST LIKE IN DA, IF I WAS CHOSEN TO SHARE, I'D LEAVE ON A SPIRITUAL HIGH.

IF I DIDN'T GET CHOSEN, I'D FEEL CRUSHED, ABANDONED, BETRAYED! SOMETIMES I LEFT FEELING WORSE THAN WHEN I GOT THERE.

FUCK ALL OF YOU ASSHOLES!

I GOT A SUGGESTION TO TRY THE 7TH-STEP PRAYER. IT HELPED A LITTLE.

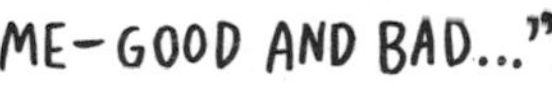
"MY CREATOR, I AM NOW WILLING THAT YOU SHOULD HAVE ALL OF ME—GOOD AND BAD..."

I ALSO FOCUSED ON EXPANDING MY SOCIAL CIRCLE IN SLAA, SO I'D HAVE MORE FRIENDS TO SHARE WITH BY PHONE AND AFTER MEETINGS.

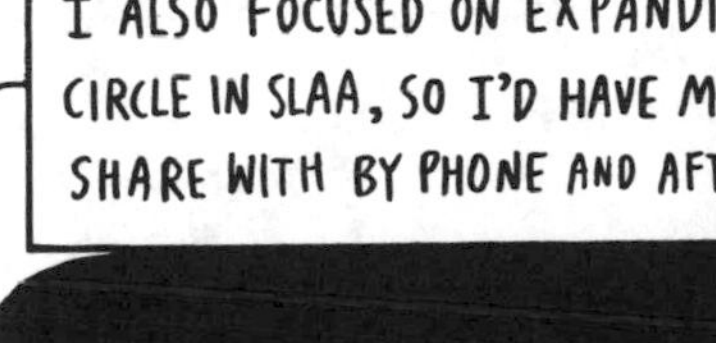

AMONG OTHERS, THERE WAS LARRY.

I DIDN'T LIKE HIM AT ALL AT FIRST.

WHY DOES HE ALWAYS HAVE THAT SILLY SMIRK ON HIS FACE?

INSTEAD OF A NORMAL UPDATE DURING THE DAY-COUNT SECTION OF THE MEETING, i.e., "39 DAYS OFF PORN," LARRY WOULD SHARE:

I'M RECLAIMING MY CHILDHOOD THROUGH SOFTBALL.
UGH!

ONE WEEK HE SHARED THAT HE WAS "EATING CONSCIOUSLY." THAT PHRASE CAUGHT MY ATTENTION.

WHAT DID IT MEAN TO EAT CONSCIOUSLY? I HAD NO IDEA.

CAN I GET YOUR NUMBER?

I STARTED SHARING WITH LARRY ABOUT MY MYSTERIOUS STOMACH TROUBLE.

I'M ADDICTED TO ANT-ACID PILLS AND I WAKE UP IN THE MIDDLE OF THE NIGHT ALL THE TIME IN AGONY.

WE WERE BOTH OF MIXED IRISH AND ITALIAN HERITAGE.

WE MUST HAVE THE SAME STOMACH!

HE ENCOURAGED ME TO GIVE UP WHEAT, DAIRY, AND SOY.

SUGAR WOULD BE NEXT IF I COULD MANAGE IT.

I DID AS HE SAID AND IMMEDIATELY FELT BETTER.

YOU CAN THROW OUT THOSE ANTACID PILLS NOW. YOUR SYSTEM IS STARTING TO RIGHT ITSELF.*

WHEN I'D SEE HIM AT MEETINGS, HE'D GIVE ME A SPOT CHECKUP.

YOUR EYES LOOK NICE AND CLEAR... YOU MUST BE EATING WELL.
I FEEL AMAZING!

* IT WOULD ACTUALLY BE ANOTHER SEVEN YEARS BEFORE I STOPPED TAKING THEM.

THE HEAVY CRASH AFTER A MEAL, THE IRRITABILITY, MOOD CHANGES, AND MOST OF THE REFLUX PAIN WERE GONE.

THANK YOU, GOD!
NOT GROGGY

NEXT, I STOPPED EATING BEEF, BANANAS, AND PEANUTS.

ALL THE COMMON ALLERGENS.

I ALWAYS THINK, "GREAT! ANOTHER FOOD I CAN JUST LET GO OF!"

BETTER IN THE GARBAGE CAN THAN ROTTING AWAY IN MY STOMACH.

HA
HA

REBECCA WAS IRRITATED AT FIRST, THEN ALARMED.

I NEVER KNOW WHAT TO COOK FOR YOU!

I GREW SKINNIER, BUT I FELT HEALTHY AND ENERGIZED BEYOND BELIEF.

THIS IS GOD'S WILL FOR ME! WHY CAN'T YOU JUST SUPPORT ME?!?

I TOLD MYSELF THAT REBECCA WAS A FEARFUL PERSON. I DIDN'T NEED TO LET HER DICTATE THE COURSE OF MY RECOVERY.

WHENEVER I GOT TO SHARE, MY FOCUS SHIFTED AWAY FROM SEX TO TALKING ABOUT FOOD.
IT'S ALWAYS BEEN A PROBLEM FOR ME- HATING MY BODY AND EATING COMPULSIVELY.
AFTER ONE MEETING...
I HAVE SOME THOUGHTS ABOUT WHAT YOU SHARED.
?

ISSUES WITH FOOD ALMOST ALWAYS CORRELATE WITH SEXUAL ABUSE. IS THAT PART OF YOUR STORY?
NOT THAT I'M AWARE OF!
UGH! NO SENSE OF BOUNDARIES!

HIS QUESTION RATTLED AND HAUNTED ME.
AM I NOT REMEMBERING SOMETHING?
AT HOME I WAS FEELING EDGIER THAN EVER. THE HONEYMOON PERIOD OF HAVING A NEW BABY WAS OVER. IT WAS NOW GRUELING.
WAAAAAAA!
WAAAAAAAA!

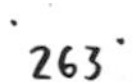

REBECCA AND I WENT BACK TO OUR ARGUING. IT HAD NOW BEEN A YEAR SINCE WE HAD ANY SEXUAL CONTACT.

I HATED HAVING TO COMPETE WITH THE KIDS FOR SCRAPS OF HER ATTENTION.

MOMMY? MOMMY? MOMMY!

EVEN WHEN I DID GET TO BE HEARD, EVERY TOPIC OF CONVERSATION WAS A MINEFIELD: GOD, FOOD, 12-STEP MEETINGS.

I OFTEN NEEDED TO BOOKEND MY TIME WITH REBECCA AND THE KIDS WITH PROGRAM CALLS BEFORE AND AFTER.

MY INTENTION IS TO BE LOVING AND KIND AND TO BE OF SERVICE TO MY FAMILY.

WHAT WAS THE SECRET OF THE MEN WHO EXUDED A SENSE OF LASTING PEACE? I WANTED **THAT.**

SHH...
IT'S TIME FOR SLEEP NOW.

I OFTEN FELT IT IN THE ROOMS, BUT I WANTED IT EVERYWHERE IN MY LIFE.

GO TO SLEEP!!!
WAAA

THE "INNER CIRCLE" OF THE MEN'S MEETING HAD ALL BEEN ON "EMOTIONAL RELEASE" RETREATS TOGETHER.

MMMH!

I DID A HUGE PIECE OF WORK AT THE RETREAT THIS WEEK.

THESE WERE SPIRITUAL, THERAPEUTIC WEEKENDS NOT AFFILIATED WITH SLAA.

TODAY I FEEL LIKE I'M **ENOUGH!**

CLAP CLAP

CLAP CLAP

BUT THE ORGANIZER WAS A LONG-TERM MEMBER NAMED MOSHE.

IT DIDN'T TAKE ME LONG TO SAVE UP THE $500.

DAVID, YOU'LL SEE... THIS IS A LIFE-CHANGING EXPERIENCE!

I CAN'T WAIT!

BUT NOW I HAD TO ADMIT TO REBECCA THAT I HAD JOINED A THIRD PROGRAM—THAT I WAS A SEX AND LOVE ADDICT.

POUND
POUND
POUND
POUND
HI...
HI... WHAT'S UP?

SHE DIDN'T TAKE THE NEWS WELL.

YOU REALLY SEE YOURSELF AS ONE OF THOSE MEN?!?

PEOPLE WHO SEE PROSTITUTES AND WATCH PORN 15 HOURS IN A ROW?!?
ARE YOU CRAZY?*

I WENT ON A TIRADE, ADMITTING TO ALL THE SEXUAL FANTASIES I'D HAD IN MY LIFE AND ALL THE TIMES AND PLACES I'D MASTURBATED IN HIGH SCHOOL AND COLLEGE.

WHILE DRIVING A CAR!

I FINALLY CONVINCED HER.

MAYBE I WAS SICK AFTER ALL.

MAYBE I DID NEED THOSE MEETINGS.

*YES.

IT WAS HARD FOR HER TO SWALLOW THAT SHE WOULD HAVE TO WATCH BOTH OUR TWO-YEAR-OLD AND SIX-MONTH-OLD WHILE I WAS OFF ON A THREE-DAY "RETREAT," BUT SHE GAVE IN.
IT WAS MID-OCTOBER.
I PACKED MY BAGS AND HEADED UP TO A CAMP IN COLD SPRING, NY...
...TO JOIN MY BROTHERS IN THE MYSTERIOUS RITUAL OF EMOTIONAL RELEASE.

YOU
WITHIN...
Alcoholics Anonymous
4TH ST
THE POWER OF NOW
Tolle
Twelve Steps
10
...SHINES...
...THE
DON'T BE AFRAID OF...

MY FIRST THOUGHT WHEN I ARRIVED WAS THAT THE PLACE LOOKED JUST LIKE MY CHRISTIAN SUMMER CAMP.

FUCK!

THERE WERE THE SAME DANK, DINGY CABINS.

AND THE SEPARATE OUTDOOR BATHROOM.

"GREENIES"

I DROPPED MY STUFF ON A STAINED, SQUEAKY MATTRESS AND WALKED OVER TO THE LODGE.

THIS WAS WHERE WE WOULD MEET EVERY DAY TO DO OUR "RELEASE WORK."

IT WAS WHERE I MET DAN JONES.

HE HAD BECOME SOMETHING OF A LEGEND TO ME.

THAT'S HIM?

AT THE MEN'S MEETING, PEOPLE SPOKE OF HIM WITH AWE AND REVERENCE.

HE LOOKS SO GOOFY.
HA HA

HE HAD THOSE CULTY, "LIT FROM WITHIN" EYES AND A PERPETUAL SMILE ON HIS FACE.

OKAY! LET'S GET STARTED.

FIRST: WELCOME TO A SAFE PLACE.

YOU'LL EACH GET A TURN TO COME UP, USUALLY FOR A HALF HOUR, BUT IT CAN GO AS LONG AS AN HOUR.

NO ONE WILL INTERRUPT YOU WHILE YOU DO YOUR WORK. YOU'LL ONLY SPEAK TO ME.

HE WRAPPED UP HIS INTRODUCTION. I WAS ANXIOUS TO START, BUT IT WAS LATE.

HEY, GUYS, I'LL BE CHAIRING AN SLAA MEETING HERE IN TEN MINUTES. ANYONE IS WELCOME.
MOSHE

EVERYONE STAYED EXCEPT ME. I WAS EXHAUSTED AND NEEDED SLEEP.

TWO HOURS LATER, I WOKE UP TO LIGHTS SWITCHING ON AND VOICES CHATTERING THROUGHOUT THE CABIN.

BUMP
CLANG
WHAT A GREAT MEETING. I LOVED YOUR SHARE!

IT WAS RAINING AND THE CABIN HAD ONLY SCREEN WINDOWS, SO MY SLEEPING BAG WAS DAMP.

I WAS WIDE AWAKE AND COULDN'T FALL BACK ASLEEP ALL NIGHT.

THIS IS MISERABLE!

THE NEXT MORNING I WAS WORN OUT WHEN WE GOT TO THE LODGE. DAN JONES ASKED FOR A VOLUNTEER TO GO FIRST.

WE NEED A LEADER, SOMEONE UNAFRAID TO DIVE IN.

OF COURSE ANDREW RAISED HIS HAND.

CLAP CLAP CLAP

WOO!

HE HAD BROUGHT A DRAWING ALONG WITH HIM.*

I HAVEN'T LOOKED AT THIS YET.

MY THERAPIST DREW THIS WITH MY PERMISSION. SHE'S ALSO AN AMAZING ARTIST. IT'S A SCENE OF ME AND MY MOTHER THAT I HAD DESCRIBED TO HER.

?

WITHIN A MINUTE, HE WAS CRYING. I SQUIRMED WITH EMBARRASSMENT.

CHOKE MOMMY WITH HER PILLS...

DID SHE CALL YOU ANDY?

I WANTED TO RUN OUT THE DOOR.

THIS WAS A MISTAKE.

SOB SOB SOB

* HE LIVED JUST DOWN THE HILL.

DAN JONES GUIDED HIM UNTIL HE HIT UPON THE RIGHT PHRASE.

MOMMY, LOOK AT ME!
STAY THERE!
LOOK AT ME!

MOMMY, LOOK AT ME!!!!!
SOB SOB SOB
SQUEEZE MY HANDS.

AFTER A FEW MINUTES OF THIS, ANDREW REACHED HIS CRESCENDO AND THEN HIS FACE SETTLED.

HE LOOKED TRANSFORMED, AT PEACE.
CLAP CLAP CLAP CLAP
CLAP
CLAP

I WAS GLAD I STAYED.
CLAP
CLAP
CLAP
SO THAT'S EMOTIONAL-RELEASE WORK...
WOO!
CLAP
CLAP

WE ALL LINED UP TO GIVE HIM HUGS.
GREAT WORK!
THANKS, MAN.

THREE MORE MEN CAME UP AND DID THEIR WORK BEFORE LUNCH.

ONE GUY WAS A TALL, BURLY CONSTRUCTION MANAGER. HE TALKED ABOUT A HORRENDOUS MEMORY FROM SUMMER CAMP.

CHOKE

A GROUP OF FOOTBALL JOCKS ANALLY RAPED HIM WITH A BROOMSTICK HANDLE.

I WAS GROANING IN PAIN AND THEY LAUGHED AND SAID, "LOOK, HE LIKES IT!" SOB SOB

SOB SOB SOB
SOB SOB

AFTER HIM, A MIDDLE-AGED MAN TALKED ABOUT HIS SHAME AND OBSESSION WITH BONDAGE PORN AND HIS DESIRE FOR WOMEN TO DOMINATE HIM.

I DON'T IMAGINE ANYONE HERE CAN RELATE TO THAT. YOU ALL SEEM REALLY MASCULINE TO ME.

I BET YOU'D BE SURPRISED.

AS THE DAY WORE ON, I GOT IRRATIONALLY AFRAID I'D GET SKIPPED.

IS THERE ANY TIME LEFT TODAY?

YES. I CAN SQUEEZE YOU IN TONIGHT. YOU'LL GO LAST.
OKAY.

FOR THE REST OF THE EVENING I WAS A WRECK.

WHAT WILL COME OUT OF ME?
SOB
SOB
SOB

I KEPT WATCHING THE CLOCK.

WHEW THAT ONE WAS ONLY A HALF HOUR
CLAP
CLAP

RIGHT BEFORE MY TURN, A YOUNG DOCTOR FROM LONG ISLAND STARTED HIS SESSION.

SINCE HE WAS GETTING MARRIED THE FOLLOWING WEEKEND, THE GROUP WAS BEING EXTRAINDULGENT.

I HOPE YOU GUYS DON'T MIND—I LIKE TO STAND WHILE I DO MY WORK.

HE CLEARLY WANTED US TO KNOW HOW EXPERIENCED HE WAS.

MOST OF YOU KNOW MY STORY...

I FOUND EVERYTHING ABOUT HIS SESSION TO BE EXCRUCIATING.

GOD GRANT ME THE SERENITY...

IT TOOK HIM AN HOUR OF TALKING BEFORE HE FOUND HIS RELEASE-WORK PHRASE.

I'M SO TIRED OF BUILDING THINGS UP THEN DESTROYING THEM.

GOOD. STAY THERE.

BUILDING THINGS UP... DESTROYING THEM!

HE GOT ON THE FLOOR AND SOBBED WITH HIS HEAD BURIED IN A PILLOW.

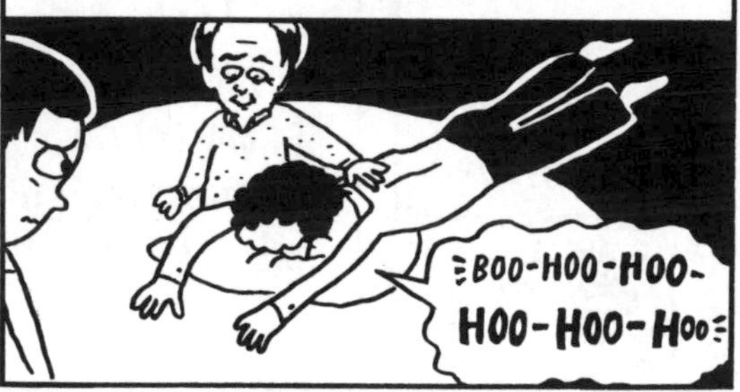
BOO-HOO-HOO-HOO-HOO-HOO

YOU KNOW? IT'S SO GOOD THAT THIS IS HAPPENING!

HE WENT ON FOR ANOTHER 20 MINUTES.

AND NOW... I'M REALLY GETTING MARRIED!

I WAS CONSUMED WITH ANGER.

GOD, **PLEASE** TURN MY THOUGHTS...

BLAH BLAH BLAH

HE HAD SUCKED ALL THE ENERGY OUT OF THE ROOM.

THANK YOU, GUYS! I LOVE YOU ALL!

CLAP
CLAP
CLAP
CLAP

EVERYONE WAS RED-EYED, EXHAUSTED FROM THE DAY.

THAT WAS AMAZING!
THERE'S NOTHING LEFT FOR ME.

DAN JONES ASKED THAT WE KEEP OUR COMMENTS BRIEF SINCE WE HAD GONE OVER TIME.

THAT WAS LIKE A BROADWAY SHOW, ESPECIALLY WHEN YOU WERE ON THE FLOOR WITH THE PILLOW! HA HA HA

FINALLY IT WAS MY TURN.

WE HAVE ONE MORE TONIGHT. COME ON UP, DAVID!

CLAP
CLAP
CLAP
POUND
POUND
POUND
POUND
POUND
POUND
CLAP
CLAP

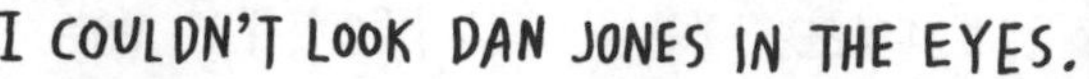
I COULDN'T LOOK DAN JONES IN THE EYES.

I'M REALLY AFRAID NO ONE WANTS TO LISTEN TO ME...

GOD, I WANT TO ASK YOU FOR GUIDANCE.

HELP ME TO SHARE THE THINGS I NEED TO SHARE.

I WOUND UP TALKING ABOUT BEING BEAT UP, CHOKED, AND EGGED IN THE FACE WHILE I WAS AT SUMMER CAMP.

I QUICKLY HIT UPON A GOOD PHRASE.
FUCK YOU!
FUUUUCK! YOOOUU!

I TALKED ABOUT MY MOM—CONTROLLING ME, COMPETING WITH ME, BELITTLING ME. THE SAME PHRASE WORKED.

FUCK YOU!!!

AAAAAHH!!!

AAAAAAAH!!!

SOB SOB SOB
SOB SOB SOB

SIGH...

I FINISHED AND FELT A POWERFUL RELEASE.

THERE WAS AN AIRY LIGHTNESS IN MY HEAD, CHEST, AND STOMACH– THE BIGGEST "GOD BURST" I'D FELT TO DATE.
IT WAS BLISS.
CLAP CLAP CLAP CLAP CLAP CLAP

EVERYONE GAVE ME HUGS AND GENEROUS, LOVING FEEDBACK.

YOUR FACE LOOKS DIFFERENT. LIKE WHEN A BOY GOES THROUGH PUBERTY.

WOW!

THERE HAD BEEN ENOUGH FOR ME AFTER ALL!

AFTER WE WRAPPED UP, ANDREW OFFERED TO LET A FEW OF US STAY OVER AT HIS HOUSE INSTEAD OF THE CABIN.

I'D LOVE TO!
ME, TOO!
LEV

LEV WAS SOMEONE I'D SEEN IN DA. WE'D BE SHARING ANDREW'S SMALL FINISHED BASEMENT WITH TWO MATTRESSES ON THE FLOOR.

WE HIT IT OFF RIGHT AWAY.

THIS BEATS THE SHIT OUT OF THE CABIN!
MAYBE IT'S OUR DA RECOVERY... NO DEPRIVATION FOR US!
HA
HA HA HA
HA
HA

AFTER WE DROPPED OFF OUR STUFF, ANDREW DROVE US ALL TO THE LODGE FOR MOSHE'S SLAA MEETING.

BIZARRELY, ANDREW BROUGHT A BLOW-UP SEX DOLL AS A PRANK.

MEET MY FRIEND!
HA HA HA
!

A COUPLE OF PEOPLE LAUGHED, BUT ONCE THE MEETING STARTED, THE BONDAGE-PORN GUY SPOKE UP.

HEH
HEH
I'M DISTRACTED BY THE OBJECTIFICATION TOOL. CAN YOU PUT THAT AWAY?

HE SHEEPISHLY PUT IT UNDER HIS CHAIR.

THANK YOU.

AFTER THE MEETING, ANDREW INVITED EVERYONE BACK TO HIS HOUSE.

HA
HA

HE PUT ON LOUD DANCE MUSIC.

BOOM BOOM BOOM

AS ANOTHER PRANK, HE PASSED AROUND HIS LAPTOP, WHICH WAS LOADED TO A FETISH PORN SITE, "HOGTIED BITCHES."

HAHA
IS SHE UP IN A TREE?
???

PORN WASN'T ON HIS BOTTOM LINE. HE WAS ABSTAINING FROM "UNAVAILABLE WOMEN."

I'M GOING TO BED.
HAHA

THE NEXT MORNING, THE LAST FEW MEN DID THEIR WORK. DAN JONES WRAPPED THINGS UP AND THEN DEBRIEFED US ALL.

YOU'VE JUST BEEN THROUGH EMOTIONAL SURGERY.

YOU NEED TO TREAT YOURSELF LIKE YOU'RE RECOVERING FROM A HOSPITAL STAY.

HE RISKED SHARING A PERSONAL EXAMPLE OF SELF-CARE THAT WE COULD TRY.

SOMETIMES WHEN I'M ALONE, I'LL PUT ON MY FAVORITE SONG AND I'LL SING AND DANCE...

I'M IN LOVE, I'M IN LOVE ♫ I'M IN LOVE... ♫

♪... I'M IN LOVE WITH A WONDERFUL ME! ♫

YOU SHOULD TRY THAT WEARING A DRESS AND HEELS.
HA HA

DAN LOOKED WOUNDED FOR A SPLIT SECOND... AND THEN:

HA!

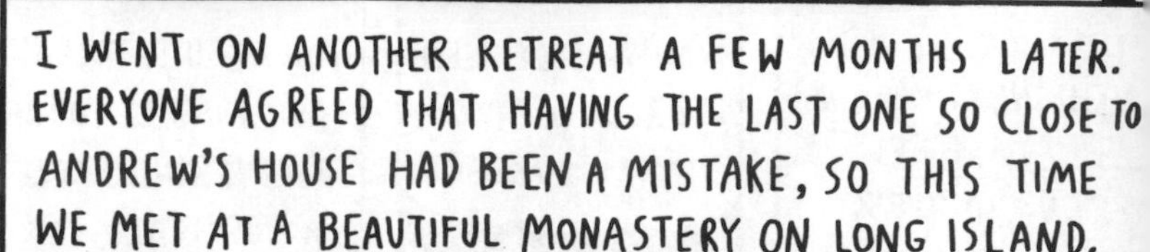
I WENT ON ANOTHER RETREAT A FEW MONTHS LATER. EVERYONE AGREED THAT HAVING THE LAST ONE SO CLOSE TO ANDREW'S HOUSE HAD BEEN A MISTAKE, SO THIS TIME WE MET AT A BEAUTIFUL MONASTERY ON LONG ISLAND.
WOW!

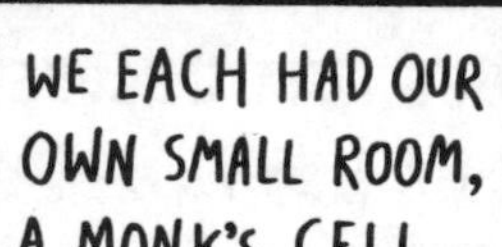
WE EACH HAD OUR OWN SMALL ROOM, A MONK'S CELL.

THE MAIN ROOM WHERE WE WOULD DO OUR WORK WAS JUST DOWNSTAIRS. IT WAS COMFORTABLE, SPACIOUS, AND BRIGHT.

I HAD ARRIVED EARLY AND MET SOMEONE NAMED TONY SITTING IN HIS CAR IN THE DRIVEWAY.

OH, HI. I DIDN'T NOTICE YOU WERE IN THERE. I'M DAVID.

I DISLIKED HIM RIGHT AWAY.

HOW YA DOIN'?

HE HAD THE SAME WORKING-CLASS ITALIAN ACCENT AS MY MOM'S FAMILY.

BLAH BLAH BLAH BLAH BLAH

BUT THERE WAS SOMETHING ABOUT HIS FACE.

BLAH BLAH BLAH

IT WAS AS IF HIS CHILDHOOD FACE WAS STILL TRAPPED ON HIS ADULT FACE, SITTING RIGHT INSIDE THE FRAME OF HIS HEAD.

HA
HA

IT GAVE HIM A STRANGE, FEMININE QUALITY.

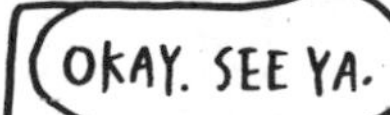
I'M GONNA EXPLORE THE GROUNDS.

OKAY. SEE YA.

I WALKED DOWN TO A PRIVATE BEACH, THEORIZING THAT MAYBE EVERYONE WHO'S BEEN SEXUALLY ABUSED HAS THIS "INSET" CHILD'S FACE.

DO I HAVE IT?

WHEN EVERYONE ELSE ARRIVED, TONY VOLUNTEERED TO GO FIRST, EVEN THOUGH HE HAD NEVER BEEN ON A RETREAT.

OH BOY...
CLAP
CLAP
CLAP
CLAP

HE LAUNCHED RIGHT INTO HIS STORY, HIS VOICE DRIPPING WITH ANGER.

I GUESS I'LL JUST SAY IT.

THIS FAGGOT ABUSED ME WHEN I WAS LITTLE.

DAN JONES LISTENED FOR A FEW MINUTES, THEN:

WELL, IF WE HAD BEEN THERE, WE WOULD HAVE KILLED HIM. WOULD YOU LIKE TO KILL HIM NOW?

YEAH, OKAY...
!

YOU MOTHERFUCK-ING FAGGOT!!!
WHAM!

I'LL FUCKIN' KILL YOU, YOU FAGGOT!
WHAM
WHAM
WHAM
WHAM

IT WAS TERRIFYING, HE WENT ON AND ON.

WHAM!
WHAM!
WHAM!
WHAM!

IF I EVER CAUGHT A REAL PEDOPHILE, I THINK I REALLY WOULD KILL HIM.

HUFF
HUFF

OKAY, ONE MORE STAB AND I SEND YOU TO HELL FOREVER.

WHAM

HE DIDN'T SEEM ANY LESS ANGRY.

HUFF
HUFF
I HAVE TO GET THE FUCK OUT OF HERE.
CLAP
CLAP
CLAP
CLAP

DURING A BREAK, I BONDED WITH A SWEET GUY NAMED HERMAN WHO WAS FEELING EQUALLY FREAKED OUT.

THAT WAS PRETTY PSYCHOTIC.
HA
HA

I SHARED MY FEARS WITH MOSHE, TOO. HE LISTENED PATIENTLY.

LISTEN, DO I THINK TONY IS VIOLENT AND EVEN DANGEROUS? YES.

BUT HE'S BETTER OFF DOING THIS WORK WITH US THAN OUT ON THE STREET.

YOU DON'T NEED TO BE FRIENDS WITH HIM. IF YOU NEED TO KEEP YOUR DISTANCE, DO THAT.

BUT STAY FOCUSED ON WHAT **YOU** WANT TO GET OUT OF THIS RETREAT!

THANK YOU, MOSHE!
YOU'RE WELCOME.

AFTER LUNCH, WE GOT BACK TO WORK. THREE MORE MEN CAME UP. THEN THINGS TOOK A DARK TURN WHEN GREG VOLUNTEERED TO DO HIS WORK.

I GUESS I'LL GO NEXT.
CLAP CLAP
CLAP

GREG HAD A GLAZED, MEDI-CATED LOOK. HE SEEMED ANGRY AT DAN JONES.

HE COMPARED DAN'S PROCESS TO OTHER RETREATS HE'D ATTENDED.

I FIND THIS TO BE REALLY LACKING.

USUALLY THERE'S MORE INTERACTION BETWEEN THE AT-TENDEES, NOT JUST WITH THE THERAPIST.

A FEW MINUTES INTO HIS SHARE, GREG VIOLENTLY FLUNG OFF HIS SHIRT.

THEN HE DID THE SAME WITH HIS SHOE, BUT IT ACCIDENTLY SLAMMED INTO A MAN NAMED ADAM.

GREG MUMBLED AN APOLOGY, BUT DAN JONES STOPPED THE SESSION.

I THINK I'M IN SHOCK RIGHT NOW. I CAN TELL BECAUSE MY HANDS ARE COLD AND MY THROAT IS TIGHT. I THINK WE'RE PROBABLY ALL IN SHOCK.

WE'RE GOING TO GO TO DINNER, AND THEN WE'LL COME BACK AND TALK ABOUT WHAT JUST HAPPENED.

DINNER WAS QUIET AND TENSE, WITH GREG DISAPPEARING TO HIS ROOM TO AVOID US.

FINALLY, WE GOT BACK INTO OUR CIRCLE.

OKAY!
I'M READY TO WORK.
CLAP

THIS IS NOW LIKE A HOSPITAL ROOM, AND I'M GOING TO STAY UP AS LONG AS IT TAKES TO TREAT EVERYONE WHO HAD A PIECE OF WORK OPENED UP BY WHAT HAPPENED.

ADAM, WOULD YOU LIKE TO GO FIRST?

ADAM SHARED A HARROWING STORY ABOUT BEING RAPED BY HIS GRANDFATHER WHEN HE WAS FIVE.

POP-POP, IT HURTS...

HOW COULD ANYONE DO THAT TO A FIVE-YEAR-OLD?

STAY THERE.

TWO MORE MEN SHARED STORIES OF SIMILAR ABUSE AT SIMILAR AGES. I WEPT LISTENING TO THEM AS MOSHE HELD ME.*

SOB
SOB
SOB
SOB
SOB
SOB

* I CRIED AGAIN JUST NOW DRAWING THIS PAGE.

DAN JONES CAME OVER TO ME NEXT.

I JUST KEEP THINKING ABOUT MY KIDS.

IF ANYTHING EVER HAPPENED TO THEM...
CHOKE
SOB
SOB
SOB
SOB
SOB

OH GOD! **PLEASE!** PLEASE KEEP THEM SAFE! **PLEASE**, GOD!

ADAM SHARED WITH ME DURING FEEDBACK.
SEEING YOU PRAY FOR YOUR CHILDREN'S SAFETY TOUCHES ME SO DEEPLY.

NEXT WAS JULIO, A MAN WHO HAD ABUSED HIS OWN SISTER WHEN THEY WERE BOTH LITTLE.

HE HOWLED IN PAIN AND BEGGED OUR FORGIVENESS. WE SURROUNDED HIM AND HUGGED HIM AND TOLD HIM HE WAS FORGIVEN.*

SOB SOB
SOB SOB

*JULIO HIMSELF HAD BEEN SEXUALLY ASSAULTED MULTPLE TIMES SINCE CHILDHOOD. I DON'T KNOW WHAT KIND OF AMENDS HE MADE OR IF HIS SISTER EVER FORGAVE HIM, BUT HE FOUND LOVE AND ACCEPTANCE IN OUR GROUP.

I WENT TO BED COMPLETELY SPENT, EMPTIED OUT OF PAIN...

AND FILLED UP WITH THE MYSTERY AND GRACE OF GOD.

THE NEXT DAY WHEN I DID MY SESSION, I DIDN'T HAVE MUCH ANGER OR SADNESS LEFT TO EXPRESS. I TALKED ABOUT MUSIC.

IT WAS CENTRAL TO MY LIFE AS A TEENAGER, BUT I LET IT FALL AWAY.

I'VE BEEN ACHING TO SING AND WRITE SONGS AGAIN, BUT I'M STUCK.

DAN GUIDED ME TO MY PHRASE.

NO ONE CAN STOP ME!!!
YES!

MY MOUTH OPENED AND MUSIC NOTES CAME OUT OF ME.

THEY FILLED THE WHOLE ROOM UP TO THE CEILING.

IT WAS THE LOUDEST I HAD EVER LET MY VOICE GO.

I FELT A TREMENDOUS GOD BURST AS I TOOK IN THE FEEDBACK AND HUGS.

YOUR VOICE IS INCREDIBLE!

JULIO WAS THE LAST TO COME UP TO ME.

NOW I KNOW A RELEASE DOESN'T HAVE TO BE SCREAMING. IT CAN BE MUSIC!

2007-2008

OF ALL THE MEN FROM THE RE-TREATS, I RELATED BEST TO LEV. WE KEPT IN TOUCH.

HE WAS HAVING A MOMENT IN HIS CAREER. WE SPOKE AFTER HE SIGNED TO A MAJOR TALENT AGENCY.

I WANT TO FEEL THE SUCCESS, BUT WITHOUT THE EUPHORIA. IT'S LIKE A DRUG THAT'S A BIT TOO STRONG.

WE MET EVERY FEW WEEKS FOR COFFEE. HE BECAME LIKE A BIG BROTHER TO ME.

YOU NEED TO MAN UP!

YOU HAVE TO FIGHT FOR YOUR ARTISTIC DREAMS. THE UNIVERSE ISN'T TOO PICKY ABOUT WHO GETS THE SPOTLIGHT.

WE TALKED ABOUT BASKETBALL.

I'VE ALWAYS WANTED TO PLAY WITH A REGULAR GROUP.

WITH HIS ENCOURAGEMENT, I JOINED A WEEKLY GAME NEAR MY HOME, CALLING HIM FOR SUPPORT ON MY WAY THERE.

I'M SCARED I'LL GET BEAT UP.
IF ANYONE STARTS SOME SHIT, YOU JUST PUNCH HIM IN THE FACE!

I TALKED TO LEV ABOUT MY BOOK DEAL AND RESENTMENTS THAT WERE COMING UP AT WORK.

MY FIRST ADVANCE WAS $37,000, BUT THAT'S NOT REALLY "QUIT MY JOB" MONEY YET... SIGH

WHAT DOES "QUIT YOUR JOB" MONEY LOOK LIKE? DO THE NUMBERS...

I GOTTA TELL YOU, THE WAY YOU TALK ABOUT OGILVY, IT'S LIKE YOU'RE A KID SUCKING ON MOMMY'S TIT.

DOES OGILVY MAKE UNDERGROUND COMICS? DO THEY CARE ABOUT YOU MAKING YOUR MUSIC? NO? THEN **FUCK** OGILVY.

GIGGLE

I DID THE NUMBERS AND TALKED IT OVER WITH REBECCA.

HONEY, YOU HAVE TO QUIT! HOW OFTEN DOES ANYONE GET A BOOK DEAL LIKE THAT?

BA!
REALLY?

I MADE A SECRET PLAN TO GIVE MY NOTICE IN JUNE. I'D SPEND THE SUMMER FINISHING MY BOOK AND HAND IT IN THAT FALL.

THERE WAS NO ONE IN MY LIFE WHO SPOKE TO ME LIKE LEV. I WORKED UP THE NERVE TO ASK HIM IF HE WOULD BE MY SPONSOR.
SURE. I LIKE DOING THIS WORK WITH YOU.
YES!!!
I WAS ECSTATIC.
FINALLY, AFTER YEARS OF LOOKING, I HAD FOUND SOMEONE WHO COULD TAKE ME THROUGH THE STEPS!
THANK YOU, GOD!

I LOVED SHARING THE NEWS AT MEETINGS. IT MADE ME HIGH.
I'M WORKING WITH MY SPONSOR THIS WEEK!

AS OUR FIRST MEETING APPROACHED, I GOT NERVOUS.
WHAT IF HE CHANGES HIS MIND?

RIGHT AWAY I WAS DISAPPOINTED.
BUY A COPY OF A GENTLE PATH THROUGH THE 12 STEPS.*

DO THE FIRST TWO CHAPTERS. THEN WE CAN MEET.
OH... OKAY.

I ONLY REMEMBER MEETING UP TWICE. THE FIRST TIME WAS AT A PACKED RESTAURANT. I FELT EMBARRASSED SHARING SUCH PERSONAL DETAILS IN A PUBLIC PLACE.

THE SECOND TIME WAS AT HIS APARTMENT. HIS GIRLFRIEND WAS IN THE NEXT ROOM.
I'M FEELING ALL THIS GRIEF ABOUT MY BOOK DEAL. I'M SO AFRAID OF SURPASSING MY DAD.

IT'S SUCH A HEAVY FEELING. I'VE GOT SOME BIG TEARS AROUND THIS ONE.

* A DO-IT-YOURSELF 12-STEP WORKBOOK

SIGH MAYBE YOU'RE EXCITED! THAT FEELS LIKE SUCH AN OLD FEELING FOR YOU... "GRIEF AND TEARS..."

I LEFT FEELING SHUT DOWN.

HE COULDN'T DEAL WITH ME CRYING!

I RESISTED DOING ANY MORE STEP WORK AFTER THAT. I DIDN'T UNDERSTAND WHAT I WAS FEELING TOWARD LEV, JUST THAT I HATED WRITING IN THE WORKBOOK.

FUCK THIS.

I WAITED TWO MONTHS FOR HIM TO CALL AND CHECK ON ME. HE DIDN'T.

DADDY? DADDY?

FINALLY, ONE DAY I GOT A VOICEMAIL.

DAVID, I FEEL LIKE OUR WORK TOGETHER IS DONE.

I FEEL LIKE YOU'RE ACTING OUT IN MY DIRECTION, AND I DON'T HAVE TIME FOR THAT KIND OF DRAMA.

I WAS HURT, BUT I KNEW HE WAS RIGHT.

I UNDERSTAND...

I'D LIKE TO KEEP IN TOUCH. CALL ME ANY TIME AND GIVE ME AN UPDATE.

OKAY, I WILL.

A MONTH LATER, I CALLED HIM TO CHECK IN.

I'VE BEEN MOVING AWAY FROM THE 12 STEPS...

HAVE YOU HEARD OF THE LAW OF ATTRACTION?*

IT'S KIND OF LIKE DA VISION WORK, BUT ON STEROIDS.

SOMETHING ABOUT IT REALLY WORKED FOR LEV. RIGHT AFTER HE LEFT THE PROGRAM, HIS CAREER BEGAN TO SKYROCKET!

* ESTHER HICK CLAIMS THAT SHE CHANNELS A BEING OF "INFINITE INTELLIGENCE" SHE CALLS "ABRAHAM." I TRIED LISTENING TO HER TALKS ON THE "LAW OF ATTRACTION," BUT SHE SOUNDED COMPLETELY INSANE TO ME.

I WAS SKYROCKETING, TOO.
AFTER QUITTING OGILVY, MY ILLUSTRATIONS WERE APPEARING REGULARLY IN THE NEW YORK TIMES.
AND I LANDED A NEW YORKER COVER, THE HIGHEST PROFILE PROJECT I'D EVER DONE.
MY BOOK WAS ALMOST FINISHED.
I WAS SLOWLY GETTING BETTER AT BASKETBALL, AND I MADE SOME FRIENDS AT THE WEEKLY GAME.
GOOD DEFENSE, DAVE!!!

BUT AS I GOT CLOSER TO COMPLETING MY BOOK, MY STOMACH TROUBLE RETURNED.

BUT YOU DIDN'T EAT ANYTHING BAD!

THE REFLUX AT NIGHT WAS UNBEARABLE.

IT GOT SO BAD THE WEEK WE CHOSE MY BOOK'S PUB DATE THAT MY STOMACH ACID SERIOUSLY BURNED MY ESOPHAGUS.

I HAD TO TAKE PRESCRIPTION PAINKILLERS FOR SEVERAL DAYS JUST TO SWALLOW.

OWW!

I REMEMBERED DARYL BELONGED TO A BRANCH OF OA CALLED "GREY-SHEETERS." I TOOK A RISK AND CALLED HIM.

I'VE BEEN ABSTINENT IN THAT PROGRAM FOR 8 YEARS. I GOTTA WARN YOU— IT'S NOT FOR EVERYONE.

THAT SAID, IF IT'S A GOOD FIT FOR YOU... GET READY FOR A WHOLE NEW LEVEL OF FREEDOM!

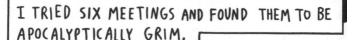

I TRIED SIX MEETINGS AND FOUND THEM TO BE APOCALYPTICALLY GRIM.

EVERYONE RECITED THIS WHOLE THING BEFORE SHARING

I'M LAURIE AND I'M A COMPULSIVE OVEREATER. I WEIGH AND MEASURE THREE MEALS A DAY FROM THE CAMBRIDGE GREY SHEET, WRITE THEM DOWN, COMMIT THEM TO A SPONSOR OR ANOTHER QUALIFIED PERSON. I DON'T EAT IN BETWEEN NO MATTER WHAT. ABSTINENCE IS THE MOST IMPORTANT THING IN MY LIFE.

ROBOTIC

THE QUALIFICATIONS WERE DARK.

WHEN I GOT TO GREY-SHEETER, I WAS A FALL-DOWN DRUNK WITH FOOD...

IT WAS TRULY "THE LAST HOUSE ON THE BLOCK" AS THEY SAY IN AA.

EVERY DAY IS A BRUTAL STRUGGLE FOR ME, BUT I'M ABSTINENT.

I SAW FRANCINE FROM THE DA WRITERS MEETI

IF YOU WANT, I CAN BE YOUR TEMPORARY SPONSOR UNTIL YOU FIND ONE. HERE'S A COPY OF THE GREY SHEET.

THANKS.

I PROMISED FRANCINE I'D CALL HER EACH NIGHT AND LIST OUT THE INGREDIENTS OF ALL MY MEALS.

YOU CAN LEAVE IT ON MY VOICEMAIL IF I DON'T PICK UP.

I DIDN'T WANT TO FIGHT WITH REBECCA MORE THAN WE ALREADY WERE, SO I KEPT IT A SECRET.

DAY 1 WAS EXCITING.

I'M FINALLY TAKING CHARGE OF THIS!

IT WAS A RELIEF TO HAVE SOMEONE ELSE DECIDE WHAT AND HOW MUCH I SHOULD EAT. ON MY OWN IT WAS TOO BAFFLING.

"EXACTLY 1 TSP OF OLIVE OIL AND 4 OZ OF MEAT."

WHEN I CALLED FRANCINE THAT NIGHT, I TOLD HER I WAS FEELING GREAT AND LISTED MY MEALS IN ORDER.

OKAY... BUT PEAS AREN'T ON THE GREY SHEET.
OH!

THAT FIRST DAY WOULDN'T COUNT AS ABSTINENT.

FUCK.

REBECCA STARTED TO GET SUSPICIOUS WHEN I WOULDN'T EAT THE MANGOES SHE BOUGHT.* IT WAS OUR NIGHTLY RITUAL.

TV AND MANGO TIME?
I'M TOO FULL.

AFTER A FEW DAYS, THEY STARTED TO ROT ON THE COUNTER.

THIS IS OUR LOVE... ROTTING AWAY IN FRONT OF ME.

AFTER THAT FIRST NIGHT, EVERY OTHER TIME I CALLED FRANCINE, I GOT HER VOICEMAIL.

♫ HI, THIS IS FRANCINE. LEAVE A MESSAGE. ♫ BEEP

HI, IT'S DAVID. I'M CALLING TO TURN OVER MY FOOD.

AROUND DAY 4, I WAS GETTING HUNGRIER AND LESS SURE OF THE FOOD PLAN. I HAD A CONSTANT HEADACHE. FRANCINE'S DISCONNECTED VOICE GOT EERIER AND EERIER.

♫ HI, THIS IS FRANCINE. LEAVE A MESSAGE. ♪
BEEP

THAT NIGHT, REBECCA CAUGHT ME MEASURING.

WHAT ARE YOU DOING?

*MANGOES WEREN'T ON THE GREY SHEET.

I CONFESSED AND FELT THE RELIEF OF A CRIMINAL GIVING HIMSELF UP FOR ARREST.

MY INSIDES ARE SHAKING.

I HAD BEEN TELLING MYSELF THAT MY BODY WAS DETOXING FROM ALL THE YEARS OF EATING POISONOUS FOODS NOT ON THE GREY SHEET.

I HAD CALLED DARYL TO ASK IF THIS HAD HAPPENED TO HIM.

DID YOU HAVE A CONSTANT PANICKY FEELING?

HE DIDN'T WANT TO BE PRESCRIPTIVE,* SO HE ANSWERED MY QUESTIONS BY REPEATING MY QUESTIONS BACK TO ME.

MAYBE I'M ADDICTED TO RICE AND I'M GOING THROUGH WITHDRAWAL?

SO YOU'RE SAYING YOU THINK YOU'RE ADDICTED TO RICE?

THE WAY HE ASKED, IT WAS LIKE THE CORRECT ANSWER WAS "YES," BUT I HAVE NO IDEA WHAT'S RIGHT ANYMORE.

I'M WORRIED ABOUT YOU! BOTH OF OUR MOMS TOLD ME YOU LOOK TOO SKINNY!

* AL-ANON RECOVERY IN ACTION

I TOLD REBECCA ABOUT THE ARTICLE I HAPPENED TO HAVE READ THAT MORNING.
Controversial Websites Celebrate Anorexia

THROUGH SOCIAL MEDIA, THE SITES WERE BEING SHARED BY TEENAGE GIRLS.

ONE IMAGE HAUNTED ME.
EMBRACE THE SKELETON

WHERE WAS I HEADED...?
OH, HONEY.

REBECCA MADE ME EAT A PLATE OF RICE AND I WAS RESTORED TO SANITY.

I CALLED FRANCINE TO TELL HER I WAS QUITTING AND I GOT HER VOICEMAIL.
I'M HAPPY TO TALK MORE IF YOU CALL ME BACK.

SHE TEXTED BACK A HALF HOUR LATER.
Francine
No need to talk. Good luck.

OA WASN'T FOR ME AFTER ALL AND DA STARTED TO FEEL WEIRDER AND WEIRDER.

I WAS **BORN** A DEBTOR!
MMMMMH

IT SEEMED LIKE THE HEALTHIEST MEMBERS TRIED TO AVOID THE SICK ONES, REFUSING TO SPONSOR THEM OR GIVE PRGs.

MOST MEETINGS I WENT TO HAD TROUBLE FILLING BASIC SERVICE POSITIONS LIKE CHAIRPERSON, TREASURER, AND SECRETARY.

I NOMINATE GINA.
SORRY, I'M ALL FULL UP WITH COMMITMENTS.
PLEASE DON'T NOMINATE ME.
I NOMINATE RON.
I LOST MY SOLVENCY.

SOME OF THE SHARES WERE CHILLING, TOO.

DA TAUGHT ME TO "DO THE NUMBERS."

IF I DIE, MY WIFE GETS HALF A MILLION DOLLARS. IF SHE DIES, I GET LESS THAN 12 GRAND. I'M NOT PUTTING A PRICE ON HER LIFE. IT JUST HIGHLIGHTS HER UNDER-EARNING, AND I'M NOT SURE I CAN LIVE WITH IT ANYMORE.

DID I REALLY BELONG HERE?

REALLY, THE MOST ACUTE PAIN I FELT WAS WHENEVER WE HAD TO SEE MY "FAMILY OF ORIGIN."* IT USUALLY REQUIRED MEETINGS OR PROGRAM CALLS BEFORE, DURING, OR AFTER EACH VISIT.

I'LL BE RIGHT BACK...
DESSERT I COULDN'T EAT

MY BROTHER LUKE WAS ESPECIALLY TOXIC.

HIS UNRELEASED ANGER WAS PALPABLE AND I WAS AFRAID HE'D LOSE HIS MIND AGAIN.

MOM, THIS PIE IS **ICE COLD!**

MY MOM AND I AT LEAST SPOKE THE SAME PROGRAM LANGUAGE, BUT SHE COULDN'T HELP COMPETING WITH ME.

I TOTALLY IDENTIFY WITH THAT, DAVID, BUT FOR ME "DETACHING WITH LOVE" MEANS BLAH BLAH BLAH BLAH...

SHE HAD RECENTLY LEFT ALL HER PROGRAMS AND WAS NOW JUST GOING TO AA.

BUT SHE DOESN'T DRINK...
I KNOW!

*MORE PROGRAM LANGUAGE

MORE AND MORE, I FOUND THE BOOKS ON MY SHELVES, THE NEWS, MOST MOVIES AND TV SHOWS TO BE "SPIRITUALLY TOXIC."
I SPENT MY LEISURE TIME READING PROGRAM LITERATURE AND OTHER SPIRITUAL GUIDES.
THREE DIFFERENT 12-STEP DAILY-MEDITATION BOOKS
EVERYTHING ELSE WAS "UNCHECKED DISEASED THINKING." I DIDN'T WANT IT POLLUTING MY PURE ECOSYSTEM.
AT THE END OF THE SUMMER, WE HAD PLANS TO CELEBRATE MY DAD'S BIRTHDAY. MY MOM WAS INVITED. I HADN'T SEEN EITHER OF THEM IN MONTHS.
I REALLY DON'T WANT TO GO. I'LL NEED TO MAKE SOME CALLS AS SOON AS WE GET THERE.
NO ONE I USUALLY CALLED WAS HOME.
HA HA HA
GOD, PLEASE GUIDE ME.

I FELT LED TO REACH OUT TO DARYL. HE PICKED UP AFTER ONE RING AND I LAUNCHED INTO A RANT ABOUT MY PARENTS.

WHOA, WHOA! LET ME JUST STOP YOU RIGHT THERE.

FIRST, I WANT TO REMIND YOU THAT YOU'VE REACHED A LIVE PERSON, NOT AN ANSWERING MACHINE.
HA HA
SORRY.

AND SECOND, I WANT TO ASK YOU IF YOU'VE EVER WORKED THE STEPS WITH A SPONSOR.

I DID STEPS 1, 2, AND 3 WITH MY SPONSOR IN SLAA.

SO YOU HAVEN'T DONE A 4TH-STEP INVENTORY?

NO.

HE OFFERED TO WALK ME THROUGH IT IF I CALLED HIM LATER.

THANKS, DARYL. I FEEL SO MUCH BETTER JUST KNOWING THAT.

HOW ARE YOU DOING? YOU SOUND GROGGY.

HE ADMITTED THAT HE HAD BEEN OUT LATE AT A MASSAGE PARLOR, ACTING OUT IN A NEW, DANGEROUS WAY WITH A FEMALE MASSEUSE. HE ASKED ME TO PRAY FOR HIM.

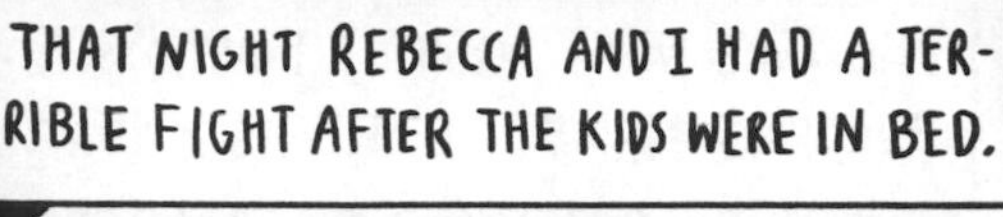
THAT NIGHT REBECCA AND I HAD A TERRIBLE FIGHT AFTER THE KIDS WERE IN BED.

I CAN SLEEP AT A FRIEND'S HOUSE IF YOU WANT!

I CALLED DARYL AND HE WALKED ME THROUGH A BIT OF THE 4TH STEP.
I'M EMAILING YOU AN EXCEL DOCUMENT.

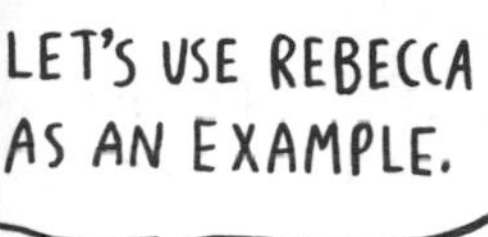
LET'S USE REBECCA AS AN EXAMPLE.

WHAT'S A RESENTMENT THAT YOU HAVE TOWARD HER RIGHT NOW?
WE HAVEN'T HAD SEX SINCE BEFORE MY SON WAS BORN.

HE HAD ME FILL IN BLANK CELLS ACROSS THE DOCUMENT, STARTING WITH MY RESENTMENT, AND THEN FOCUSING ON MY PART IN IT.
THIS IS WHERE YOU ASK YOURSELF, "HAVE I BEEN SELF-SEEKING?"

I WENT TO BED AFTER REBECCA WAS ASLEEP AND KEPT THE STEP WORK TO MYSELF.

THE VERY NEXT NIGHT I FOUND HER PURSUING ME IN BED. WE HAD SEX.

IT WAS A MIRACLE. THERE WAS NO OTHER EXPLANATION FOR HER TURNAROUND.

THANK YOU, GOD!

IF THE RESULTS OF DOING THE STEP WORK THE "RIGHT WAY" WERE THIS INSTANTANEOUS, THEN I WOULD DIVE IN COMPLETELY!

I TOLD DARYL WHAT HAD HAPPENED.

THAT'S GREAT!

AND I ASKED HIM TO BE MY SPONSOR. HE AGREED. GOD WAS SMILING ON ME.

DARYL HAD BEEN SOBER FOR 13 YEARS IN AA. HE'D BEEN IN AL-ANON FOR JUST AS LONG. HE WAS ABSTINENT WITH FOOD AND SOLVENT WITH MONEY.

UNITY
AA
SERVICE
RECOVERY

AL-ANON

OVEREATERS ANONYMOUS

DEBTORS ANONYMOUS

THE FACT THAT HE WAS ACTING OUT AT MASSAGE PARLORS DIDN'T FACTOR INTO MY DECISION TO WORK WITH HIM AT ALL. NO ONE WAS PERFECT!

IT AMAZED ME THAT AFTER YEARS OF SEARCHING, HERE WAS THE PERFECT SPONSOR FOR ME—RIGHT UNDER MY NOSE.

I'M FINALLY DOING THE STEPS ACCORDING TO THE BIG BOOK!
SIGNIFICANCE LOST ON HER

WITH THE PROPER STRUCTURE TO OUR RELATIONSHIP, I FELT SURE THINGS WOULD WORK THIS TIME BETWEEN DARYL AND ME.

"FOR THE NEXT FEW YEARS, FORTUNE THREW MONEY AND APPLAUSE MY WAY. I HAD ARRIVED."*

* "BILL'S STORY," BIG BOOK OF ALCOHOLICS ANONYMOUS. I HAD COME A LONG WAY IN JUST A FEW YEARS. THESE WORDS WERE NOW SACRED TO ME.

THE ONLY OBSTACLE TO JUMPING FULLY INTO THE STEP WORK WAS THE PUBLICATION OF MY BOOK. I'D BE TRAVELING TO THE WEST COAST, BARCELONA, PARIS, AND ANGOULÊME, WHERE I'D BEEN INVITED AS A SPECIAL GUEST.

DARYL SUGGESTED I FIND AN **AA** MEETING TO ATTEND EACH DAY TO STAY GROUNDED. THERE WERE LOTS TO CHOOSE FROM IN EVERY CITY I WAS VISITING.*

I ASSURED DARYL I'D STAY IN CLOSE CONTACT BY EMAIL AND PHONE UNTIL I GOT BACK.

AS I HEADED TO MY GATE, I WAS BEYOND EXCITED. THIS WAS WHAT I'D BEEN WORKING TOWARD FOR SO LONG. MY DREAM WAS COMING TRUE.

*THERE WERE NO DA OR SLAA MEETINGS AND VERY FEW AL-ANON.

UNITY
SERVICE
AA
RECOVERY
11
♫ I GOT A RIGHT TO FEEL
HIGH...
AFTER A LIFE OF FEELING LOW ♪

2008-2009

MY WEST COAST EVENTS WERE, ON THE WHOLE, SPARSELY ATTENDED.

JESUS...

NO ONE SEEMED TO CARE THAT MY BOOK HAD BEEN PUBLISHED.

HI, EVERYONE...

I HAD BOUGHT MYSELF SPECIAL DESIGNER CLOTHES AND HAD PREPARED A MULTIMEDIA SLIDE SHOW HIGHLIGHTING MY BOOK'S THEMES.

HERE I AM USING A DILDO ON MYSELF.

I INTERSPERSED A FEW LIVE SONGS BETWEEN THE STORIES.*

♫ I GOT A RIGHT TO FEEL HIGH... AFTER A LIFE OF FEELING LOW... ♫

AND I ROUNDED IT ALL OUT WITH SOME BREAK DANCING.

♫ JAM ON IT..
JAM ON IT..

* WRITTEN SOON AFTER MY LAST EMOTIONAL-RELEASE RETREAT

I PERFORMED AT THE GOOGLE CAMPUS IN MOUNTAIN VIEW TO 15 OR 20 DISTRACTED WORKERS ON THEIR LAPTOPS DURING LUNCH.

♫ MY BRAIN IS HANGING UPSIDE DOWN! ♫

VEGAN

GF

THEN I ATE ALL THE COMPLIMENTARY DAIRY-, SOY-, AND GLUTEN-FREE FOOD I WANTED IN THEIR INSANE CAMPUS CAFETERIA.

ORGANIC VEGETABLE GARDEN FOR CAFETERIA MEALS

← FEELING EXISTENTIAL DESPAIR

IN SANTA CRUZ, THE SLIDE PROJECTOR DIDN'T WORK AND ONLY EIGHT PEOPLE SHOWED UP. I HELD UP THE PAGES OF MY BOOK AND IMPROVISED A TALK.

THEY WERE MOSTLY SENIOR CITIZENS. I PLAYED ONE QUIET SONG AND SKIPPED THE DANCING.

"STORY TIME"

THANKS, EVERYONE.
CLAP CLAP

IN SAN FRANCISCO, NINE PEOPLE CAME, THREE OF WHOM WERE FRIENDS. I SIGNED FOUR BOOKS.

IN LOS ANGELES, THERE WERE FIVE PEOPLE. I KNEW TWO OF THEM.

OKAY. HI, EVERYONE
JOE MATT

THE WHOLE TRIP WAS NOTHING LIKE I'D IMAGINED. IT WAS AN EMBARRASSMENT.

ALONE IN MY HOTEL ROOM. CAN'T DRINK OR MASTURBATE.

THANK GOD FOR THE AA MEETINGS.

THEY HELPED RE-FOCUS MY ATTENTION AWAY FROM MY BRUISED EGO.

GOD, GRANT ME THE SERENITY...

OTHERWISE I WOULD HAVE CRATERED INTO A DANGEROUS DEPRESSION.

AS LONG AS I'M BREATHING, I'M GRATEFUL. I AIN'T SUPPOSED TO EVEN BE HERE AFTER EVERYTHING I DONE.
MMHH

POSSIBLY AS A REWARD FOR MY HUMILITY, MY LAST EVENT AT POWELL'S IN PORTLAND WAS A FULL HOUSE. THEY LOVED ME!

CLAP CLAP CLAP
WOO!
THANK YOU SO MUCH!
CLAP CLAP
WHISTLE

SOME CUTE INDIE ROCKER GIRLS CHATTED WITH ME AFTERWARD.

UMM... YOU'RE AWESOME...
HA HA

IT KNOCKED ME OFF BALANCE AGAIN.

I TRIED CALLING REBECCA THE NEXT MORNING AND WOUND UP LOSING MY PATIENCE IMMEDIATELY. I SCREAMED AT HER IN THE MIDDLE OF THE STREET.

WHY THE **FUCK** DO YOU **ALWAYS** INTERRUPT ME?!?

BEEP

SHE HUNG UP ON ME.

AAARRGH!!!

MY BOOK EVENTS CONTINUED ON THE UPSWING, EVEN AS I WAS ESTRANGED FROM REBECCA. PARIS WAS GLORIOUS! A BEAUTIFUL WOMAN NAMED EMMANUELLE WAS ASSIGNED BY MY FRENCH PUBLISHER TO SHOW ME AROUND.
♫ BON JOUR, DAVID! ♪
SHE ORDERED ALL MY MEALS FOR ME REQUESTING THE CHEF TO AVOID USING DAIRY, WHEAT, AND SOY.
I FELT SO CARED FOR.
I GAVE AN INTERVIEW TO A "BANDE DESSINÉE" JOURNALIST IN A PICTURESQUE CAFE.
THEN I WALKED AROUND MONTMARTRE UNTIL IT WAS TIME FOR MY ART SHOW AND BOOK SIGNING.

I HAD A FANTASTIC TIME SINGING SOME SONGS AND SIGNING BOOKS FOR THE DOZEN OR SO FANS WHO CAME TO THE COMIC-BOOK STORE.
♪ AUX... CHAMPS-ÉLYSÉES ♫
HA HA HA
HA HA HA
ONLY LEARNED ONE VERSE AND THE CHORUS

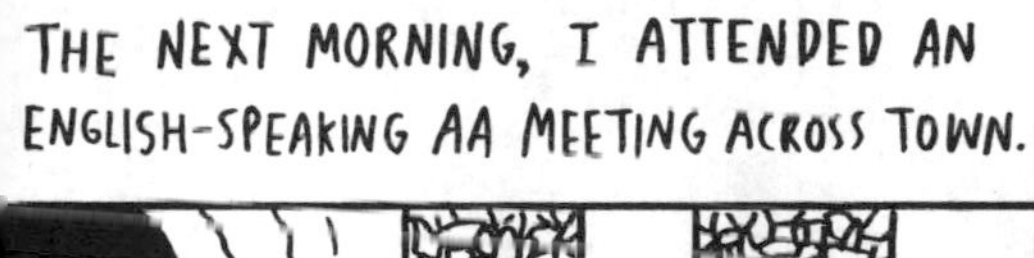
THE NEXT MORNING, I ATTENDED AN ENGLISH-SPEAKING AA MEETING ACROSS TOWN.

I HIT IT OFF WITH AN OLDER WOMAN NAMED ALISON.
I HAVE ZE SAME DIET AS YOU!

SHE INSISTED ON DRIVING ME TO A HEALTH-FOOD STORE FOR LUNCH.
WE PASSED THE EIFFEL TOWER AND SHE STOPPED AND TOOK MY PICTURE.

WE ATE OUR HEALTH FOOD AT HER SURREAL, PALATIAL FLAT. HER HUSBAND WAS A BUSINESS MOGUL AND A HUNTER. HE DIDN'T KNOW SHE WENT TO AA WHEN HE WAS OUT OF TOWN.

HER SPECIAL-NEEDS GRANDSON SHOWED ME SOME OF HIS BRILLIANT DRAWINGS.

DAVID IS AN ARTIST, TOO!
DINOSAURS AND ROBOTS

I'LL NEVER FORGET HER KINDNESS OR HER DEEPLY STRANGE AND EXOTIC HOME.

BARCELONA WAS EVEN MORE EXCITING.
HOLA!
¡DAVID!
A YOUNG EDITOR NAMED ARNAU WAS ASSIGNED BY MY SPANISH PUBLISHER TO BE MY GUIDE. HE QUICKLY BECAME MY FRIEND.
I SAW A FEW SIGHTS WITH ARNAU, BUT MAINLY IT WAS A SOLID TWO DAYS OF INTERVIEWS WITH NEWSPAPERS, RADIO, AND EVEN TELEVISION STATIONS.
"SEX HISTORY..." I LOVE IT! TELL ME HOW YOU STARTED THIS!
HA HA
ALL THE JOURNALISTS HAD THOROUGHLY READ MY BOOK AND HAD THOUGHTFUL, COMPLEX QUESTIONS, WHICH WERE A PLEASURE TO ANSWER.
THE INTERVIEWS WERE BROKEN UP WITH LEISURELY MEALS ON THE PUBLISHER'S DIME.

I GAVE A TALK THAT WAS TRANSLATED LIVE TO A HALL FULL OF PEOPLE AT A DOWNTOWN BOOKSTORE.
CUTE FAN

THEN I PLAYED A SET OF MY SONGS AT A TRENDY LITTLE BAR NEARBY.

TWO GORGEOUS YOUNG WOMEN WAITED TO MEET ME AFTERWARD.

THEY HAD COPIES OF MY BOOK AND WANTED MY AUTOGRAPH.
¡GRACIAS!
HA HA
DE NADA.

SO FAR I HAD MANAGED TO STAY GROUNDED THANKS TO AN ENGLISH-SPEAKING AA MEETING EARLIER IN THE DAY. THE QUALIFICATION WAS INCREDIBLE.

MY NAME IS MATEO AND I'M AN ALCOHOLIC.

BUT AFTER THE SHOW, MY HEAD WAS SWIRLING AGAIN WITH SEXUAL FANTASIES. I COULDN'T SLEEP.

GOD, PLEASE TURN MY THOUGHTS.
NO MASTURBATION

AT 5AM, I CREPT OUT AND WENT TO THE MERCADO DE LA BOQUERIA.

I WATCHED THE MERCHANTS SET UP THEIR STALLS.

I SAW MY PICTURE IN THE NATIONAL NEWSPAPER.

AFTER THAT I MET MATEO AT A CAFE FOR A TWO-PERSON AA MEETING BEFORE I LEFT TOWN.

HE SAID SO MANY THINGS THAT SPOKE TO MY SOUL, BUT I REMEMBER MOST HIS RESPONSE TO MY LONGING FOR FAME.

AS AN ALCOHOLIC, I CAN BE IN A GIANT STADIUM FULL OF SCREAMING FANS, GIRLS RIPPING OFF THEIR CLOTHES FOR ME! AND I MIGHT **STILL** WANT TO KILL MYSELF. NONE OF THAT CAN EVER MAKE ME FEEL WHOLE.

THE LAST STOP ON MY "INTERNATIONAL BOOK TOUR" WAS A PRESTIGIOUS COMICS FESTIVAL IN ANGOULÊME, FRANCE.
HI, EMMANUELLE!
♫ DAVID! ♪
THREE MORE DAYS OF NONSTOF
SIGNINGS, INTERVIEWS, PANEL'
AND GOURMET FRENCH MEALS.
TAXI AT MY BECK AND CALL
I WAS STAYING AT A NEARBY BED-AND-BREAKFAST UP A COUNTRY ROAD, NESTLED IN VERDANT HILLS, JUST PAST THE LARGEST CRUCIFIX I'D EVER SEEN.

THERE WAS ONLY ONE AA MEETING THAT WAS ANYWHERE NEAR ANGOULÊME. LUCKILY, A FELLOW CARTOONIST NAMED HUGO WAS ALSO IN AA.
I'LL DRIVE US AFTER YOUR SIGNING.
ANGOULÊME FESTIVAL
DELCOURT

WE BONDED DURING THE CAR RIDE.
HA HA

THE LOCATION WAS IN SOME KIND OF CHILDREN'S COMMUNITY ART CENTER, FILLED WITH COLORFUL SCULPTURES, PAINTINGS, AND MOSAICS.
THIS IS A SIGN.

THANK YOU, GOD! I'M EXACTLY WHERE I'M SUPPOSED TO BE!
BIENVENUE AUX ALCOOLIQUES ANONYMES...

AS THE MEETING STARTED, I SETTLED IN AND LISTENED.

EVEN THOUGH I COULDN'T UNDERSTAND A WORD OF ANYONE'S SHARES, I COULD SENSE SOMETHING OF THEIR STORIES— WHERE THEY WERE IN THEIR SPIRITUAL DEVELOPMENT.

WOULD YOU LIKE TO SHARE? I CAN TRANSLATE FOR YOU.

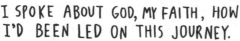

I SPOKE ABOUT GOD, MY FAITH, HOW I'D BEEN LED ON THIS JOURNEY.

I'M SO GRATEFUL!

IT WAS A TYPICAL SHARE, TAME BY AMERICAN STANDARDS.

BUT IN THE CAR, HUGO TOLD ME MOST OF THEM WERE SPOOKED BY ME.

REALLY?

FRANCE HAS AN UNEASY RELATIONSHIP WITH GOD FOR OBVIOUS HISTORICAL REASONS.

OH.

YOU SOUNDED LIKE A "JESUS FREAK" TO THEM!

HA HA

THE NEXT MORNING, THE OWNER OF THE B-AND-B CAME BY AS I WAS EATING BREAKFAST.
ARE YOU FINDING EVERY-THING OKAY?
YES. THANK YOU!
I HAVE SOMETHING TO ASK IF YOU DON'T MIND...?
?
SURE.

MY DAUGHTER LÉONIE WAS CURIOUS WHEN I TOLD HER YOU WERE AMERICAN, SO SHE LOOKED YOU UP ON THE INTERNET.
WOULD YOU MIND TERRIBLY IF I BROUGHT HER OVER HERE TO MEET YOU?
OF COURSE NOT!

A MINUTE LATER...

SHE SAT NEXT TO ME AND WE TALKED.

I WANT TO BE A FILMMAKER SOME DAY LIKE JAMES CAMERON.

WOW!

EITHER THAT OR MAYBE A SINGER.

WHY DON'T YOU SING HIM A SONG, LÉONIE?
YES, PLEASE! I'D LOVE IT!
OKAY.

SHE HAD THE VOICE OF AN ANGEL.
♫ ... SAYS YOU WERE HALF NOW YOU'RE WHOLE... ♪

♫ NO MORE HUNGER AND THIRST... FIRST BE A PERSON WHO NEEDS PEOPLE! ♪

MY DAD SANG THIS SONG ALL THE TIME. I HELD BACK TEARS.
♪ PEOPLE WHO NEED PEEEE-EEOPLE ♫

♫ ARE THE LUCKIEST PEOPLE IN THE WORLD! ♪
CLAP
CLAP
CLAP
CLAP
CLAP
THAT WAS AMAZING!

WILL YOU SING FOR US NOW?
OH!
UMM... DO YOU HAVE A GUITAR?

I FOLLOWED THEM OUT OF THE GUEST COTTAGE AND INTO THEIR OWN HOUSE.

LÉONIE'S FATHER LOOKED FOR A GUITAR.

EXCUSE ME... DO YOU MIND...?

?

I HAD TWO FRIENDS STAY OVERNIGHT.

CAN THEY LISTEN TO YOU SING, TOO?
HA HA
SURE!

HERE IT IS!
WHAT ON EARTH IS HAPPENING?!?

I PLAYED MY TWO BEST SONGS AND REALLY SANG MY HEART OUT.

HEE HEE
GIGGLE

BRAVO!
CLAP
CLAP
WE LOVE YOUR VOICE!
HEE HEE
CLAP
GIGGLE
CLAP
CLAP

I WANTED TO PLAY MORE, BUT MY TAXI WAS WAITING OUTSIDE.

THANK YOU.
BEEP
BEEP

IN THE CAR RIDE TO TOWN, I FELT CRAZY. ALL THAT ADMIRATION HAD BEEN INTOXICATING.

CLAP CLAP CLAP CLAP

I HAD TO TELL SOMEONE WHAT HAD JUST HAPPENED.

HUGO!

I SPILLED MY GUTS.

AH! YOU SHOULD HA AN AFFAIR WITH THIS GIRL, NO? SIXTEEN IS NO PROB LEM. YOU AMERICANS ARE SO REPRES

MAYBE SHE IS TOUCHING HERSELF RIGHT NOW THINK ABOUT YOU AND YOUR GUIT

IT WAS A BIG MISTAKE.

HE TOLD ME ALL ABOUT HAVING SEX WITH UNDERAGED PROSTITUTES IN AFRICA AND TRANSSEXUAL PROSTITUTES IN PARIS.

I FROZE UP AND TRIED TO EXCUSE MYSELF.

SHIT. HE'S AN ACTIVE SEX ADDICT!
HA HA

I CAN FUCK ANYONE.
HA HA HA

WHAT WAS **THAT**?

I THOUGHT MY FEELINGS HAD BEEN PURE AND INNOCENT.

BUT HUGO SEXUALIZED MY STORY AND PROJECTED HIS FANTASY ONTO ME. NOW I FELT DIRTY AND ASHAMED.

I HAD A LARGE DRAWING TO COMPLETE THAT NIGHT FOR A PARISIAN ART MAGAZINE.

THERE WERE NO AA MEETINGS, BUT AT LEAST THE DRAWING WOULD KEEP ME BUSY.

WHEN I GOT BACK TO THE COTTAGE, THE DINING ROOM WHERE I WAS PLANNING TO DRAW WAS OCCUPIED BY OTHER GUESTS.

MAYBE LÉONIE'S PARENTS WOULD LET ME WORK IN THEIR HOME.

KNOCK
KNOCK
KNOCK

I'M SORRY TO BOTHER YOU...

I HAVE TO WORK ON A LARGE DRAWING THAT'S DUE TOMORROW MORNING, BUT THE DINING ROOM IS OCCUPIED RIGHT NOW.

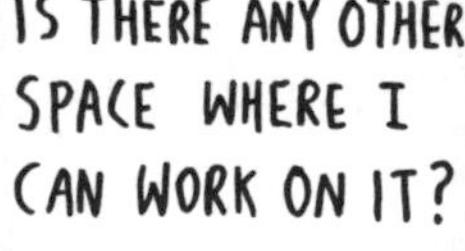
IS THERE ANY OTHER SPACE WHERE I CAN WORK ON IT?

SHE INVITED ME INSIDE.

OF COURSE. DO YOU WANT TO USE OUR DINING TABLE?

OH! LÉONIE...

THIS IS SO KIND. THANK YOU! I CAN GO BACK AS SOON AS THE ROOM NEXT DOOR IS FREE.

IT'S NO TROUBLE.

I SET UP MY DRAWING TOOLS AND STARTED WORKING. I HOPED LÉONIE WOULD ASK IF SHE COULD SIT WITH ME AND SHE DID.

WE TALKED FOR AN HOUR AS I DREW. I SOAKED IN THE PLEASURE OF HER ATTENTION. IT WAS BLISS.

BEFORE LONG, LÉONIE WAS TOLD IT WAS TIME FOR BED. WE SAID GOOD NIGHT.

I DREW FOR A BIT LONGER AND HER FATHER CAME AND SAT WITH ME.

YOU DON'T MIND...?

HE TOLD ME THAT WHEN HE TUCKED HER IN, LÉONIE WAS BESIDE HERSELF WITH EXCITEMENT.

SHE KEPT SAYING, "THANK YOU, PAPA, FOR ENCOURAGING ME TO MEET HIM AND SING FOR HIM!" HA HA

IT WAS MY ABSOLUTE PLEASURE! IT REALLY MEANT THE WORLD TO ME TODAY!

I NOTICED A WORRIED EXPRESSION ON HIS WIFE'S FACE.

IT'S GETTING LATE.
YES.

I THANKED THEM AGAIN AND RETURNED TO THE COTTAGE. THE DINING ROOM WAS EMPTY.

SIGH!

A FEELING OF SEARING, NOSTALGIC LONGING CONSUMED ME.

I WISHED I COULD HAVE BEEN LÉONIE'S BOYFRIEND WHEN I WAS 16. INSTEAD I WAS 35 AND MARRIED.

I SUDDENLY REMEMBERED I COULD CALL DARYL. IN THE RUSH OF ACTIVITY, I HAD FORGOTTEN TO KEEP IN TOUCH.

I TOLD HIM MY STORY, BLAMING THE TORTURED ROMANTIC FANTASIES ON HUGO.

I HAD NO IDEA HE WAS AN ACTIVE SEX ADDICT!

DARYL TOTALLY MISUNDERSTOOD ME. HIS TONE GOT STERN AND PATERNALISTIC.

LOOK, I KNOW WORDS DON'T DO MUCH TO SWAY AN ADDICT WHEN HE'S CAUGHT UP LIKE YOU ARE NOW.

HE TREATED ME LIKE I WAS ABOUT TO SNEAK INTO HER BEDROOM OR SOMETHING.

I WOULD NEVER HAVE DONE THAT!

ASIDE FROM THE DAMAGE TO YOUR MARRIAGE AND YOUR CHILDREN, THERE IS THE **LAW** YOU'D BE BREAKING.

HE TOLD ME TO PRAY INCESSANTLY, THAT I WAS IN THE GRIP OF MY DISEASE.

MAYBE HE'S RIGHT. I CAN'T TRUST MYSELF!

OD, PLEASE TURN MY THOUGHTS TO WHAT YOU WOULD HAVE ME DO.

I WOUND UP STAYING AWAKE ALL NIGHT, CHANNELING MY EMOTIONS INTO THE DRAWING.

EARLY THE NEXT MORNING, I GAVE IT TO HUGO AND BOARDED MY TRAIN TO THE AIRPORT.

GOOD BYE!

WHEN I LANDED IN NEW YORK, IT WAS LATE.
HI.
HI.
I CAME HOME TO A QUIET HOUSE. THE KIDS WERE IN BED AND REBECCA WAS WAITING UP FOR ME.
I TOLD HER EVERYTHING.
I DON'T UNDERSTAND... IS THIS A BIG DEAL OR NOT?!?
I GUESS IT WAS NOTHING.
FOR ONCE WE DECIDED NOT TO FIGHT AND BOTH GOT INTO BED.
I QUIETLY SOBBED MYSELF TO SLEEP.

THE NEXT MONTH WAS PURE PAIN AS I CRASHED BACK DOWN TO EARTH.

SOME TANTALIZING MEETINGS ABOUT TV DEVELOPMENT DEALS AND A FILM ADAPTATION OF MY BOOK ALL FIZZLED OUT TO NOTHING.

THE NUMBERS CAME IN FROM MY PUBLISHER.

MY BOOK HAD SOLD LESS THAN 2,000 COPIES.

RIP
FUCK!

IT WAS A FLOP.

FIVE YEARS OF MY LIFE **WASTED!**

WORSE, I HAD TO FACE THE REALITY THAT WE WERE BEHIND ON OUR BILLS AGAIN. I NEEDED TO FIND A FULL-TIME JOB.

I DON'T WANT TO GO CRAWLING BACK TO THE AD AGENCY WORLD!
THEN DO SOMETHING ELSE!

REBECCA STARTED TEACHING AGAIN. HER JOB COVERED OUR HEALTH CARE. I WOULD HAVE TO WATCH THE KIDS.

BYE, HONEY.
DON'T LEAVE.

I WAS ON EDGE. MY PATIENCE WAS AT AN ALL-TIME LOW.

BAM!
WAAAA!
PLEASE, GOD!

MAYA AND SAM WERE GOING THROUGH WILLFUL, TANTRUM-FILLED TODDLER PHASES.

NO! BABY SAM **GWABBED** IT!

WAAAAAAA!

STOP IT! STOP BOTH OF YOU!

I CARRIED SAM TO HIS ROOM AND DROPPED HIM FACE DOWN ONTO HIS CRIB MATTRESS.

WAAAA!

SECONDS LATER, I WAS FULL OF SELF-HATRED AND REMORSE.

WAAAAAAA
WHAT DID YOU DO?!?

I RAN TO HIM AND SAVAGED MYSELF FOR BEING A TERRIBLE FATHER.

WAAAAAA

WHAT'S WRONG WITH YOU?!? YOU THREW HIM IN THERE LIKE A PIECE OF GARBAGE!

WAAAA

SHH...

I'M SO SORRY, BUDDY... **SHHHH**... I'M SORRY...

CHOKE SNIFF

YOUR DISEASE IS COMPLETELY OUT OF CONTROL. YOU NEED A MEETING!

I COULDN'T GET THE IMAGE OF ME DROPPING HIM OUT OF MY HEAD.

"ON MONDAY HE ATE THROUGH ONE APPLE. BUT HE WAS STILL HUNGRY."

I MADE SOME PROGRAM CALLS.

I THREW MY SON DOWN INTO HIS CRIB. I COULD HAVE REALLY HURT HIM!*

* I'M NOT EXCUSING THIS AWFUL BEHAVIOR, WHICH STILL FILLS ME WITH SHAME, BUT SAYING IT THIS WAY MADE IT SOUND SO MUCH WORSE.

ONE PROGRAM FRIEND WAS REALLY WORRIED.
WHEN I HEAR THAT, I'M AFRAID SOMETHING REALLY TERRIBLE IS GOING TO GO DOWN AT YOUR HOUSE. LIKE SOMETHING INVOLVING THE POLICE.
SHIT!

ANOTHER ONE...

YOU MIGHT WANT TO GET HIM CHECKED OUT FOR BRAIN DAMAG

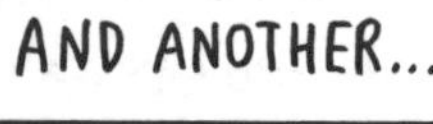
AND ANOTHER...

IT'S SHOCKING TO HEAR YOU SAY THAT.

IT'S THE COMPLETE OPPOSITE OF WHO I KNOW YOU TO BE IN THE ROOMS.

HA HA HA

I KNOW... IT'S MY DISEASE!

THIS WAS THE LOWEST "BOTTOM" I HAD EVER HIT. MY BEHAVIOR WAS MONSTROUS. I HAD TO CHANGE SOMETHING ABOUT MY LIFE IMMEDIATELY. NO MORE TALKING ABOUT IT— I HAD TO WORK THE STEPS!

♫ HAPPY HEALTHY MONSTERS ♪
HA
HA
HI, DARYL. I WANT TO COMMIT TO DOING THIS WORK WITH YOU. WHEN CAN WE START?

IT WAS THROUGH TALKING WITH MY FRIEND JUDAH THAT I BEGAN FORMULATING A NEW STORY ABOUT MY DISEASE.
"ALCOHOLISM" IS A MISLEADING TERM.

IT'S LIKE CALLING A HEADACHE "ASPIRINISM."

ALCOHOL IS JUST ONE "CURE" ADDICTS SEEK FOR THEIR DISEASE.
AND FOR A WHILE IT WORKS!
BUT THE CORE OF OUR DISEASE IS "RESTLESSNESS, IRRITABILITY, AND DISCONTENTMENT" ACCORDING TO THE BIG BOOK.
I DEFINITELY HAVE ALL THREE OF THOSE!

I WAS AS OUT OF CONTROL AS A RAGING DRUNK, JUST WITHOUT THE ALCOHOL.*

THE ONLY REPRIEVE FROM THIS DISEASE WAS STEP WORK AND DAILY MEETINGS.
DARYL
THAT MAKES SENSE TO ME. YOUR THOUGHTS AND BEHAVIORS ARE CERTAINLY "ALCOHOLIC." YOU'RE BASICALLY A "DRY DRUNK."

* MANY "TRUE ALCOHOLICS" TAKE ISSUE WITH THIS. THEY SEE EXACTLY THIS KIND OF THINKING AS WATERING DOWN AA.

I PRAYED ABOUT IT AND TRIED TO LISTEN FOR ANSWERS.

YOU NEED TO TRUST THE CIRCUMSTANCES THAT LED YOU TO THOSE AA MEETINGS ON THE BOOK TOUR. IT WAS GOD'S WILL!

TRUST THE FEELING OF IDENTIF CATION YOU HAVE WITH ALCOHOLI

BUT I REALLY ONLY HAVE ONE OR TWO DRINKS PER MONTH!

AM I JUST COPYING MOM?

"THE ONLY REQUIREMENT FOR AA MEMBERSHIP IS A DESIRE TO STOP DRINKING."

I DON'T HAVE A STRONG NEED OR DESIRE TO STOP.

BUT I DO HAVE AN OVERPOWERING DESIRE TO BELONG.

IF THE PRICE OF ADMISSION TO AA WAS SIMPLY GIVING UP ALCOHOL, I'D GLADLY DO IT.
WHEN I HAD FINALLY MADE UP MY MIND, I TOLD REBECCA.
I'M GOING TO JOIN AA AND GO TO A MEETING EVERY DAY WHILE WORKING THE STEPS WITH DARYL. THIS IS THE ONLY THING THAT WILL WORK FOR WHAT I HAVE.
BUT YOU'RE NOT AN ALCOHOLIC!!!
NO MATTER HOW MANY TIMES I TRIED TO EXPLAIN IT TO HER, SHE DIDN'T UNDERSTAND. SO I STOPPED TRYING.
I'M GOING TO BED.
I'D HAVE TO PROVE THAT I WAS DOING THIS FOR HER.

12
NO MORE MUST I STRIVE
THIS IS THE END OF FAITH
IT'S TIME TO PUT GOD AWAY... I PUT GOD
Elia Kazan
A LIFE

010-2011

THIS WAS IT! MY SPIRITUAL PATH HAD BEEN BUMPY AND FRUSTRATING, BUT NOW I WAS EXACTLY WHERE I NEEDED TO BE—AA.

ONCE I COMMITTED TO WORKING THE STEPS WITH DARYL, I GOT A JOB RIGHT AWAY.

YOU CAN START MONDAY.

THIS WORKS FASTER THAN DA!

GREAT!

MORE MIRACULOUS THAN THAT, I FELT HAPPY TO BE WORKING AT AN AD AGENCY. I BELIEVED IT WAS GOD'S WILL.

NOW I JUST NEEDED AN AA HOME GROUP.

"PERRY STREET" WAS A TINY MEETING NEAR MY NEW JOB. ALL THE SEATS FILLED UP 20 MINUTES BEFORE IT STARTED.

I OFTEN SPENT THE MEETING STANDING IN THE DOORWAY OR NEXT TO THE BATHROOM, BUT I DIDN'T MIND. I LOVED JUST BEING THERE.

OKAY, LET'S GET STARTED.

FLUSH!

THE QUALIFICATIONS WERE OFF THE CHARTS.

HI, I'M KATE AND I'M AN ALCOHOLIC.

HI, KATE

HI, KATE

HI, KATE

HI, KATE

EACH DAY AN AA MEMBER SHARED FOR 30 MINUTES.

HA HA
AT ONE POINT, I HAD A MODELING CAREER. YOU CAN GUESS WHAT HAPPENED TO THAT...
HA
HA
HA HA

THEY WOULD SHARE THEIR DRINKING STORY AND THEN HOW THEY LANDED IN AA.

MY FRIEND JUST REFUSED TO GIVE UP ON ME. CHOKE

I WAS CAPTIVATED.

FOR WEEKS I GOT MY "MORNING SPIRITUAL ADJUSTMENT," AND THEN I'D LEAVE FEELING AT PEACE WITH THE WORLD.

THANK YOU, GOD!

KATE THE MODEL WAS THERE EVERY DAY. IT ALWAYS MOVED ME TO SEE HER CLEANING UP AFTER THE MEETING WITH TOTAL HUMILITY.

SHE HAD COME OUT OF THE CLOSET LATE IN LIFE. IT MADE ME LOVE HER MORE.

SIGH
I GUESS I LIKE GIRLS...

I ONCE REFERRED TO HER IN ONE OF MY SHARES.

...I THOUGHT, "WHO IS THIS BEAUTIFUL WOMAN SWEEPING THE FLOOR?"

HA HA

AFTER THAT, SHE HAD A SOFT SPOT FOR ME.

HI, KATE.
HI, HONEY!

ANOTHER FRIEND FROM DA NAMED ALESSIA SHOWED UP ONE MORNING.

DAVID! YOU GO TO AA NOW? THIS IS LIKE MY FAVORITE MEETING!
HEY! WATCH IT. HE'S MY BOYFRIEND!

I KNEW HIM FIRST! HE'S MY BOYFRIEND
HA
HA
HA
HA

THERE WERE OTHER PEOPLE I CONNECTED WITH, TOO.

GIL THE GUITARIST

WE'D WALK TOGETHER AFTER THE MEETING OR GET COFFEE.

CARTER THE FILMMAKER

I LOVE HEARING YOU SHARE, DAVID. YOU'RE REALLY CHANNELING SOMETHING POWERFUL.

I FELT SO PROTECTED BY MY FRIENDS THAT I DIDN'T GET RATTLED BY LENA, THE UNMEDICATED BI-POLAR WOMAN.

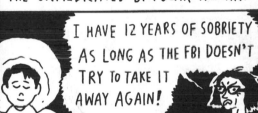

I HAVE 12 YEARS OF SOBRIETY AS LONG AS THE FBI DOESN'T TRY TO TAKE IT AWAY AGAIN!

I DIDN'T STOP AT PERRY STREET. THERE WERE DOZENS OF DAILY AA MEETINGS THROUGHOUT THE CITY. I TRIED THEM ALL.

"NEW BUST WEST" WAS A MONDAY MEN'S MEETING NEAR TIMES SQUARE.

IT WAS EVERY BIT AS POWERFUL AS THE SLAA MEN'S MEETING I'D LEFT BEHIND.

I TRIED NOT TO LET MY EGO GET FED IF I SAW ANYONE FAMOUS. IT WAS HARD.

DAVID CARR IS LISTENING TO ME SHARE!

HA HA

I USED TO THINK I WAS "TOO AD-VANCED FOR AA."

I NEVER GOT TO INTERACT WITH CARR BEFORE HE DIED, BUT I WAS A BIG FAN OF HIS BOOK.*

ONE OF HIS SHARES HAUNTED ME.

THERE'S ONE THING I'LL NEVER UNDERSTAND.

THERE ARE PEOPLE WHO COME TO THESE MEETINGS WHO CLEARLY AREN'T ADDICTS, BUT **WISH** THEY WERE! IT'S BAFFLING!

IS HE TALKING ABOUT ME?!?

AT NYU, I FOUND A MEDITATION MEET-ING CALLED "NOW YOU UNDERSTAND." IT BECAME A FAVORITE.

SOMETIMES I SAW DARYL THERE.

HOWDY, PARTNER!

HEY!

* THE NIGHT OF THE GUN

AN ENORMOUS MEETING IN BROOKLYN WAS FILLED TO THE BRIM WITH OVER 100 WELL-DRESSED, ATTRACTIVE HIPSTERS.

HA

I KNOW SOME PEOPLE CALL THIS MEETING "90 OUTFITS IN 90 DAYS," BUT THERE'S REAL PEOPLE HERE GETTIN' SOBER!

HA HA

I LOVED IT. IT WAS JUDAH'S HOME GROUP.

SO GOOD TO SEE YOU HERE!

IN QUEENS, I WENT TO SPARSELY ATTENDED WORKING-CLASS MEETINGS. THE SHARES WERE PLAIN AND DIRECT AND TOUCHING. I'M SURE MOST OF THEM WERE RIGHT WINGERS, BUT WE AVOIDED POLITICS.

THIS IS JUST LIKE MY FIRST AA MEETING IN HACKENSACK!

I'M FILLED WITH GRATITUDE TODAY!

WE SHARED SOMETHING DEEPER. THEY ALWAYS MADE ME FEEL LIKE I BELONGED.

I WANNA PICK UP ON SOMETHING DAVE JUST SHARED.

THE ONLY THING THAT TRIPPED ME UP WAS THE WORD "ALCOHOLIC." I COUNTED MY DAYS OF SOBRIETY AND INTRODUCED MYSELF WHEN I SHARED, BUT THE WORD CAUGHT IN MY THROAT.

HI, I'M DAVID AND I'M AN ALCOHOLIC.
HI, DAVID
NO, YOU'RE NOT!
HI, DAVID

CALLING MYSELF A "GRATEFUL MEMBER OF THIS GROUP" WOULDN'T CUT IT. NO MADE-UP BOTTOM-LINE DAY-COUNTS EITHER.

YOU WERE EITHER DRINKING ALCOHOL OR YOU WERE 100% SOBER.

TODAY IS DAY 75 OF SOBRIETY FOR ME.
KEEP COMIN' BACK

IT FELT WRONG ANNOUNCING SOMETHING THAT WASN'T HARD FOR ME TO GIVE UP. IT WAS LIKE ANNOUNCING TO THE GROUP THAT I'D GIVEN UP BUNGEE JUMPING.

WOO!
CLAP
CLAP
STOP CLAPPING!
CLAP
CLAP

A FEW PEOPLE SENSED MY AMBIVALENCE AND KEPT THEIR DISTANCE.

ONLY ONE MAN WAS OUTRIGHT HOSTILE.

I DON'T COME HERE FOR FUN, Y'KNOW... THIS IS LIFE OR DEATH FOR ME!

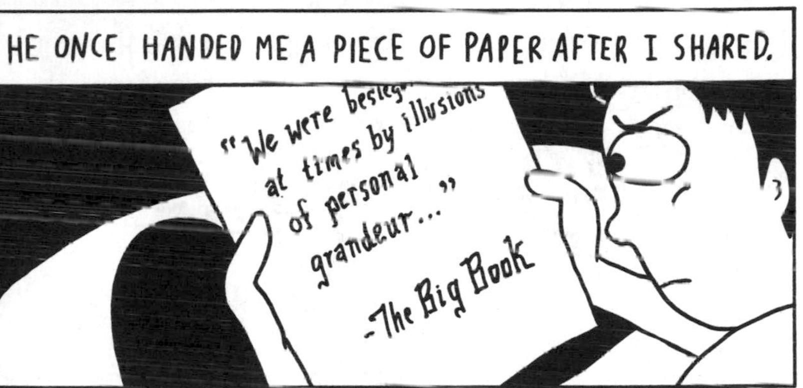
HE ONCE HANDED ME A PIECE OF PAPER AFTER I SHARED.
"We were besieg... at times by illusions of personal grandeur..."
-The Big Book

AFTER 90 DAYS, I WAS ASKED TO QUALIFY AT PERRY STREET.
POUND
POUND
POUND
POUND
POUND
POUND
YOU'RE UP NEXT WEEK, DAVID!
OH! OKAY!

I TRIED NOT TO REHEARSE OR PREPARE TOO MUCH, BUT THIS WAS MY FIRST AA QUALIFICATION. I HAD TO GET MY STORY STRAIGHT!

I LOOTED MY PAST FOR THE MOST SALACIOUS DETAILS I COULD SHARE.

• ADDICT PARENTS
• TEEN DRUG USE
• STEALING
• DRIVING DRUNK ONCE
• DRAMA AROUND MONEY
• INAPPROPRIATE SEXUAL FANTASIES

I BUILT UP TO THE STORY OF "THROWING" SAM INTO HIS CRIB.

MMMH
MY DISEASE WAS OUT OF CONTROL.

AND THEN I ENDED BY DESCRIBING MY TALKS WITH JUDAH.

THAT'S WHAT GOT MY ATTENTION AND BROUGHT ME TO AA.

AFTERWARD, I FELT NONE OF THE USUAL RELIEF, JUST A SEARING, SHAMEFUL SENSE OF BEING A FRAUD.

CLAP CLAP CLAP CLAP

I WAS TOLD IT WAS COMMON TO FEEL THAT WAY...
...THAT FEELING LIKE A FRAUD IS ONE OF THE SIGNPOSTS OF AL-COHOLISM. EVERYONE FELT IT.
DESPITE WHATEVER YOU'RE TELLING YOURSELF, HONEY, IT REALLY IS A BIG DEAL TO PUT TOGETHER 90 DAYS IN AA. I'M PROUD'A YOU!
I GUESS YOU'RE RIGHT.
I PUSHED DOWN MY DOUBTS AND FOCUSED ON DOING THE STEP WORK WITH DARYL.

STEP 1

ADMITTED WE WERE POWERLESS OVER ALCOHOL, THAT OUR LIVES HAD BECOME UNMANAGEABLE.

STEP 2

CAME TO BELIEVE THAT A POWER GREATER THAN OURSELVES COULD RESTORE US TO SANITY.

DARYL KNEW HOW LONG I'D BEEN IN PROGRAM, SO WE COVERED THESE FIRST THREE STEPS IN ONE CONVERSATION.

OVER WHICH THINGS ARE YOU POWERLESS? WHAT MAKES YOUR LIFE UNMANAGEABLE?

MONEY, SEX, FOOD, OTHER PEOPLE, AND THE EFFECT OF ALCOHOL ON ME AND MY FAMILY.
GOOD.

STEP 3

MADE A DECISION TO TURN OUR WILL AND OUR LIVES OVER TO THE CARE OF GOD AS WE UNDERSTOOD HIM.

I JUST WANT TO POINT OUT THAT IT SA
THE "CARE" OF GOD. GOD IS CARIN
ALSO, "OUR WILL AND OUR LIVES"—FOR ME IT'S EASIER T
SAY "MY THOUGHTS AND ACTION

STEP 4

MADE A SEARCHING AND FEARLESS MORAL INVENTORY OF OURSELVES.

THIS WAS THE STEP THAT "SEPARATED THE MEN FROM THE BOYS," AS THE BIG BOOK SAID.

HANG ON TIGHT... THIS ONE'S GONNA CHANGE YOUR LIFE!

I USED DARYL'S EXCEL SPREADSHEET, AND I LISTED EVERYONE I'D EVER RESENTED IN MY ENTIRE LIFE.

HERE GOES...

THE DOCUMENT GREW TO 231 LINES TOTALING 12 PAGES. IT TOOK 6 MONTHS.

I PUT AN X UNDER ANY PART OF MY LIFE THE RESENTMENT AFFECTED.

Self-esteem	Pride	Personal relations	Sex relations	Ambition	Money	Emotional security
X	X	X	X	X		X

THIS EXERCISE WAS MEANT TO DRIVE HOME HOW THE RESENTMENT WAS REALLY HURTING **ME**.

AS AA MEMBERS LIKED TO SAY:

HAVING A RESENTMENT IS LIKE ME DRINKING A BOTTLE OF POISON AND HOPING **YOU** DIE FROM IT!
HA
HA HA HA
HA

I WENT DOWN THE LIST FROM REBECCA TO MY IMMEDIATE FAMILY TO EVERY FRIEND, CO-WORKER, AND EVEN ACQUAINTANCE I COULD THINK OF.

IT INCLUDED OLD, DEEP WOUNDS...

Mom

Competes with me, turns the focus back to herself whenever I share anything.

... AND MINOR ANNOYANCES.

Ella, co-worker

Showed up depressed to all our meetings and work sessions.

IT TOOK A WHILE TO ASSESS THE IMPACT THEY HAD ON ME.

DID THIS AFFECT MY SELF-ESTEEM OR MY PRIDE?

THEN I WAS ASKED TO THINK ABOUT MY PART IN THE RESENTMENT.

HERE'S WHERE DARYL SAID I WOULD FEEL THE MOST RESISTANCE.

I BOILED DOWN MY PART TO A SINGLE SENTENCE AND TRIED TO NAME A "CHARACTER DEFECT" TO WHICH THE RESENTMENT CORRESPONDED.

FUCK! THIS IS HARD!

I ASKED MYSELF, WAS I BEING "SELFISH, DISHONEST, FRIGHTENED, SELF-SEEKING, OR INCONSIDERATE" IN MY BEHAVIOR?

WHAT'S THE DIFFERENCE BETWEEN BEING "SELFISH" AND "SELF-SEEKING"?

SOME AAERS FELT THERE SHOULD ONLY BE SEVEN POSSIBLE DEFECTS TO CHOOSE FROM.

I KEEP IT SIMPLE. THERE'S SEVEN DEADLY SINS: LUST, GLUTTONY, GREED, SLOTH, WRATH, ENVY, AND PRIDE.

BUT DARYL LET ME BE MORE CREATIVE.

I'LL CALL THIS ONE "JUDGE, JURY, AND EXECUTIONER"!

FINALLY, SINCE DARYL WAS STEEPED IN AL-ANON, HE BELIEVED IN AN "EASY DOES IT" APPROACH.* HE HAD ME THINK OF A STRENGTH WORTH KEEPING THAT WAS HINTED AT IN THE DEFECT.

I GUESS I'M A GOOD JUDGE OF CHARACTER...?

*HA.

THE WORK WAS GRUELING, EXHAUSTING, LONELY.* DARYL MOSTLY COMMUNICATED WITH ME EACH WEEK BY PHONE AND EMAIL.

I FUCKING HATE THIS!
EVERYBODY ASLEEP

THE FEW TIMES WE MET IN PERSON, I FELT A BURST OF GOD ENERGY.

WHY WON'T HE MEET WITH ME MORE OFTEN? I PROBABLY ANNOY HIM.

BETTER NOT ROCK THE BOAT. I'M LUCKY TO HAVE A SPONSOR AT ALL!

SOMETIMES I'D DROP OUT OF TOUCH FOR A WEEK OR TWO BECAUSE THE WORK WAS SO UNPLEASANT. BUT DARYL GENTLY NUDGED ME BACK ON TRACK UNTIL I FINISHED IT ALL.

KEEP GOING!

*A BIT LIKE WORKING ON THIS BOOK!

WITH THE MONEY COMING IN FROM MY AD AGENCY JOB, I WAS ABLE TO RENT A SMALL ART STUDIO NEARBY. IT ALLOWED ME TO DO MY 4TH-STEP WORK WITHOUT FAMILY DISTRACTIONS.
VROOM
THE LAST DAY I WORKED ON IT WAS DURING A BLIZZARD, LATE AT NIGHT, ALONE IN MY STUDIO.
MOST PEOPLE DON'T DO THIS WORK. BUT YOU'RE A SPIRITUAL WARRIOR, WORKING ON HAVING FREEDOM IN THIS LIFETIME.
File
Save
I FILLED IN THE LAST ROW ON THE SHEET AND SENT IT OFF TO DARYL. MY 4TH-STEP INVENTORY WAS FINISHED. BUT I COULDN'T REST ON MY LAURELS. I STILL HAD EIGHT STEPS TO GO.
4thstep.xl
SEND

STEP 5

ADMITTED TO GOD, TO OURSELVES, AND ANOTHER HUMAN BEING THE EXACT NATURE OF OUR WRONGS.

FOR THIS STEP, I'D BE SHARING MY FULL INVENTORY WITH DARYL. WE PLANNED FOR AN ENTIRE DAY IN EARLY SPRING.

YOUR LIFE IS ALREADY CHANGING AND WILL CONTINUE TO CHANGE IN DRAMATIC WAYS.

IT WAS JUST LIKE THE PROMISES IN THE BIG BOOK. NOW THEY WERE COMING TRUE FOR ME AS THEY HAD FOR SO MANY OTHERS.

"A NEW FREEDOM AND A NEW HAPPINESS"

"WE WILL NOT REGRET THE PAST."

"WE WILL KNOW PEACE."

"LOSE INTEREST IN SELFISH THINGS."

"WE WILL SEE HOW OUR EXPERIENCE COULD BENEFIT OTHERS."

"GAIN INTEREST IN OUR FELLOWS."

"INTUITIVELY KNOW HOW TO HANDLE SITUATIONS WHICH USED TO BAFFLE US."

"FEAR OF PEOPLE AND ECONOMIC INSECURITY WILL LEAVE US."

"GOD IS DOING FOR US WHAT WE COULDN'T DO FOR OURSELVES."

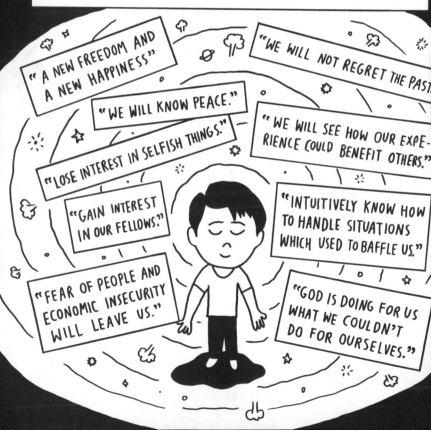

DARYL WENT EVEN FURTHER:

YOU'LL BEGIN TO SEE TEARS IN THE FABRIC OF REALITY. LIFE IS ILLUSORY. WE'RE ALL SPIRITUAL BEINGS.

HMM.

HE PROMISED MY RELATIONSHIP TO TIME WOULD TRANSFORM. I'D SEE THERE WAS AN ABUNDANCE OF TIME—MORE THAN I COULD POSSIBLY NEED.

IF THE STEPS DON'T PROFOUNDLY IMPROVE YOUR LIFE, THEN YOU SHOULD LEAVE THE PROGRAM. THAT'S HOW CERTAIN I AM THAT THIS STUFF WORKS!

HA
HA

THE BIG DAY ARRIVED. WE MET IN A BEAUTIFUL STATE PARK UNDER A SECLUDED LEAN-TO WITH PICNIC TABLES.

I BROUGHT MY GUITAR SO I COULD SING DURING OUR BREAKS. DARYL LOOKED IRKED.

IT OPENS MY HEART AND ALLOWS MY FEELINGS TO FLOW.

OKAYYY...

DARYL WARNED ME THAT HE'D NEED TO STOP FOR LUNCH AT 12:30 AND A SNACK AT 3:00.

NO PROBLEM.

TIME PASSED IN A STRANGE WAY—NOT FAST OR SLOW. MORE "LIQUID." WE BOTH FELT IT.

WE SPENT THREE HOURS ON THE FIRST TWO PAGES OF MY INVENTORY.

A REMINDE
I NEED TO EAT IN 15 MINUT

DARYL WAS ULTRA-PRESENT, LOOKING ME SOULFULLY IN THE EYES AND TAKING LUXURIOUS AMOUNTS OF TIME WITH EACH RESENTMENT AND HOW IT AFFECTED ME.

IT WAS SO HEALING TO UNBURDEN MYSELF OF ALL THESE OLD FEELINGS.

HA HA HA
EXHALE

THERE WAS SOME TENSION, TOO. I WAS SNACKING ALL DAY AND AT ONE POINT I SLIPPED, HALF-FORGETTING DARYL'S ABSTINENCE.
DO YOU WANT SOME?

NO, I DON'T WANT TO **EAT** WHILE WE DO THIS WORK.

RIGHT, SORRY!

AT EXACTLY 12:30, DARYL TOOK HIS LUNCH BREAK. I HADN'T REALIZED HE SPACED OUT HIS MEALS DOWN TO THE MINUTE.
I'M GONNA PLAY SOME GUITAR.
COOL.

HE VISIBLY BRISTLED, BUT I SANG MY HEART OUT ANYWAY WHILE HE ATE.
♫ I NEED SOME INTERVENTION ♪

AFTER LUNCH, DARYL REALIZED WE STILL HAD TEN PAGES LEFT. HE HADN'T SEEN THE WHOLE STACK.
OH...

HE SUGGESTED WE PICK UP THE PACE.
I ONLY HAVE 'TIL 4:00.
OH. OKAY

FOR THE REST OF THE DAY, IT FELT LIKE WE WERE TICKING OFF A GROCERY LIST TOGETHER. THE MAGIC WAS GONE.

UMM... THIS ONE AFFECTS MY SELF-ESTEEM.
GOOD!
POP!
PACING-
BACK AND FORTH

INSTEAD OF SPEAKING UP, I PRETENDED IT WAS STILL WORKING FOR ME.
THIS ONE IS THE SAME AS THE LAST DEFECT-ENVY.
GREAT! KEEP GOING.
GOTTA CRAM IT ALL IN!

WE GOT TO THE BOTTOM OF THE LIST ALMOST EXACTLY AT 4:00. I TOLD HIM I ALREADY FELT A CHANGE HAPPENING IN ME.

I THANKED DARYL AND GOT IN MY CAR, BADLY WANTING TO BELIEVE THAT WHAT WE'D SPENT ALL DAY DOING HAD WORKED.

I THINK I'M DIFFERENT NOW.

TIME PASSED SO STRANGELY TODAY.

I KNOW I'LL BE MORE SPIRITUALLY CONNECTED FROM NOW ON.

STEP 6

WERE ENTIRELY READY TO HAVE GOD REMOVE ALL THESE DEFECTS OF CHARACTER.

THANKS TO MY MOM, STEP 6 WAS MUCH EASIER THAN THE GRUELING STEPS 4 AND 5.

I HAVE THE PERFECT BOOK FOR YOU, ANGEL.

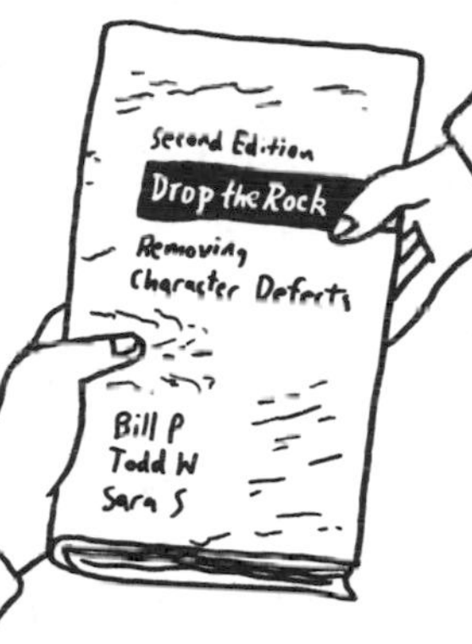
Second Edition
Drop the Rock
Removing Character Defects
Bill P
Todd W
Sara S

IT WAS A REVELATION. I TOLD DARYL.

AS ALCOHOLICS, WE ACTUALLY LOVE OUR CHARACTER DEFECTS. WE CLING TO THEM LIKE A DROWNING MAN CLING-ING TO A BOULDER, BUT WE CAN "DROP THE ROCK" AND BE FREE!

GREAT!

I LIKE TO GO TO THE LATIN ROOTS OF WORDS. "CHARACTER" AND "DEFECTS" MEAN "TOOLS" AND "BROKEN."
THAT'S BRILLIANT!
THESE ARE BROKEN TOOLS YOU DEVELOPED TO SURVIVE IN AN ALCOHOLIC HOME. YOU DON'T NEED THEM ANYMORE.

STEP 7

HUMBLY ASKED HIM TO REMOVE OUR SHORTCOMINGS.

STEP 7 WAS SIMPLY THE PRAYER WE RECITED WHEN WE WERE READY FOR GOD TO TAKE OUR DEFECTS FROM US.

I FINALLY UNDERSTAND THIS PRAYER I'VE BEEN SAYING FOR FIVE YEARS!

"MY CREATOR, I AM NOW WILLING THAT YOU SHOULD HAVE ALL OF ME, GOOD AND BAD. I PRAY THAT YOU NOW REMOVE FROM ME EVERY SINGLE DEFECT OF CHARACTER WHICH STANDS IN THE WAY OF MY USEFULNESS TO YOU AND MY FELLOWS.

GRANT ME STRENGTH AS I GO OUT FROM HERE TO DO YOUR BIDDING."

STEP 8

MADE A LIST OF ALL PERSONS WE HAD HARMED AND BECAME WILLING TO MAKE AMENDS TO THEM ALL.

BEGINNING WITH MANY OF THE NAMES ON MY 4TH STEP, I MADE A LIST OF "HARMS DONE."

ALCOHOLICS ARE FUNNY. OFTEN THE PEOPLE WE RESENT THE MOST ARE THE ONES WE OURSELVES HARMED!

HUH...

HALF OF MY "HARMS" LIST CAME TO ME THIS WAY.

⌘
COPY

THEN THERE WAS THE STEALING.

SIGH
• FOOD FROM CAMP DINING HALL
• ART SUPPLIES FROM THE STORE WHERE I WORKED
• TAPES, CDs, BOOKS
• CASH FROM STUDENT GROUP AT COLLEGE

AS I PUSHED MYSELF THROUGH ANOTHER GRUELING EXERCISE, I FELT TWINGES OF DOUBT.

IS DOING THIS REALLY GOING TO BRING ME LASTING PEACE?

CLACK
CLACK
CLACK
CLACK

I LISTED AS MANY HARMS AS I COULD POSSIBLY REMEMBER AND GOT READY FOR STEP 9.

STEP 9

MADE DIRECT AMENDS TO SUCH PEOPLE WHEREVER POSSIBLE, EXCEPT WHEN TO DO SO WOULD INJURE THEM OR OTHERS.

OVER THE NEXT THREE MONTHS, DARYL AND I DISCUSSED EACH PERSON OR INSTITUTION I'D HARMED AND HOW I'D APPROACH EACH OF THEM TO MAKE AN AMENDS.

SHOULD I SEND A FACEBOOK MESSAGE OR IS THAT WEIRD?

LET'S BOTH PRAY ABOUT IT.

I VOLUNTEERED TO WORK AT A FOOD PANTRY FOR THE DIOCESE THAT OPERATED THE CAMP WHERE I STOLE FOOD.

YO, THIS DUDE'S **KILLIN'** THE POTATOES!
HA HA

I MAILED CHECKS TO THE ART-SUPPLY STORE, THE STUDENT ORGANIZATION, AND FOUND CREATIVE WAYS TO MAKE UP FOR THE TAPES AND CDs I'D STOLEN.

I FELT WAVES OF JOY, INSIGHT, SOMETIMES GRIEF WASH OVER ME WITH EACH AMENDS I MADE.

IT GAVE ME POWERFUL STORIES TO SHARE AT MEETINGS, TOO.

I WROTE TO A GUY NAMED KEVIN WHO I BULLIED IN MIDDLE SCHOOL. HE SAID HE'D BEEN WAITING 20 YEARS TO HEAR MY APOLOGY.
GOOD SHARE!

THE MOST PERSONAL AND PROFOUND AMENDS I MADE WAS TO MY BROTHER LUKE.

CAN I TAKE YOU TO LUNCH?
POUND
POUND
POUND
POUND

WE MET ONE SUMMER AFTERNOON, NEAR HIS OFFICE.

HEY, DAVE!

AFTER WE ORDERED, I LAUNCHED RIGHT IN.

I NEED TO APOLOGIZE FOR SOME THINGS I'VE DONE TO YOU.

I ACKNOWLEDGED PUNCHING HIM AND CALLING HIM "FAGGOT" WHEN WE WERE YOUNG, EXCLUDING HIM WITH MY FRIENDS.

I FORGIVE YOU. I BARELY REMEMBER, TO BE HONEST.

FINALLY, I BROUGHT UP THE SUMMER I FOOLED AROUND WITH HIS CAMP GIRLFRIEND WHILE HE WAS AWAY.
THAT I **DO** REMEMBER. THAT ONE REALLY HURT...
SNIFF
I JUST NEVER UNDERSTOOD HOW YOU COULD DO THAT TO ME.
I'M SO SORRY! I DON'T HAVE ANY EXCUSE FOR WHAT I DID. I WAS AN ASSHOLE AND I HOPE YOU CAN FORGIVE ME.
SNIFF
WE TALKED ABOUT CALIFORNIA.
IT'S TAKEN ME YEARS TO SEE HOW SICK I REALLY WAS.
THAT MUST HAVE BEEN SO SCARY FOR YOU.
WE COVERED EVERYTHING WE NEEDED TO TALK ABOUT. AND UNLIKE SOME OTHER PARTS OF THE PROGRAM, STEP 9 TRULY TRANSFORMED MY RELATIONSHIP WITH LUKE AND SET US BOTH FREE.
LOVE YOU, BRO.
LOVE YOU, TOO.

STEP 10

CONTINUED TO TAKE PERSONAL INVENTORY AND WHEN WE WERE WRONG, PROMPTLY ADMITTED IT.

DARYL'S PRESCRIPTION FOR HOW TO WORK STEP 10 WAS TO DO A NIGHTLY INVENTORY, BASICALLY A MINIATURE 4TH STEP.

I OPEN THE NOTEBOOK NEXT TO MY BED NIGHTLY.

EVERY NIGHT?!?

I TAKE A FEW MINUTES TO ASK MYSELF IF I'VE BEEN SELFISH, SELF-SEEKING, DISHONEST, FRIGHTENED, OR INCONSIDERATE AND, IF SO, TO WHOM?

WHAT AMENDS DO I OWE THEM?

I DUTIFULLY WROTE MY NIGHTLY LIST FOR TWO WEEKS.

THEN AN OVERWHELMING FEELING OF RESENTMENT HIT ME IN THE GUT.

WHY AM I PUTTING MY-SELF THROUGH THIS?!?

IN THE MIDDLE OF THIS STEP, I GOT FIRED FROM MY AD AGENCY JOB AND FOUGHT WITH REBECCA AGAIN.

I RESENTED DARYL.

IS ANY OF THIS WORKING? ISN'T IT JUST ACTIVATING MY PERFECTIONISTIC, CONTROLLING TENDENCIES?

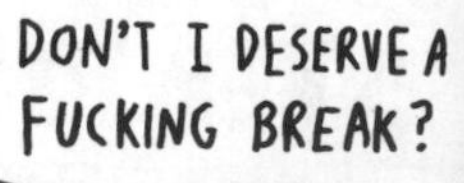
DON'T I DESERVE A FUCKING BREAK?

MAKING IMMEDIATE AMENDS IF I'VE HARMED SOMEONE MAKES SENSE.

BUT A NIGHTLY TALLY?!?

I BUCKED UNDER THE REINS.

I'M NOT DOING THAT ANYMORE!

THIS OPENED UP A SERIES OF DOUBTS.

THE AA PROMISES HAVEN'T COME TRUE FOR ME.

GOD, GRANT ME THE SERENITY

I DON'T FEEL ANY MORE SERENE. I STILL HAVE TO WORK SO HARD AT IT.

ISN'T GOD SUPPOSED TO **REMOVE** OUR DEFECTS?

HELP ME WELCOME OUR SPEAKER...

SHOULDN'T GOD BE "DOING FOR ME WHAT I COULDN'T DO FOR MYSELF" AS LONG AS I DID THE STEPS IN AA?
NOW WE'LL GO TO SHARING... YES, YOU!

DID IT COUNT AS A MIRACLE IF I WAS SCANNING MYSELF FOR DEFECTS AND LOGGING THEM EVERY NIGHT?

WHAT ABOUT ALL THE AAERS WHO SHARED THAT "RECOVERY WAS AN UNENDING FLOW OF GIFTS" AS LONG AS WE SIMPLY STAYED SOBER AND WENT TO AA MEETINGS? THINGS WERE AS BAD AS EVER FOR ME.

I LOST MY JOB AND I CAN'T STOP FIGHTING WITH MY WIFE! I'M AFRAID WE'LL WIND UP GETTING DIVORCED!

MMMH!!

IT WAS STARTING TO LEAK OUT IN FRONT OF THE KIDS.

GOD, IF ANYTHING IN MY LIFE FELT LIKE AN ADDICTION, IT WAS OUR FIGHTS!

SOB

DESPERATE FOR SOMETHING TO SHAKE ME OUT OF MY DOUBTS, I TRIED A NEW MEETING.

I'M GOING TO ANOTHER AA MEETING RIGHT NOW!
FINE!

I HEARD A MAN NAMED SPIRO QUALIFY. HE WAS INCREDIBLY SMART.

DURING MY SHARE I POURED MY HEART OUT.

I'M DAVID. I'M AN ALCOHOLIC.

NO YOU'RE NOT.

HI, DAVID

I TALKED ABOUT MY JOB SITUATION, DISAPPOINTMENT WITH MY BOOK, AND FIGHTING WITH REBECCA.

I'M SO TIRED!

I DIDN'T TRY TO HAVE A "GOOD" SHARE. I JUST LET ALL MY PAIN OUT.

THINGS **SUCK** RIGHT NOW!

I EVEN TALKED ABOUT DOUBTING DARYL, THE 10TH STEP, AND AA ITSELF. I DIDN'T CARE.

IT'S ALL SO CONTROLLING! IT REMINDS ME SO MUCH OF MY MOM!

SPIRO WAS INTERESTED IN MY DILEMMAS AND WE EXCHANGED PHONE NUMBERS.

LET'S GET COFFEE NEXT WEEK.

HE'S A THERAPIST.

A FEW DAYS LATER, WE SAT ON A PARK BENCH AND TALKED.
I RECENTLY ATTENDED A TALK BY A JUNGIAN ANALYST NAMED MAX.

IT WAS INTRIGUING. HIS SPECIALTY IS WORKING WITH CREATIVE PEOPLE WHO SUFFER FROM "NARCISSISTIC INJURY."

I HAD NEVER HEARD THE PHRASE.
MAYBE THAT'S WHAT I HAVE!

READING THROUGH MAX'S WEBSITE, I WAS CONVINCED HE COULD HELP ME.

I have a special interest in treating injuries to self-esteem, for example, the daughter or son of a narcissistic mother or father.

I CALLED HIM AND MADE AN APPOINTMENT.

OK, THANKS. SEE YOU MONDAY!

STEP 11

SOUGHT THROUGH PRAYER AND MEDITATION TO IMPROVE OUR CONSCIOUS CONTACT WITH GOD AS WE UNDERSTOOD HIM, PRAYING ONLY FOR KNOWLEDGE OF HIS WILL FOR US AND THE POWER TO CARRY THAT OUT.

MY RELATIONSHIP WITH GOD WAS OBVIOUS TO PEOPLE IN THE ROOMS.

OH, COOL... YOU HAVE THE "AA EYES..."
I DO?

PRAYER AND MEDITATION HAD BEEN PART OF MY LIFE SINCE MY AWAKENING IN CALIFORNIA.

I OFTEN THOUGHT ABOUT AN AA SAYING:

IF I DON'T FEEL CLOSE TO GOD TODAY, WHICH ONE OF US MOVED?
HA HA
HA

I WAS COMPLETELY RESPONSIBLE FOR MY HAPPINESS- MY SENSE OF CONNECTION! I JUST NEEDED TO REACH OUT TO GOD.

EVEN AS MY FAITH IN DARYL AND AA WAS WOBBLING, MY CONNECTION TO GOD WAS AS STRONG AS EVER.

EVERY MORNING I PRAYED TO KNOW GOD'S WILL.

AS LONG AS I TRUSTED GOD COMPLETELY. HE WOULD LEAD ME TO THE NEXT STEP. THERE WAS NEVER A QUESTION WHETHER IT WAS THE "RIGHT" STEP.

GOD WAS INFALLIBLE.

I NO LONGER TRIED TO "LISTEN" FOR GOD'S WILL WHILE MEDITATING. IT COULD EASILY BE MY DISEASED MIND TALKING. INSTEAD, I TRIED TO ACCESS AN EMPTY, TIMELESS SPACE, DEVOID OF ALL THOUGHTS.

LATER IN THE DAY, I MIGHT HEAR A WHISPER IN MY MIND WHEN I LEAST EXPECTED IT. **THIS** WAS GOD'S WILL.

I FELT SURE GOD HAD LED ME TO MAX.

WHY ELSE WOULD I HAVE CHOSEN THAT MEETING WHERE SPIRO SPOKE?
BZZZZ

AND WHY DID WE GET COFFEE JUST AFTER HE HEARD MAX SPEAK?

HI. COME IN.

THE FUNNY THING WAS THERE WAS NO "GOD BURST" WHEN WE MET IN MAX'S OFFICE.

IT WAS CALM AND SOOTHING—A SPACE WHERE A SAFE, OLDER MAN GAVE ME HIS UNDIVIDED ATTENTION. BUT HE DIDN'T LET ME SAY WHATEVER I WANTED WITHOUT INTERRUPTION. HE CHALLENGED ME.

I'D HAVE TO MAKE PEACE WITH HAVING "CROSS TALK" BACK IN MY LIFE.

IT WAS DISORIENTING AT FIRST, BUT I LIKED MAX AND TRUSTED HIM. I KEPT COMING BACK.

I FEEL MORE CONFIDENT AND CREATIVE.

I WROTE TWO MORE SONGS THIS WEEK!
WOW!

I'D LIKE TO HEAR THEM AT SOME POINT IF YOU FEEL LIKE SHARING THEM.*

I COULD SENSE THAT MAX HAD DOUBTS ABOUT THE WORK I'D DONE IN PROGRAM.
I GET SO TONGUE-TIED TRYING TO EXPLAIN IT TO YOU.

HE NEVER HURRIED ME ALONG TO ANY REVELATIONS. HE JUST ENCOURAGED ME TO REFLECT DEEPLY ON WHY I FELT I NEEDED THE 12 STEPS IN MY LIFE.

I FEEL LIKE I'M PROTECTING REBECCA AND THE KIDS FROM MYSELF.

I HAVE A FEELING THIS IS RELATED TO WHAT YOU TOLD ME ABOUT YOUR FATHER.

* THESE WERE WORDS I HAD LONGED TO HEAR SINCE I WAS A TEEN.

STEP 12

HAVING HAD A SPIRITUAL AWAKENING AS A RESULT OF THESE STEPS, WE TRIED TO CARRY THIS MESSAGE TO ALCOHOLICS AND TO PRACTICE THESE PRINCIPLES IN ALL OUR AFFAIRS.

DARYL HAD BEEN GROOMING ME TO BE A SPONSOR MYSELF.

I KNOW YOU'RE READY!

LIKE THE OTHER "MAINTENANCE STEPS," THIS ONE HAD NO END GOAL. I'D BE GIVING SERVICE TO ALCOHOLICS FOR LIFE.

CLAP CLAP CLAP

I HAD JUST FINISHED MY 11TH MONTH IN AA AND I WAS ALREADY DOING PLENTY OF SERVICE WHENEVER I COULD.

I CLEANED UP WITH JANE EVERY MORNING AFTER THE PERRY STREET MEETING.

I QUALIFIED AROUND TOWN WHEN I WAS ASKED.

AND I WAS CO-CHAIR AT AN ANNIVERSARY MEETING AT NYU.

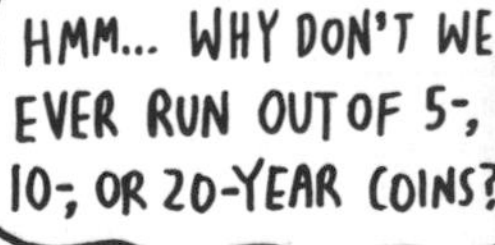

HMM... WHY DON'T WE EVER RUN OUT OF 5-, 10-, OR 20-YEAR COINS?

ON TOP OF THAT WAS PARENTING TWO PRE-SCHOOLERS WHILE I HUSTLED UP FREELANCE JOBS.

THE THOUGHT OF ADDING SPONSEES TO MY LOAD WAS COMPLETELY OVERWHELMING.

I'M REALLY NOT SURE...

TWO WEEKS BEFORE MY ONE-YEAR ANNIVERSARY, I WAS BARRAGED AGAIN BY THOUGHTS OF BEING A TOTAL FRAUD.

GOD, GRANT ME THE SERENITY...
WHAT AM I DOING HERE? I'M NOT AN ALCOHOLIC!

I SHARED ABOUT IT AND GOT THE SAME ENCOURAGEMENT AS BEFORE.

YOU BELONG HERE WITH US!

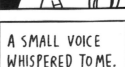

DO YOU KNOW HOW **INSANE** YOU'D HAVE TO BE TO COME TO THESE MEETINGS EVERY DAY FOR A YEAR IF YOU **WEREN'T** AN ALCOHOLIC?!?
HA
HA HA
HA HA

A SMALL VOICE WHISPERED TO ME.

I MIGHT JUST BE THAT INSANE!
HA
HA

ANOTHER VOICE PLAGUED ME WHENEVER I CHAIRED A MEETING.
CONGRATULATIONS! YOU'RE NOW A PERFECT AA ROBOT!
UCK STOP!!!

I HAD TO CONFESS TO DARYL THAT I WAS HAVING DOUBTS ABOUT BEING A SPONSOR, SO I SENT HIM AN EMAIL.

HE WANTED TO TALK THROUGH IT WITH ME ON THE PHONE.
Let me know when you can talk. I'd rather not do this over email. I'm free on
I HAD A FEELING IF WE SPOKE, HE'D CONVINCE ME TO DO IT.
I'M NOT RESPONDING TO THA

I PUT HIM OFF AS LONG AS I COULD, FINALLY EMAILING HIM THAT I WOULD DECIDE AFTER MY SUMMER VACATION WITH REBECCA AND THE KIDS.
SEND

MY DOUBTS WERE TEARING ME APART.

I CAN'T TELL REBECCA. SHE'LL POUNCE ON IT. BESIDES, WHAT IF IT'S JUST MY DISEASE TRYING TO SABOTAGE ME?

I DIDN'T FEEL FULLY COMMITTED, BUT I ALSO COULDN'T IMAGINE LIFE WITHOUT AA.

"MY CREATOR, I AM NOW WILLING THAT YOU SHOULD HAVE ALL OF ME..."

TO REBECCA'S HORROR, I INSISTED ON FINDING MEETINGS EVERY DAY OF OUR VACATION.

WHAT?!?

LUCKILY, THERE WERE PLENTY OF MEETINGS ALL OVER NEW ENGLAND.

THAT MUST BE THE CHURCH.

EVEN IN THE MOST RURAL TOWN IN MAINE NEAR THE CANADIAN BORDER, THERE WERE PACKED DAILY AA MEETINGS.

I HEARD AMAZING SHARES AND GOT THAT DEPENDABLE "GOD BURST."

THERE'S A LOT OF PEOPLE IN THE CEMETERY WHO WOULD **LOVE** TO HAVE MY PROBLEMS!
HA HA
HA HA HA HA

BUT TRYING TO RELATE TO REBECCA ON OUR TRIP WAS TORTURE.

HI, I'M BACK!

YOU REALLY JUST WANT TO GET AWAY FROM US, DON'T YOU?!?
NO! I'M DOING THIS FOR ALL OF YOU!
POP!

AFTER SIX DAYS OF THIS, THINGS TOTALLY DETERIORATED. REBECCA FOUND OUT OUR BANK ACCOUNT WAS OVERDRAWN. SHE LOST IT.

I HAVE THREE FREELANCE CHECKS COMING! I JUST HADN'T PLANNED ON ALL THESE SUMMER EXPENSES!

IF YOUR JOB PAID OVER THE SUMMER, THIS WOULDN'T BE AN ISSUE!!!

WE HAD TO BORROW FROM OUR FRIENDS TO GET THE KIDS ICE CREAM. IT WAS MORTIFYING.

JUST LET ME TREAT YOU.
MELA

ON THE LAST NIGHT OF VACATION, WE HAD THE WORST FIGHT OF OUR MARRIAGE.

THIS WAS THE LAST STRAW FOR REBECCA.

SHE WAS DONE.

SOB SOB SOB

CREDIT CARDS STEP WORK GOD SEX ASSHOLE DEBT AA UCK MONEY ZERO JOB FAMILY OF ORIGIN ALCOHOLIC ABA UNDEREARNING JESUS SHIT SHIT SHIT

WHEN WE GOT BACK HOME, SHE TOLD ME:

I'M SICK OF MY LIFE REVOLVING AROUND YOU. I NEED A BREAK. I DON'T WANT TO HEAR ANYTHING ABOUT YOU FOR A WHILE.

SCARILY CALM

OKAY.

NO SEX, NO TALKING ABOUT OUR DAYS, NO MANGOES IN FRONT OF THE TV, NO FIGHTS.

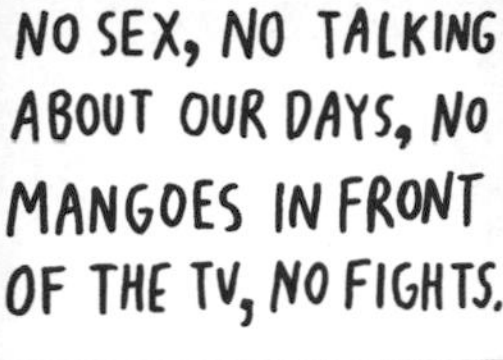

WE CO-EXISTED AS PARENTS, BUT SPENT NO OTHER TIME TOGETHER. THIS WOUND UP LASTING MONTHS.

IT WAS AGONY.

DARYL CALLED ME AND ASKED POINTEDLY IF I WANTED TO BE A SPONSOR.

I'M STARTING TO DOUBT THAT I'M EVEN AN ADDICT.

THAT'S NOT INSIGNIFICANT!

HE LISTENED TO ALL MY CRYSTALIZING DOUBTS, INCLUDING HOW MY COMMITMENT TO PROGRAM HAD DESTROYED MY MARRIAGE.

HMM... I THINK YOU MAY JUST BE BALKING AT TAKING THIS LAST STEP - THE ONE THAT'LL CEMENT YOUR RECOVERY AND GIVE YOU LASTING FREEDOM.

INSTEAD YOU'RE SELFISHLY FILLING YOURSELF UP ON SPIRITUAL JUICE AND THEN LEAVING BEFORE PAYING ANY OF IT BACK.

I PRAYED ABOUT WHAT DARYL SAID TO ME.
HAVEN'T I BEEN "PAYING IT BACK" ALL ALONG THE WAY?

MAYBE I SHOULD BE PAYING REBECCA BACK FOR ALL THE PAIN I'D CAUSED HER!

HE DOESN'T HAVE A WIFE AND CHILDREN. HE HAS NO CLUE!

WAS IT FREEDOM I'D BE GAINING FROM TAKING STEP 12 OR A LIFETIME OF SERVITUDE TO MEETINGS AND SPONSEES?

DARYL TOLD ME TO TAKE A FEW MORE DAYS TO DECIDE WHAT I WANTED TO DO.

I have six spots available for sponsees. Please decide if you want to continue this work together before I offer your spot to someone else.

IT WAS OBVIOUS TO ME THAT I DIDN'T WANT TO WORK WITH DARYL ANYMORE.

COLD BASTARD!

BUT I DREW THINGS OUT AS LONG AS I COULD.
THREE-PAGE EMAIL EXPLAINING ALL MY REASONS FOR DOUBTING THE PROGRAM

HE DIDN'T WANT TO ENGAGE ANYMORE ON THE TOPIC, SO WE MADE A TIME TO HAVE ONE LAST CALL.

THIS IS IT...
RING

I READ YOUR EMAIL AND SAW THAT YOU ASKED ME IF WE COULD REMAIN FRIENDS.

I'VE NEVER BEEN MORE SURE THAT THE 12 STEPS WORK FOR ME IN MY LIFE. OUR CONNECTION ISN'T REALLY A FRIENDSHIP. I REMEMBER WE TRIED ONCE TO JUST HANG OUT AND IT WAS REALLY UNCOMFORTABLE FOR BOTH OF US.*

I THANKED HIM FOR ALL THE WORK WE DID TOGETHER AND THEN HUNG UP.
BEEP

FOR DAYS I SUFFERED A BROKEN HEART, BUT NEVER DOUBTED I HAD MADE THE RIGHT DECISION.

*TRUE

FOR A FEW WEEKS, I WENT THROUGH THE MOTIONS OF ATTENDING MY DAILY MEETINGS, BUT MY HEART WASN'T IN IT.

THANK GOD I HAD MAX TO TALK TO.

HI.

SOB SOB
SOB

I'M REALLY AFRAID THAT IF I DON'T GO TO A MEETING EVERY DAY I'LL LOSE MY MIND!

SEE, THAT'S A POWERFUL ILLUSION YOU'RE OPERATING UNDER.
BUT THAT'S ALL IT IS.
AN ILLUSION.

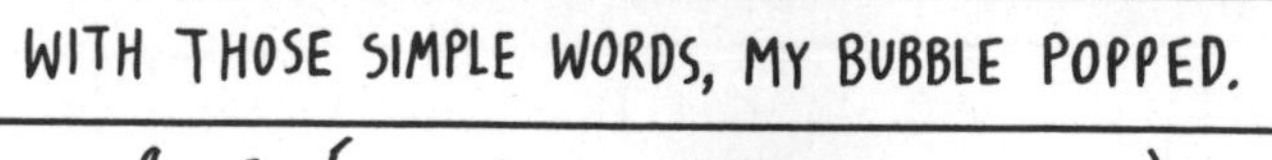
WITH THOSE SIMPLE WORDS, MY BUBBLE POPPED.

I CALLED AND RESIGNED FROM MY AA SERVICE POSITION.

I DIDN'T CELEBRATE MY YEAR OF SOBRIETY.

I DIDN'T DO THE 12TH STEP.

I NEVER RETURNED TO ANY OF MY OTHER 12-STEP PROGRAMS AGAIN. I WAS OUT.

2012
I SLOWLY RE-INTRODUCED HAVING A GLASS OF WINE ON OCCASION.
NONE TOMORROW NIGHT.
I STARTED MASTURBATING AGAIN AND SOMETIMES WATCHED PORN.
IT'S OKAY THAT YOU'RE DOING THIS.
MY LIFE DIDN'T FALL APART.
I DIDN'T LOSE MY MIND.

THERAPY WITH MAX GROUNDED ME.

I'M OKAY THIS WEEK.
GOOD.

IN MY FIRST YEAR WITH MAX, I SAW MORE PERSONAL GROWTH THAN IN ALL MY YEARS WORKING THE PROGRAM.

YOU CAN INTERNAL-IZE A PERSONAL RELATIONSHIP...

...BUT YOU CAN'T INTERNALIZE A PROGRAM.

THAT'S WHY WITH THE WORK WE'RE DOING, YOU ACTUALLY GET BETTER.

I WORKED ESPECIALLY ON NOTICING AND SHRINKING MY OWN NARCISSISM.

JUST SIT HERE AND LISTEN TO THEM.

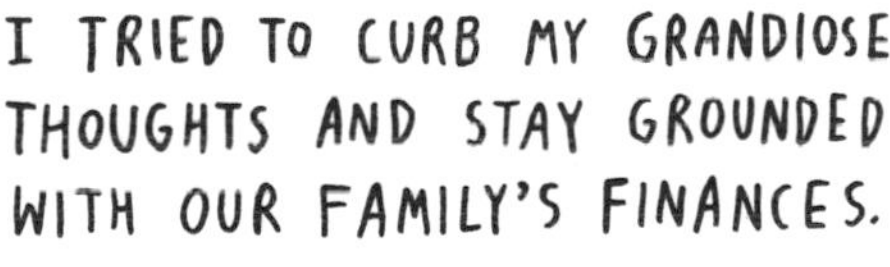
I TRIED TO CURB MY GRANDIOSE THOUGHTS AND STAY GROUNDED WITH OUR FAMILY'S FINANCES.

WE'RE UP TO DATE NOW.
THANKS.

WITH MAX'S GENTLE GUIDANCE, I UNCOVERED AND PUT INTO CONTEXT THE MOST PAINFUL MEMORIES OF MY DAD'S BEHAVIOR.

KISSING MY NAKED ASS WHEN I WAS TEN AS WELL AS A DOZEN OTHER WAYS HE SEXUALIZED OR ROMANTICIZED OUR CONNECTION.

IT EXPLAINED WHY I ALWAYS RELATED TO STORIES OF ABUSE.

OWW!

AND SOME OF WHY I'D ALWAYS HAD TERRIBLE STOMACH TROUBLE.

A YEAR AFTER WORKING WITH MAX, I CONFRONTED MY DAD ABOUT THE MEMORIES IN AN EXCRUCIATING PHONE CALL.

POUND
POUND
POUND
POUND
POUND
DO YOU REMEMBER DOING THAT? IT'S DONE LASTING DAMAGE TO ME.

HIS FIRST RESPONSE WAS IRRITATION.

UHH... OKAY... THIS IS VERY TOUGH TO HEAR.

I WOULD HAVE THOUGHT SOMETHING LIKE THIS WOULD HAVE COME UP YEARS AGO.

BUT AS I HELD MY GROUND, HE CHANGED HIS RESPONSE.

I'M TELLING YOU NOW!!!

MAYBE AS A WAY OF SHUTTING ME UP, HE ADMITTED TO HIS BEHAVIOR AND APOLOGIZED.

I THINK YOU'RE RIGHT. I DID DO THAT AND I'M SORRY. YOU AND YOUR BROTHERS ARE THE MOST IMPORTANT THING IN MY LIFE. I TOTALLY REGRET ANYTHING I DID TO HURT YOU.

THEY WERE ALL THE RIGHT WORDS. THE ONLY THING MISSING WAS A GENUINE FEELING OF REMORSE.

FOR A YEAR OR SO, I DISINVITED HIM FROM HOLIDAY EVENTS WITH MY IN-LAWS.

I'M JUST NOT COMFORTABLE HAVING YOU THERE! IT'S TOO PAINFUL TO SEE YOU.

BUT IT BECAME SO CUMBERSOME TO SEE HIM SEPARATELY THAT I EVENTUALLY GAVE IN, AT LEAST FOR THE BIG HOLIDAYS.

I USUALLY ONLY SAW HIM 4-5 TIMES A YEAR.

I'LL BE WATCHING THE KIDS ON SATURDAY. WE COULD COME OUT FOR LUNCH.

HE LIVED IN SENIOR COMMUNITY HOUSING.

HI, DAD. WE'RE HERE.
BE RIGHT DOWN.

HE COULD BARELY WALK. HE TOLD US HE "GOT SICK" A FEW YEARS BEFORE WITH A BAD CASE OF "EXHAUSTION."

JESUS. HE LOOKS WORSE.

BUT THERE WAS NO OFFICIAL DIAGNOSIS FOR WHATEVER HE HAD.

THANK YOU, DAVE.

HIS FINGERNAILS WERE OFTEN GROTESQUELY LONG.

TAP
TAP

THE LITTLE HAIR LEFT ON HIS HEAD WAS UNKEMPT.

TAPPITY
TAPPITY

HIS FACE WAS COVERED IN WHITE STUBBLE.

SO, HOW'S MISS MAYA AND MISTER SAM?

WORST OF ALL, HE WOULD COVER UP A LACK OF HYGIENE BY DOUSING HIMSELF IN COLOGNE, SOMETHING I HAD TO SPEAK TO HIM ABOUT MORE THAN ONCE.

SNIFF
SNIFF
HA
HA
WHIRR
GOOD! HOW'RE YOU?

HIS RESPONSE:

I HAVE NO VANITY LEFT.
HA
HA

DAD HAD STOPPED GOING TO AA.

I LIVE MY LIFE ACCORDING TO THE 12 STEPS. I'D NEVER DRINK!

HE PRAYED INCESSANTLY AND SOMETIMES LET SLIP THAT HE LONGED FOR THE WORLD TO END SO "JESUS CAN TAKE US ALL TO BLISS."

DAD, CAN WE KEEP IT LIGHT, PLEASE?!?
HAHA OKAY, I'LL TRY.

I WANTED MY CHILDREN TO KNOW THEIR GRANDFATHER, BUT COULDN'T STAND BEING AROUND HIM.
MY STOMACH HURTS.
HA HA
HA
TALKING ABOUT SCI-FI OR TOLKIEN
HA HA
WE NEVER LINGERED LONGER THAN AN HOUR AND WE ALWAYS STUCK TO OUR ROUTINE—A QUICK DINER MEAL, THEN RIGHT BACK HOME.
I SOMETIMES WISHED HE WAS ALREADY GONE.
WE HAVE TO GET GOING.
OKAY, I'M READY.
THEN I'D BE ABLE TO SUM UP HIS LIFE, SORT THE GOOD FROM THE BAD, FORGIVE AND MOVE ON.
I'LL BE THERE EVENTUALLY.
HA HA
FOR NOW, I'D HAVE TO ENDURE MY FATHER DYING IN SLOW MOTION.
THANK YOU, DAVE. THAT WAS WONDERFUL!
NO, IT WASN'T.
I JUST WANTED HIS DOWNWARD SLIDE TO FINALLY END.

SINCE I STARTED THIS BOOK, A FEW THINGS HAVE HAPPENED. I GOT A CALL FROM THE DIRECTOR OF THE SENIOR HOME WHERE HE LIVED.

DAD HAD LET HIS ROOM LAPSE TO THE POINT WHERE IT VIOLATED NJ HEALTH CODES.

THERE'S A NOXIOUS ODOR COMING INTO THE HALLWAY. HE WON'T LET ANYONE IN.

WORSE THAN THAT, HE HAD ESCALATING SCREAMING FIGHTS WITH A FEW RESIDENTS, ONE OF WHICH HAD JUST TURNED VIOLENT.

CUT HER ARM

DURING LUNCH ONE DAY, HE TURNED OFF SOMEONE'S OXYGEN TANK BECAUSE THE SOUND ANNOYED HIM.

HE NEEDED TO MOVE OUT IMMEDIATELY. LUKE AND I SCRAMBLED TO GET HIM INTO A MEDICAID FACILITY.*

WE TOOK TURNS CLEANING OUT HIS ROOM.

DID YOU SEE THE PISS BOTTLES?!?
DAVE, THERE WAS LITERALLY A **TURD** IN A NAPKIN ON THE FLOOR!
HA HA
OH MY FUCKING GOD!!!
HA HA

* VICTOR HAS BEEN LIVING IN LOS ANGELES WITH HIS WIFE AND TWO KIDS FOR THE LAST FIVE YEARS. THEY WERE IN AUSTRALIA FOR SIX YEARS BEFORE THAT. WE'RE NOT CLOSE.

WE GOT DAD A SPOT IN A NEARBY FACILITY, BUT HE HAD BROUGHT TOO MUCH STUFF WITH HIM. I SPENT A FULL DAY SORTING THROUGH ALL OF HIS BELONGINGS. A LOT OF IT WAS GARBAGE.

BAG OF EMPTY TOOTHPASTE TUBES
WOW, HE REALLY IS SICK.
BAGS OF EMPTY AIR FRESHENERS

THERE WAS ALSO A LEATHER FOLDER CONTAINING A LETTER.

?

To the people I love the most in this world:

Victor, Luke, and David

In case something should happen to me...

Please forgive me. I never wanted to hurt you.

SOB SOB SOB
SOB SOB SOB

NOW THAT HE'S GETTING THE CARE HE NEEDS, A TRANSFORMATION HAS OCCURRED—IN BOTH OF US.

HE'S BEEN HUMBLE, GRATEFUL, EVEN DOCILE.

THANK YOU AGAIN FOR ALL YOUR HELP.

SINCE FINDING THAT LETTER, I'VE BEEN AMAZED TO WITNESS MY RESENTMENTS MELTING AWAY. IT FEELS MIRACULOUS.

I'VE BEEN SET FREE.

I DON'T HATE MY FATHER!

I'M REMINDED OF A BIBLE VERSE THAT JAMES QUOTED FOR ME IN CALIFORNIA.

"THE PEACE OF GOD, WHICH PASSES ALL UNDERSTANDING, WILL GUIDE YOUR HEARTS AND MINDS."

"THE PEACE WHICH PASSES ALL UNDERSTANDING" HAS SWEPT OVER MY RELATIONSHIP WITH MY MOM, TOO.

DURING A RECENT STAY IN THE HOSPITAL, SHE WANTED TO CLEAR THE AIR.

EVER SINCE YOU LEFT PROGRAM, YOU DON'T CALL ME TO SHARE ABOUT YOUR LIFE. I WANT TO KNOW WHAT'S GOING ON!

SIGH

YOU REALLY WANT TO HAVE THIS CONVERSATION NOW?
I DO.

I TOOK A LEAP OF FAITH.
MOM, YOU DON'T REALLY **LISTEN** TO ME.

AND YOU HAVE THIS RIGHTEOUS TONE WHEN YOU TALK TO ME.

YOU'RE SO SURE YOU KNOW WHAT MY PROBLEMS ARE, HOW TO FIX THEM, AND HOW QUICKLY I SHOULD COME TO THE SAME CONCLUSION AS YOU. IT'S COMPLETELY ALIENATING!
HMM... OKAY. I CAN OWN THAT!
EXHALE

FOR ONCE, NEITHER OF US GOT ANGRY. MAYBE WE'VE BOTH AGED OUT OF OUR MUTUALLY COMBATIVE TENDENCIES.
I HEARD EVERYTHING YOU SAID. I WANT TO TELL YOU SOMETHING, TOO.
I'M NOT GOING TO THE PROGRAM ANYMORE EITHER.
!

I HAD TO GIVE UP HOPE OF EVER HAVING THE MOTHER I NEEDED AS A YOUNG CHILD...
I'M FOCUSED ON REJOINING THE CATHOLIC CHURCH.

...IN ORDER TO SEE MY MOM FOR THE PERSON SHE IS.
I WANT TO BE A THORN IN ITS SIDE AND HELP IT TO GROW!

MOM AND I DEBATED THE MERITS OF THE 12 STEPS NOW THAT WE BOTH HAD SOME DISTANCE. WE DIDN'T SEE EYE TO EYE, BUT THERE WAS ENOUGH OVERLAP.
I LEARNED HOW TO LEAD WITH MY VULNERABILITY AND LET OTHERS MEET ME WHERE I REALLY AM.
IT USUALLY INSPIRES THEM TO OPEN UP TO ME IN RETURN AND IT BRINGS US BOTH CLOSER TO HOW GOD MIGHT SEE US.

WHEN I LEFT AA, I PUT GOD AWAY- OR AT LEAST I GOT WAY LESS SURE OF HIS OR HER EXISTENCE.

IN THE LIGHT OF DAY, ALL THAT PRAYING AND VISUALIZING IN MY OWN HEAD LOOKED LIKE ITS OWN FORM OF INSANITY— THOSE "GOD BURSTS" A NARCISSISTIC FEEDBACK LOOP.

REBECCA WAS COMPLETELY SHOCKED THAT I WAS WILLING TO LET THE PROGRAM GO. AFTER SIX YEARS, SHE HAD RESIGNED HERSELF TO THE FACT THAT I'D BE GOING TO MEETINGS FOR LIFE.

WHAT?!?

SHE SPENT THE BETTER PART OF THE NEXT YEAR WORKING ON FORGIVING ME FOR DRAGGING HER THROUGH SUCH A HELLISH ROLLER-COASTER RIDE.

I'M SORRY.
I STILL CAN'T.

IT ULTIMATELY TOOK MONTHS OF ROCKY COUPLES-THERAPY SESSIONS FOR OUR FRIENDSHIP AND SEX LIFE TO FULLY RETURN.

POST-THERAPY DATE

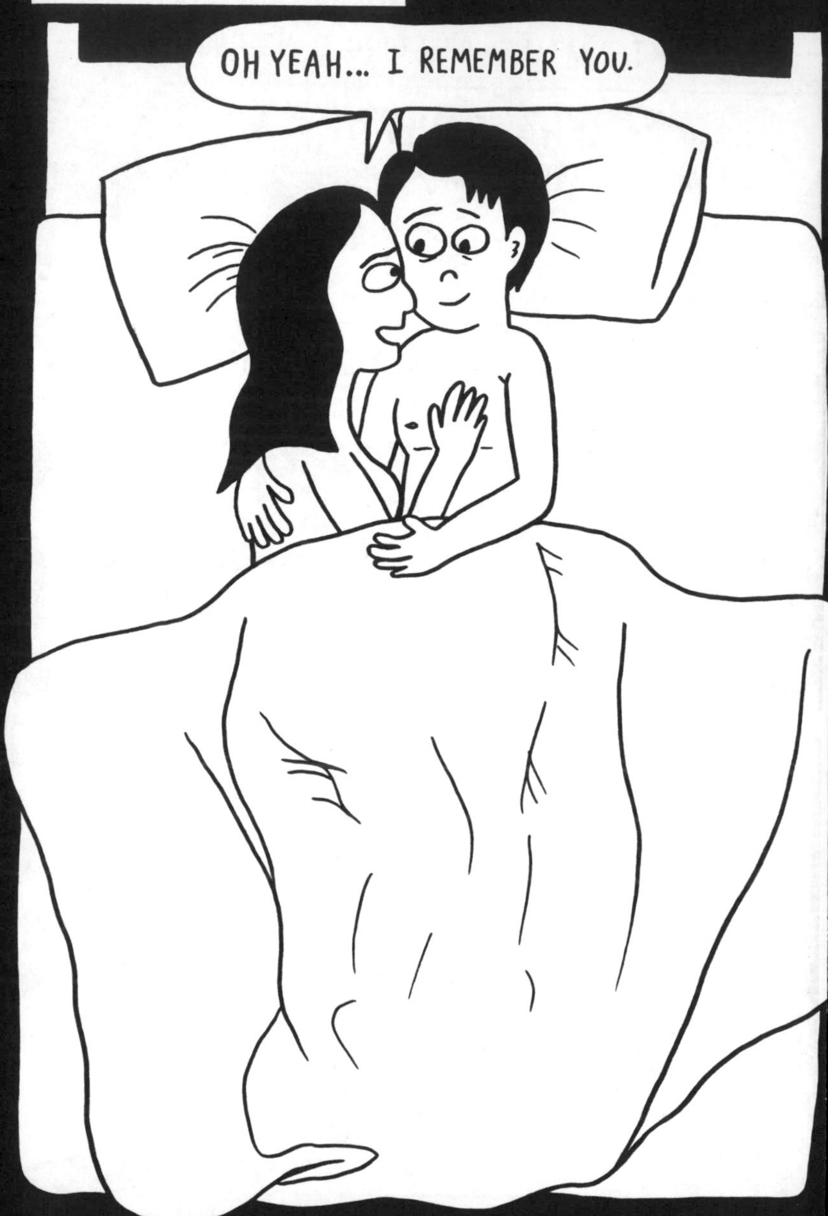
AND THEN ONE NIGHT.
OH YEAH... I REMEMBER YOU.

ONCE I HAD SOME DISTANCE AND COULD SEE WHAT I HAD PUT HER THROUGH, MY GRATITUDE FOR REBECCA OVERWHELMED ME.

YOU REALLY ARE THE BEST THING THAT EVER HAPPENED TO ME. THAT'S NOT AN EXAGGERATION!
OH, GO ON...

I STILL MARVEL AT HER AND WONDER WHAT SHE SAW IN ME THAT KEPT HER HANGING ON.

I THINK BACK TO WHEN I FIRST FELL IN LOVE WITH HER AT AGE 17.

HER PARENTS' HOUSE WITH NO ONE HOME
WHIMPER

I KNEW RIGHT AWAY HER GOODNESS RAN DEEP.

SORRY, I HAVE TO CHECK ON HER.
WHIMPER

BUT IT WASN'T BASED ON ANY MAGICAL BELIEF SYSTEM.

IT'S OKAY, MAGGIE.
DYING FAMILY DOG

SHE KNEW INTUITIVELY SOMETHING I HAD TO LEARN IN AL-ANON.

LOVE IS A VERB.

YOU **DECIDE** TO LOVE SOMEONE. YOU STICK BY THEM.

REBECCA AND I LIKE TO JOKE THAT WE'RE IN OUR GOLDEN YEARS. AFTER 20 YEARS OF LIVING TOGETHER AND 17 YEARS OF MARRIAGE, WE'VE GOTTEN THE FIGHTING OUT OF OUR SYSTEM.

SHOULD WE GO TO A MATINEE THEN GET THE EARLY-BIRD SPECIAL?
HA
HA

IT SOMETIMES AMAZES US BOTH HOW MUCH WE STILL LIKE EACH OTHER.

"ASTOUNDING ACHIEVEMENT," HONEY!

WORD GAMES IN BED

ONE TIME OUR NEIGHBOR SAW US HEADING OUT FOR A DATE.

I SEE THE WAY YOU SMILE AT EACH OTHER. IT'S DISGUSTING!
HA HA

WE'VE DONE A LOT, BUT STILL HAVE MORE TO DO TOGETHER...
MAYA, DID YOU STUDY FOR YOUR NEW YORK TIMES QUIZ?
YEAH.
OK.
SAM, YOU NEED TO PRACTICE PIANO AFTER SCHOOL.
MAKING LUNCHES
14
12
MAKING BREAKFAST
...NAMELY ALL THE THANKLESS, MUNDANE TASKS THAT GO INTO RAISING TWO BRILLIANTLY CREATIVE AND CURIOUS KIDS.
'BYE!
'BYE.
'BYE.
HAVE A GOOD DAY!
THEY'RE LIVING PROOF THAT OUR LOVE FOR EACH OTHER...
SIGH
...AS IMPERFECT AS IT MAY BE...
...WORKS.
2012 - 2019

ACKNOWLEDGMENTS

SPECIAL THANKS TO MY EDITOR, TIM O'CONNELL, AND ASSISTANT EDITOR, ANNA KAUFMAN. YOU'VE BEEN IDEAL READERS FOR ME AND HAVE SAVED ME FROM MYSELF MORE THAN A FEW TIMES.

THANKS TO PJ MARK FOR YOUR LONG-STANDING BELIEF IN MY WORK. EVERYONE SHOULD BE SO LUCKY TO HAVE SOMEONE LIKE YOU IN THEIR CORNER.

DAN FRANK, THANKS FOR YOUR PATIENCE AND YOUR LEAP OF FAITH IN BRINGING ME INTO THE PANTHEON FOLD. KNOWING THIS BOOK HAD A HOME MOTIVATED ME TO MAKE IT THE BEST IT COULD BE, EVEN IF IT TOOK ME MANY, MANY YEARS TO DELIVER.

ANDY HUGHES, THANKS FOR YOUR PRODUCTION EXPERTISE.

TO MY MOM, DAD, AND BROTHERS, THANKS FOR PUTTING UP WITH HAVING A MEMOIRIST IN THE FAMILY. THERE'S NEVER A DULL MOMENT WITH ANY OF US, GOD KNOWS.

SAM AND MAYA, HOPEFULLY YOU'RE READING THIS IN YOUR 20s, NOT YOUR TEENS. PLEASE KNOW THAT I NEVER MEANT TO HURT EITHER OF YOU, ESPECIALLY IN WRITING THIS BOOK. I'M SORRY IF IT'S HARD TO READ. BEING YOUR DAD HAS MADE ME WANT TO BE MY BEST SELF. I COULDN'T BE PROUDER OF YOU BOTH. I'M IN AWE OF THE PEOPLE YOU'RE TURNING OUT TO BE.

REBECCA, I'VE PROBABLY THANKED YOU MORE THAN YOU'RE COMFORTABLE WITH ALREADY, SO I'LL JUST END THIS WITH A QUOTE:

"IF I FIND MY HARDHEADED WOMAN, I KNOW THE REST OF MY LIFE WILL BE BLESSED." – CAT STEVENS